The Second Long Walk

Jerry Kammer

THE SECOND LONG WALK

The Navajo-Hopi Land Dispute

UNIVERSITY OF NEW MEXICO PRESS

Albuquerque

Library of Congress Cataloging in Publication Data

Kammer, Jerry, 1949–
  The second long walk.

  Includes bibliographical reference and index.
  1. Navaho Indians—Land tenure. 2. Hopi Indians—
Land tenure. 3. Indians of North America—Arizona—
Land tenure. 4. Indians of North America—Government—
relations—1934– I. Title.
E99.N3K26   333.3'1'7913   80-52273
ISBN 0-8263-0549-0

© 1980 by the University of New Mexico Press. All rights reserved. Manufactured in the
United States of America. Library of Congress Catalog Card Number 80-052273. Interna-
tional Standard Book Number 0–8263–0642–X.
Third paperbound printing 1987

To the people of the JUA

and

To my family

Contents

Preface

My first contact with the Navajo-Hopi land dispute came in the summer of 1974, when, as a reporter for the *Navajo Times*, I traveled to Washington to report on Senate consideration of legislation intended to resolve the dispute through partition of the disputed lands and large-scale relocation of Navajos. I had come to the Navajo Reservation two years previously to work as a volunteer teacher at St. Michael Mission School near Window Rock. When I was offered the chance to write about the area, I decided to stay on for a while.

On the trip to Washington I joined a group of Navajos and Hopi traditionalists who opposed the attempt of the Hopi Tribal Council to have Navajos evicted from half of the 1.8-million-acre tract that became known as the Joint Use Area in 1962, when a federal court ruled that although the land was inhabited almost exclusively by Navajos, it was owned jointly and equally by the two tribes. For me, a native of nearby Baltimore, the trip was a return to the familiar rhythms of Eastern city life. But the Navajos and Hopis were entering a world that could hardly have been more different from their quiet, expansive Arizona land. For several days they visited Senate offices, explaining to legislative aides their opposition to partition and relocation. Then they returned home, where at the end of the year they received word of the passage of the land dispute legislation.

Two years later I left my position as a reservation correspondent for the Gallup, New Mexico *Independent* to begin work on a book on the land dispute. I wanted to understand how the dispute had developed, how it had reached the point where the United States government was planning a massive program of forced relocation. I wanted to test the hypothesis that underlay passage of the land dispute legislation—that relocation was a price that had to be paid to achieve a larger good, the survival of the Hopi culture. My aim was to document how the dispute had been handled by the federal courts, the Interior Department, and, most of all, the Congress. I also sought to explain how the land dispute was affecting the people of the two tribes.

The more I learned the more I became convinced that an awful mistake had been made in 1974. I came to believe that relocation was not worth its cost, that it was unjustified, inhumane, and unworkable. My research and investigation, involving hundreds of interviews and examination of countless files, led to the unambiguous conclusion that Congress had not realized the implications of the law it passed in 1974, that it had been poorly informed and to a great extent manipulated.

Like the Cherokees' Trail of Tears and the Navajos' Long Walk of a century ago, relocation will be a blot forever on our national honor, government benefits to the relocatees notwithstanding. The United States is alienating from their land one of the few groups of traditional Indians remaining in our country, people who deserve respect and need protection and who have a historical claim on our consciences for honest and compassionate treatment. The evidence is unmistakable that relocation will indeed be devastating. It will, I am convinced, be a grave embarrassment to a nation that in recent years has done much to ease the shock of Native America's ongoing encounter with modern America.

In the fall of 1979, when I was in Washington completing research on this book, I met Ralph Reeser, who was then director of congressional and legislative affairs for the Bureau of Indian Affairs. Mr. Reeser thought the land dispute legislation was fundamentally unjust. "I just wish the Navajo-Hopi dispute had reached here five years later or the Maine claims five years sooner," he said. The reference was to the claims of the Passamaquoddy and Penobscot tribes to a minimum of 5 million acres in Maine. Federal courts had ruled that the land was still owned by the tribes because the means by which the state had acquired it in the eighteenth and nineteenth centuries were invalid. In 1979 the BIA was helping to arrange a settlement that would compensate the tribes with money and a tract of forest land. "You don't hear anybody talking about moving people in Maine, do you?" he asked rhetorically.

If we are not moving non-Indians in Maine, why are we forcing the Navajos to move in Arizona? To this unsettling question there is no acceptable answer.

I owe thanks to many people for their help in this project. Many Navajos and Hopis shared with me their personal histories and views. No individual was more important than Eric Eberhard, who not only wrote a part of chapter 2 but who made many indispensable suggestions on content and organization. My editor, Beth Hadas, was a perceptive critic who had a gentle way of prodding me along. The Reverend Theodore Hesburgh, President of Notre Dame, provided me with a grant to begin research in Washington, and a grant from the Akbar Fund, administered by the Nations Project of Santa Fe and its director John Folk-Williams, helped me complete the work. Octavia Fellin, director of the Gallup Public Library, was an amazingly consistent source of research material. Octavia's staff—especially Paula Fox, Ernestine Rohan, and Anne Weeks—put up with me with admirable patience. Professor Thayer Scudder, the Reverend John Gerber, Susan Eberhard, Jim Moran, Mike Nelson, Mike Stuhff, Sandy Stuhff, Al Taradash, Cecille Gerber, Mark Panitch, Martin Link, and Tom Harmon provided valuable comments. I haven't the space to list all those who supported me in other ways, but I am especially grateful to Mike Loughrey and Yvonne Castillo for giving me a home away from home during my many trips to Phoenix. For help over the rough spots, I am grateful to my family and friends back in Baltimore and the Pawlowski family of Gallup: Fran, Verna, Jasmine, and Jason.

A Chronology of Important Events in the Land Dispute

1882   President Chester A. Arthur issues an executive order setting aside 2.5 million acres around the Hopi mesas for the Hopis and "such other Indians as the Secretary of the Interior may see fit to settle thereon."

1891   Navajo-Hopi boundary conflicts are reported to have been brought to "a satisfactory conclusion" with the establishment of a 519,000 acre area for the Hopis.

1920   The area of Hopi use is reported to be less than 384,000 acres.

1931   The commissioner of Indian affairs and secretary of the interior say "a reasonable area of land" should be reserved for exclusive Hopi use.

1936–43   Grazing District 6 is set aside for Hopi use; subsequent expansion to 650,013 acres forces the first relocation of Navajo families.

1958   Congress passes legislation authorizing a lawsuit to determine ownership of the 1882 Reservation.

1962   A special three-judge federal court rules that 1.8 million acres of the 1882 Reservation are owned jointly by the two tribes. This area becomes known as the Joint Use Area. A year later the Supreme Court summarily affirms the district court decision.

1972   The district court in Arizona orders drastic Navajo livestock reduction to allow for Hopi use of half the JUA range; the order also bars Navajo construction in the JUA.

1974   Congress passes the Navajo-Hopi Land Settlement Act, providing for equal partition of the JUA and the relocation of members of one tribe living on land partitioned to the other.

1977   The district court in Arizona partitions the JUA; Navajo appeal delays effective date of partition to April 18, 1979.

1981 (April)   The Navajo and Hopi Indian Relocation Commission is due to submit its relocation plan to Congress.

1986   Relocation from the former Joint Use Area is to be completed.

Dramatis Personae

JAMES ABOUREZK. Democratic Senator from South Dakota who opposed settling the land dispute with large-scale relocation.

HAWLEY ATKINSON. Member of the Navajo and Hopi Indian Relocation Commission.

BILL BENJAMIN. Director of the Joint Use Administrative Office of the Bureau of Indian Affairs until his retirement in 1979.

JOHN BOYDEN. General Counsel for the Hopi Tribe.

JOHN COLLIER (1884–1968). Commissioner of Indian Affairs from 1933 to 1945.

DENNIS DeCONCINI. Democratic Senator from Arizona, elected in 1976, who disapproved of the 1974 legislation to partition the disputed Joint Use Area.

PAUL FANNIN. Republican Senator from Arizona who in 1974 played an important role in passage of the Navajo-Hopi Land Settlement Act.

J. H. FLEMING. Indian agent to the Hopis whose recommendations for a Hopi Reservation resulted in the issuance of an 1882 executive order setting aside 2.5 million acres in northeastern Arizona for the Hopis and "other Indians."

BARRY GOLDWATER. Republican Senator from Arizona and an advocate of partition and relocation as a means of settling the land dispute.

THOMAS KLEPPE. Secretary of the Interior during the administration of Gerald Ford.

NORMAN LITTEL. General Counsel for the Navajos 1947–1966. He presented the Navajo claim to the 1882 Executive Order Reservation to a special three-judge federal court in 1960.

HARRISON LOESCH. Assistant Secretary for Land Management, Department of the Interior, during the first term of Richard Nixon, he favored partition and relocation; later became vice-president of Peabody Coal Company.

PETER MACDONALD. Chairman of the Navajo Tribe elected to his third four-year term in 1978.

LLOYD MEEDS. Democratic Representative from Washington state who proposed settling the land dispute through forced arbitration.

LEE METCALF. Democratic Senator from Montana and an advocate of partition and relocation.

BILL MORRALL. Arizona hunter and environmentalist who opposed the Navajo Tribe's attempt to purchase land north of the Grand Canyon as a relocation site.

SANDRA MASSETTO. A member of the Navajo and Hopi Indian Relocation Commission; appointed in early 1979.

PHILLEO NASH. Commissioner of Indian Affairs during the administration of John Kennedy.

WAYNE OWENS. Democratic Congressman from Utah whose bill to partition the Joint Use Area was passed in 1974; later a member of John Boyden's law firm.

SAM STEIGER. Republican Congressman from Arizona and the first House sponsor of legislation to partition the Joint Use Area.

ABBOTT SEKAQUAPTEWA. Chairman of the Hopi Tribe elected to his second four-year term in 1977.

WAYNE SEKAQUAPTEWA. Hopi publisher, entrepreneur, and official of the Mormon Church; died in 1979.

RICHARD SCHIFTER. Washington counsel for the Navajo Tribe during the period Congress was considering the legislation to partition the Joint Use Area.

THAYER SCUDDER. California Institute of Technology anthropologist and authority on relocation who warned that relocation of Navajos from the Joint Use Area would have devastating consequences.

WILLIAM SIMKIN. Federal mediator whose recommended line of partition was adopted by the federal district court.

MORRIS UDALL. Democratic Congressman from Tucson who took no active role in the 1974 land dispute legislation; later, as chairman of the House Interior Committee, he opposed Navajo attempts to have the 1974 legislation repealed but favored new legislation to lessen the hardship of relocation.

GEORGE VLASSIS. General Counsel for the Navajo Tribe during the administrations of Peter MacDonald.

JERRY VERKLER. Staff director of the Senate Interior Committee in 1974; later vice-president of Texas Eastern Transmission Company.

JAMES WALSH. Federal district court judge who over a period of nearly twenty years issued several key rulings in land dispute litigation.

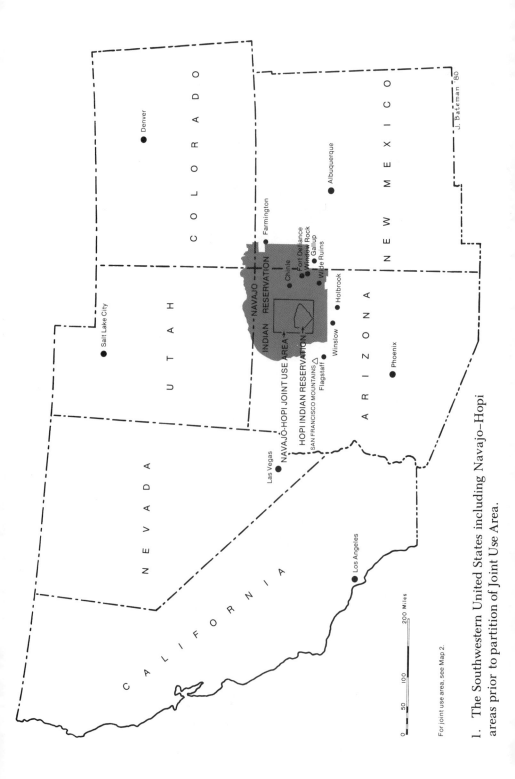

1. The Southwestern United States including Navajo–Hopi areas prior to partition of Joint Use Area.

NEVADA

UTAH

CALIFORNIA

ARIZONA

COLORADO

NEW MEXICO

J. Bateman '80

Denver

Salt Lake City

Las Vegas

Los Angeles

Phoenix

Albuquerque

Farmington

NAVAJO INDIAN RESERVATION

Chinle

Fort Defiance
Window Rock
Gallup
Wide Ruins

Holbrook

Winslow

NAVAJO-HOPI JOINT USE AREA

HOPI INDIAN RESERVATION

SAN FRANCISCO MOUNTAINS
Flagstaff

For joint use area, see Map 2.

0   50   100   200 Miles

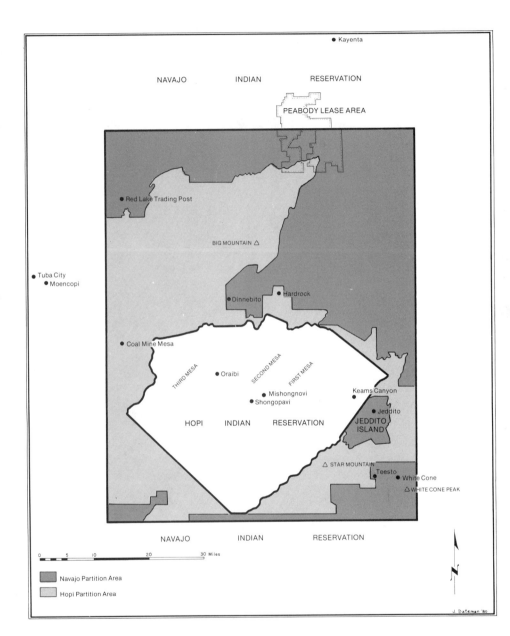

2. The 1882 Reservation After Partition.

1
Big Mountain, October–November 1977

The night here works with the slow care of a medicine man, taking a long, meditative time to conjure the darkness. As shadows poured slowly eastward from juniper trees and sagebrush and began to dissolve into the muted colors of the autumn dusk, Pauline Whitesinger set out from her one-room stucco house to gather the sheep that had been grazing since early that morning on the broad, brown earth of Big Mountain. Now she would return them to the corral, which was woven from the twisted limbs of many juniper trees.

Today, since she had the use of her son's pickup truck, she might haul water from the windmill five miles away at Sweet Water Springs, using surplus military ammunition cannisters that were distributed by the thousands in the 1950s as part of a program to improve sanitation among the Navajos. She would cook a dinner of mutton stew and fry bread on a wood-burning stove in the flaring yellow light of a kerosene lantern. Then she would spin wool for a rug she would sell to the trader at Dinnebito, twenty miles away. Finally she would sleep, relaxed in the rhythms of her forty-three years and of many years on Big Mountain before she was born.

But the crew of Navajo workmen pounding green metal fence posts into the sandy earth of Pauline Whitesinger's grazing land would make this a day like no other. Their advance over sagebrush and snakeweed, up a slope studded with juniper and pinyon, and across sandy washes and red rock canyons marked the first entry onto Big Mountain (Dził Ntsaaí in Navajo) of a law from Washington intended to fashion order out of the tangled Navajo-Hopi land dispute and bring it at last to a conclusion. For Pauline Whitesinger and her neighbors it marked the beginning of a time of fear and defiance.

"Why are you building a fence here?" she asked one of the workmen.

"We heard you were wandering off, so we're fencing you in," he replied, treating his fellow employees of the Bureau of Indian Affairs to a laugh. Mrs. Whitesinger walked away.

Later, while out in her son's pickup, Mrs. Whitesinger encountered a second work crew, one of whose members was the brother of her late husband. When she asked him the reason for the fence, a second man told her she was interfering with their work and suggested crudely that she take her brother-in-law home with her if she had any business with him.

Mrs. Whitesinger is normally a dignified woman whose bearing suggests control and serenity. But life on Big Mountain has made her tough, and this insult infuriated her. She made a run at the man with her truck, then jumped out and shoved him to the ground. "Who are you working for?" she shouted. "Why are you building this fence?"

The shaken foreman stepped in, responding defensively that the Hopis wanted the fence and that a law from Washington had ordered its construction. He warned Mrs. Whitesinger that she would be arrested if she tried to stop the fence and added for good measure that she might even die of old age in a jail cell.

Mrs. Whitesinger was not intimidated. Her eyes narrowed, her jaw stiffened, and she pointed at the foreman. "This is where I will die of old age," she replied firmly, stomping her foot on the earth. The next day, after Mrs. Whitesinger returned once more to challenge the fence makers, the foreman stalked to his truck to radio a report of interference. He received a handful of Big Mountain in the face.

With instructions from the Bureau of Indian Affairs office in Flagstaff, 120 miles to the southwest, the crew withdrew from the area for several days. They returned on the day Mrs. Whitesinger and several neighbors drove the 140 miles to the Navajo capital at

Window Rock to discuss the fence with tribal and BIA officials. They insisted they would not allow their land to be fenced, and when they returned home they tore up the day's work of the fence crew and threw the metal posts into heaps near their homes.

Then they sought the aid of Larry Anderson, a Navajo who lived, ironically, at New Oraibi, the Hopi capital, forty miles east of Big Mountain. The Hopis had been awarded over 900,000 acres inhabited by Navajos at the beginning of the year when U.S. District Court Judge James Walsh, acting with authorization provided in the 1974 Navajo-Hopi Land Settlement Act, divided 1.8 million disputed acres equally between the neighboring tribes. Big Mountain was part of the Hopi acquisition, and the fence was part of the government's program to improve the range and turn it over to the Hopis.

Navajos living on the wrong side of the fence—with the exception of a few elderly who might be allowed to live out their lives at their homes—would be relocated with federal assistance. About a hundred Hopis also faced relocation, because they lived on land partitioned to the Navajos. The partition-relocation program was Washington's attempt to end an intertribal dispute that was the legacy of nearly a century of confused federal policy. Now people like Pauline Whitesinger were to pay for the errors of the federal government by losing their homes. Where they were to go no one knew.

Larry Anderson's wife, Vicki, is a Hopi, and their two children are enrolled members of the Hopi Tribe. He is a Marine veteran of Vietnam, a former football and baseball star at Window Rock High, and a former national treasurer of the American Indian Movement. The adobe walls of the Anderson home held the symbols of an angry young American Indian. A poster depicted an American flag, which instead of a field of stars had strands of barbed wire confining two Indians. The nineteenth-century Oglala Sioux chief Red Shirt glared from another poster, and two wooden bookshelves bulged with bulky federal environmental impact statements reporting on the controversial coal-fired electrical generating stations on Navajo land near Shiprock, New Mexico. On the kitchen wall a large American flag hung upside down. On its white stripes Anderson had written slogans: Remember the Long Walk, Remember Wounded Knee I and II, Remember All Indian P.O.W., Remember the Bald Eagle, Remember Mother Earth.

Nearly three years earlier, in 1975, Anderson and other members of AIM had taken over the Fairchild Semiconductor Plant in Shiprock to protest the wages and working conditions there. Fairchild had been planning to shut the plant soon, anyway, and move to cheaper labor markets overseas, but the AIM takeover gave them a reason to hasten their departure. Although the incident ended without bloodshed after federal authorities agreed not to prosecute the militants, the plant never reopened. Many of the several hundred Navajos who lost their jobs were bitter that Anderson and the others were not punished.

After Fairchild, AIM had been a dirty word on the Navajo Reservation. Now, as he drove to Big Mountain in the caravan of six pickups that had come to Oraibi to seek his help, Anderson was determined to exercise responsible leadership. He insisted that the guns carried by several young men be kept unloaded, and he told them to keep cool heads while they set up camp along the fence line to wait for the morning and the return of the fence crews.

The crews did not return. "We've decided to back off that area, that's all," said Bill Benjamin, director of the BIA office that was supervising the fencing. Asked when the crews would be sent back to Big Mountain, Benjamin responded, "That will depend on communications from Washington."

When word of the incidents at Big Mountain reached BIA headquarters in Washington, Forrest Gerard, assistant secretary for Indian affairs in the Interior Department, met with his deputy Rick Lavis to discuss the government's response. Both men had worked on the 1974 Navajo-Hopi land dispute legislation, Gerard as a member of the Senate Interior Committee staff, and Lavis as an assistant to Arizona Senator Paul Fannin, who retired at the end of 1976.

Peter MacDonald, chairman of the Navajo Tribal Council, had sent a telegram to Gerard, warning that the situation was urgent and asking that Interior send a high-level official to the reservation for talks. Lavis flew to the western reservation community of Tuba City, then drove the eighty-five miles to Big Mountain, the last thirty miles over roads the like of which he had probably only seen in television ads for radial tires. For three hours on a chilled, windy afternoon, Lavis sat within a circle formed by 230 Navajo men and women whose ninety pickup trucks fanned out beyond. The women huddled in Pendleton shawls around small campfires; the men stood off to one side, arms folded across their chests, faces darkened by the shadows of their cowboy hats.

Lavis's pin-striped suit made him look every bit an important man from Washington. But it was poor equipment for the weather. The Navajos smiled knowingly as a young woman draped his shoulders with a blanket, a gesture of hospitality that was also a statement that he was far away from the comforts of a Washington conference room. Beside Lavis sat Peter MacDonald, BIA administrator Bill Benjamin, and Hawley Atkinson, president of the Sun City Republicans and one of the three members of the Navajo and Hopi Indian Relocation Commission. Created by the 1974 legislation, the commission had the responsibility of planning the relocation of Navajos and Hopis from partitioned lands.

The people of Big Mountain intended to make it clear that they had no intention of going anywhere. Behind Lavis they had erected the insignia of the newly formed Big Mountain Committee Against the Fence: a rifle and peace pipe crossed in an X pattern within a circular shield formed by the four sacred mountains of the Navajos. "American Indian Movement" was printed in block letters at the bottom of the shield.

There is no history of political activism on Big Mountain. People there do not decorate their homes with inverted American flags or political posters, and most have never even heard of environmental impact statements. They took little interest in state or national politics until the 1974 elections, when they were part of the record Navajo turnout to vote against Senator Barry Goldwater and Representative Sam Steiger because they had supported the land dispute legislation. Their association with Larry Anderson and AIM was a calculated political act. They knew it would draw a response from Washington that a small group of isolated, traditional Navajos could not achieve on their own. They were angry—"sore inside," as some of them said—and they saw their situation as desperate. They wanted attention from those who presumed to divide their land and expel them from it.

The people addressed Lavis with anger that was both calculated and deeply felt. Nancy Walters spoke into a microphone that had been rigged to a car battery as she read a statement from the Committee Against the Fence, charging that the federal government "has attacked our rights to live on our land as peaceful people," and pledging not to be "forced on the Long Walk of relocation."

The reference was to Navajo subjugation 114 years earlier at the hands of Kit Carson, who in 1863 directed Army troops that starved the tribe out of their mountain and canyon camps and drove them on the Long Walk of over 400 miles across the New Mexican desert to the Bosque Redondo, a sterile land in east-central New Mexico.

"It seems like Custer's last stand is coming," Walters said. "The federal government seems to continue its provocation without regard for our rights. If this has to come to a situation similar to Wounded Knee in 1973, then we are ready to stand as a people." Nancy Walters was born and raised on Big Mountain. She works as a secretary in the BIA schools at Tuba City; her mother and dozens of relatives remain on Big Mountain. She regards Big Mountain as home. Tuba City, as far as she is concerned, is just a place for work.

Ruth Benally did not come to the microphone to make her statement. She stepped abruptly into the circle and aimed a finger at Hawley Atkinson, who sat shivering under the brim of his cowboy hat. "I can see you are cold," she said in rapid-fire Navajo. "What would happen to us if we were forced from this place and had to go someplace else? We would freeze." Atkinson couldn't understand the words, but the meaning was clear even without translation.

Pauline Whitesinger's message to Lavis was a demand that Washington keep hands off. "This land means everything to us," she said through interpretation. "From now on, don't bother our land, our water, or our mountain. These things were placed here for us to use forever."

While more speakers took their turns at the microphone, Navajo women stood four deep in a line behind Samuel Pete, the director of the tribe's Land Dispute Commission, and his assistant, Jesse Thompson. The two men hunched over the hood of a pickup and wrote on yellow legal pads as the women dictated to them in Navajo. All afternoon women approached the man from Washington, solemnly shook his hand, and gave him their messages. The messages were written in a language they did not understand because they had not attended school, but they knew it was the language of the law that was exerting a powerful influence over their lives.

To the disappointment of the Navajos, Lavis spoke for less than a minute. He said he had not come to make a statement, but to listen to the people and see their land. Next day, Lavis was in Window Rock at a public meeting to discuss means of easing the angry mood at Big Mountain. He heard Peter MacDonald speak about the gap in understanding between traditional Navajos and the American Congress and courts. "We can go to them and say, 'It's written here, the Congress says it or the courts say it.' But they have no appreciation for anything that is on paper. Throughout all these years the only law they know is the law that has been handed down by the legends and the traditions of the culture in which they live. But when you say 'It's written down,' they say 'Don't talk to me about it—tell me where it is in my culture and then I'll understand.' It is a very difficult thing to go out to these communities and talk about the law, because they don't understand that. They say 'Don't talk to me about the law, I don't understand it, I probably never will.' "

In an interview with the *Navajo Times*, Lavis made it clear that he had reached a level of understanding of the land dispute not available to him when he was on Paul Fannin's staff. He said he felt that "in this case we probably didn't realize just exactly what kind of impact [the 1974 land dispute legislation] was going to have with people who are not as involved in the legislative process as we are."[1]

Terminating a Way of Life

In his office at the rear of the Dinnebito Trading Post, Elijah Blair said Pauline Whitesinger and Ruth Benally are representative of many Navajos in the Big Mountain area who "will never move off unless you go up there with the National Guard and carry them off first." Blair, who converses with his customers in Navajo, said the federal relocation program is a frequent topic of discussion in the store. "Psychologically, it has really got these people upset," he said. "It is really disturbing them. I've seen them crying in the store over it. About the time partition was made, a lady came up to me and said, 'Help us! They're going to take away our land!' And she was crying." Blair said relocation would be especially destructive to the elderly Navajos, those "who think this is really the only way of life."

The way of life for most Navajos who have grown up without a formal education was the way of life for nearly all Navajos from the sixteenth century to the middle of the twentieth century. Everything depended on the sheep. The flock provided food, clothing, and eventually—through the trading post—access to the manufactured goods of the off-reservation world. Sheep were the primary measure of wealth, security, and self-esteem.

As the tribe's population grew after release from internment at the Bosque Redondo in 1868, pressure on the land increased correspondingly. From 15,000 in 1868, the Navajos grew to 40,000 in 1940, heading toward their current level of more than 150,000. Each new family added sheep to a range which by the 1930s could no longer sustain the livestock economy. The history of Big Mountain offers a case in point.

The first family to make extensive use of Big Mountain grazing lands entered the area after their release in 1868 from the Bosque Redondo. Ashike Bizheh-e was an infant when his family received sheep, a wagon, and tools from government agents at Fort Defiance and moved west to vacant land outside the 1868 treaty reservation. In 1884, Ashike Bizheh-e's wife gave birth to twin sons in an area just south of the Dinnebito Trading Post. One of the boys died in infancy; the other became known in manhood as Hosteen Béésh Bí Woo' (Mister Goldtooth) and had five children. These five children are the core of today's grandparents at Big Mountain. Together with their children and grandchildren, they form a tightly integrated web of the Tábaah (Edge of the Water), Naakaii Dine'é (Mexican People), and Tł'ízí Łání (Many-goats) clans. Unlike many of their children and all of their grandchildren, they did not attend school, have no job skills, and speak little or no English. Their way of life has faded because of the steady diminution of the land available for grazing and because young, educated Navajo adults increasingly seek jobs away from home in the wage economy of towns both on and off the reservation.

One hundred years ago, when there were no practical alternatives to sheep raising and when the federal government encouraged them to expand their flocks, the entire tribe was living the traditional life. Beginning with the federal program of stock reduction in the 1930s and most dramatically with World War II, which introduced Navajos for the first time in large numbers to the wage economy by means of military service and war-related work and which was followed by a boom in school construction on the reservation, younger Navajos have moved inexorably away from strict dependence on livestock.

But while the Navajos' dependence on the land for economic

support has decreased in recent generations, their emotional root-edness in the land remains firm, and they have not sought to merge themselves with the mainstream of American life. This is something that non-Indian Americans have difficulty understanding. As one writer put it, many non-Indians, "believing in the melting pot, feel Indians will always be second-class citizens until they leave the reservations, move into the mainstream, and begin to enjoy the benefits offered by the majority society. Others view the separatist reservation system as contrary to an abstract American ideal of equality."[2]

The Navajos have long been known for their ability to adapt to different cultures. Several thousand of them now live in off-reservation towns and cities. Many have moved there with the help of a program operated by the BIA that until recently was called the Relocation Program. Its name has been changed to Employment Assistance because the former name smacked of government paternalism and recalled less benevolent relocations of Indians in the nineteenth century. Many, if not most, of the Navajos who leave the reservation through this program, however, eventually return home, unable to cope in an environment they find utterly alien. Once they are back home, they are willing to do almost anything to stay.

Elijah Blair said about fifty Navajos from the Big Mountain area work as seasonal laborers for railroads across the West. Perhaps another fifteen are employed at the Peabody Coal Company mine about thirty miles north on Black Mesa. Several dozen men and women work nearby at the Rocky Ridge BIA school, Blair's trading post, or the Hardrock mission and school. Others find jobs in towns on the reservation. Still others take part in government-funded, tribally administered work projects at the Hardrock chapter house, one of 104 local units of Navajo government. Many receive welfare, free commodity foods, and social security.

Sioux author Vine Deloria, Jr. explained the Indian's passionate need for a land base this way: "The tribal-communal way of life . . . views land as the most vital part of man's existence. It is THEIRS. It supports them, tells them where they live, and defines for them HOW they live. . . . it provides a center of the universe for the group that lives on it. As such, the people who hold land in this way always have a home to go to. Their identity is secure. They live with it and do not abstract themselves from it."[3]

Throughout most of the history of the United States, government agents and missionaries have opposed Indian values as unenlightened, as hindrances to progress. Then in the 1960s American public opinion for the first time began to sympathize with the Indian desire to remain Indian. President Lyndon Johnson proposed a "new goal" for Indian programs. He said Indians should be allowed "an opportunity to remain on their homelands, if they choose, without surrendering their dignity; and opportunity to move into the towns and cities of America, if they choose, equipped with the skills to live in equality and dignity."[4]

There are no easy ways to achieve the goals outlined by President Johnson. To varying degrees, all Indians are confronted with the "between two worlds" dilemma. Some, having lost their grounding in tradition and unable to adopt the values of the larger American society, are overwhelmed by confusion and despair. The significance of President Johnson's message was that it represented an important change in the official government attitude toward Indian societies. The tragedy of the government's program to settle the Navajo-Hopi land dispute is that it is bringing about societal disruption on a massive, concentrated scale. It is denying thousands of Navajos the choice and dignity President Johnson spoke of. It is forcing them to abandon the life of their fathers, compelling them to leave their homelands—regardless of their abilities or inclinations to change. The tragedy is especially acute for the middle-aged and elderly Navajos who, living in what is one of the most physically and culturally isolated regions of the United States, completely lack the skills and general cultural mobility to start a new life. Their way of life, which has been fading gradually, is being abruptly terminated by an act of Congress.

"Are They Trying to Kill Us?"

Alice Chase was the supervisor and secretary of the Comprehensive Education and Training Act (CETA) program at the Hardrock chapter house in late 1978. The program paid $2.65 per hour to thirty-seven men and women chosen for employment training from the rolls of those receiving federal general assistance funds. The CETA women weave sash belts and rugs for sale by the chapter; the men build and remodel homes. CETA provides an important boost to the depressed economy of the Hardrock chapter. But the boost is dependent on continuance of federal funding. There are no regularly available jobs in Hardrock to which CETA workers can graduate.

Alice Chase is one of those Navajo young people who have not moved away from home even after acquiring skills that would allow her to earn a living in a town. She recognizes that her position is tenuous, that if funding for CETA is cut off, the secretarial skills she learned at Lamson Business College in Phoenix would be useless at home. But home is where she hopes to stay.

Betty Wesley returned home for the summer in May 1978 after completing her sophomore year at Arizona State University, where she was majoring in health education. Betty spoke pointedly about the lack of opportunity near home. "When we were in high school, we listened to the people who said we should go to college and then come back home and help," she said. "But when you get back there's no work." The closest places of employment after graduation will be the reservation towns, Tuba City and Chinle. "But we don't know the people over there," she said.

Many young Navajos who have made the move to towns feel as strongly about the land as Alice and Betty and return home on weekends. These young Navajos are now leading the fight against the federal program to settle the Navajo-Hopi land dispute.

Fifty-two-year-old Ruth Benally is married to Joe Benally, one of Ashike Bizheh-e's sons. Three days a week she cooks for the Congregate Meals program for the elderly at Hardrock. She also performs the healing ceremony for people bothered with nightmares and for those warned of danger by the hoot of an owl. When she learned that a reporter was coming to Hardrock to talk with the people there about the land dispute, she waited all afternoon for him at the chapter house. She spoke for two hours about partition and relocation, first making a statement, then answering questions. Her hands chopped the air in front of her, helping the words express her agitation.

"When the time comes, if we don't have any other choice, we are going to use our fists," she said. "No matter how small I am, I'll fight all the way to the end. After we throw our punches, if we get clubbed to death, then they can drag us out." She said she had cooperated with the government's program to reduce livestock—

also a part of the land dispute legislation—in the hope that she would be able to stay on the land. But she drew the line there. "They told us to get rid of our stock. Now they are trying to get rid of us."

Dressed in a green velveteen blouse and brown calico skirt, and wearing a turquoise ring, bracelet, and brooch, she didn't look like a fighter. Her words to Hawley Atkinson that cold day at the end of 1977—"What would happen to us if we were forced from this place and had to go someplace else?"—offer an insight into her fear. She had no doubt that just as Atkinson shook with cold there, she would be miserable if she had to be anywhere else. "Are they trying to kill us?" she asked. "Moving away from here would be dying a slow death."

In order to remain on the land, the people of Big Mountain must export their labor and import government assistance. Ruth Benally's nephew, Danny John, drives the thirty miles one-way to the Peabody mine each day where he earns a wage with which he helps to support his entire extended family. He was one of the organizers of the Big Mountain Committee Against the Fence, which brought the attention of a national radio network to Big Mountain in late 1977.

A reporter for a Flagstaff radio station recorded Bahe Kadenahe's threat that Big Mountain would declare war on the United States if the relocation program were not stopped. Then he fed the threat to the American Contemporary Network, whose editors put it on the air. The reporter said the editors were quite excited about the story, that they had called it "great stuff."

Danny John later explained the threat as an attempt to draw attention to a situation that would otherwise have been ignored. "If you talk, no one pays attention, so we decided this would make people look at us," he said. "We never intended to get guns and put an army together." Still, John insisted the people of Big Mountain will fight to avoid eviction. He wasn't speaking for effect when he said they will "make our stand in a place we know and are known. We would rather die here quickly than in a relocated place where we are not known and not wanted."[5]

The Reverend Carlton Lucas was director of the Hardrock Mission for twenty-five years before leaving in mid 1978. During that time he saw many young Navajos bow to the pressure of economics and cultural change and leave the reservation to find work in southwestern cities and towns. Some made the adjustment; others failed or found that they didn't want to adjust. "They find that life in the city is too much for them," Reverend Lucas said. "They feel lonely and lost, and then they start drinking. After a while they come home. There's no work here, but it's home."

In 1974, while the land-dispute legislation was working its way toward enactment, Reverend Lucas corresponded with Arizona Senators Barry Goldwater and Paul Fannin, warning them that relocation would be devastating to the Navajos. Their replies offer an interesting glimpse into the minds of the two men most responsible for Senate passage of the Navajo-Hopi Land Settlement Act.

On October 21, Senator Goldwater wrote, "I am sure something will be worked out that will not cause a hardship on the Navajos and will be of justice to the Hopi." Senator Fannin said in a letter sent ten days later, "The tremendous opportunity and incentive for Navajos on the area to move should bring about the relocation, unless outside agitation encourages them to 'hold their ground.' The [area of the land dispute] is in the worst condition of any Navajo land; there are much better opportunities in other areas for farming and other employment."

Many of the senators who voted in favor of the land dispute legislation did so at the urging of Senators Goldwater and Fannin. Lacking the time to come to grips with the problem individually, they deferred to the presumed expertise of the home-state senators. As the letters to Reverend Lucas indicate, Arizona's two senators oversimplified the land dispute and were profoundly misinformed about this crisis festering in a remote corner of their state.

Relocation and the Theory of Relativity

Joseph Shelton of Hardrock enlisted in the Marines in 1967, after he received a Selective Service notice to report for a preinduction physical. Sent to Vietnam, he suffered injuries that left him with a twenty-five-percent disability. "It's behind me," he said softly, eyes downcast. "I don't want to talk about it." Following his discharge, Shelton earned an Associate of Science degree in electrical engineering from the Devry Institute of Technology in Phoenix. But the electrical generating stations on the reservation turned down his applications for employment because of his disability, he

said. In 1977, desperate for work, he was hired as a field coordina-
tor for the Navajo and Hopi Indian Relocation Commission. "I
needed the money," he said, shrugging his shoulders. "Financially, I was wiped out."

Now Shelton has to deal with the criticism of Navajo neighbors who say he is working on the side of the Hopis. He sat behind
a desk in the Relocation Commission's trailer next to the Hardrock
chapter house and explained the difficulties of his job. "Every time
we send somebody over to Big Mountain, they get chased off. We
can't even complete the enumeration [of people to be relocated]
because the people think if they fill out the form they are making
an application for relocation. They say they don't want to have anything to do with relocation." The commission's other five field
offices had nearly completed their enumerations in mid 1978, but
the list of Big Mountain families who refused to be counted had
reached several dozen.

Drawing from his technical background, Shelton said that trying
to explain the Navajo-Hopi Land Settlement Act to a traditional
Navajo is like trying to explain Einstein's theory of relativity or
Maxwell's equation to someone who has not studied physics. "But
it's the law," he said with another shrug. "It went through the
routine legislative process. I think the people need to prepare
themselves for relocation in case it becomes a reality."

The Relocation Commission is due to submit to Congress by
April 1981 its plan to move Navajos and Hopis out of partitioned
lands. Upon approval of the plan by Congress, a five-year period
will begin during which relocation is to be completed. The principal
benefit that the 1974 legislation authorized the commission to provide is a new house. The limit on the amount that may be spent for
new homes has been raised several times since 1974, primarily
because of inflation. By the beginning of 1980, a family of three or
fewer persons could receive up to $39,700 for a new house, and a
family of four or more could receive up to $57,000. In addition, the
law authorized the commission to provide a graduated bonus payment as an incentive for families to relocate early. Those who
moved in the first year of the relocation period will receive a
$5,000 bonus; those who move in the fourth year will receive
$2,000. Shelton said he expects many Navajos will still be at home
when the relocation period ends. He expects Big Mountain and
other areas to form pockets of resistance to the relocation program.

Shelton adjusted his glasses, preparing to explain why he thought the relocation program is in for trouble. "The law is supposed to solve the problem, but I think it is going to create more," he said. "The people have lived all their lives there. The land is sacred to them. It's like an altar to them. They don't see any reason for them to move. The land is in our culture; it's been drilled into us." A look of exasperation came across his thin, intellectual face. "I don't suppose we can explain it to someone else."

Maps taped to the wood panels behind Shelton had the partitioned lands plotted into neat square grids. Larger maps spread out on the desk before him assigned numbers to the homes of all Navajo families living on lands partitioned to the Hopis. Of the 276,452 acres in the Hardrock chapter, 165,871 had been awarded to the Hopis.

The Road to Big Mountain

A trip to Big Mountain in anything other than a pickup truck is an act of naive faith. The graded road that begins at the edge of Arizona Highway 264, forty-five miles east of Tuba City, runs a forty-mile northward course past the Dinnebito Trading Post and the Rocky Ridge School and on to the Peabody mine. About eighteen miles along this route it drops off into a narrow slot of a road that is nothing more than two tracks separated by a high center of grass and sagebrush, winding across a network of canyons and around boulders, trees, and sand piles. If a visitor asks how the people can move about after a bad rain or when the snow melts, he learns they sometimes cannot, because the roads become rivers of mud. In early 1978, Army and National Guard helicopters carried Navajo policemen to deliver food, water, and hay to hundreds of families stuck in the soggy earth of northeastern Arizona. The name of the exercise was Operation Mudlift.

Several miles before it reaches Pauline Whitesinger's place the road passes the sheep camp that Fannie Herbert's family shares with the family of her sister. The homestead consists of a small concrete house and three hogans, two in the old style of timber chinked with mud, and a newer one with a tarpaper roof and walls made of smoothly cut lumber. The two families share a corral for their common flock. Someone pointed out that the land here has been partitioned to the Hopis. Mrs. Herbert smiled wanly and said, "I'm a Hopi now." A young daughter hid in the folds of her voluminous skirt.

A fancy Ford XLT pickup was parked in front of the old hogans. It belonged to Mrs. Herbert's nephew, who worked seasonally for the Union Pacific Railroad and was now repairing track in Wyoming. Mrs. Herbert said she would relocate only if she could take her sheep. "If you go outside the reservation, the people there have occupations," she explained in Navajo. Mrs. Herbert guessed she was thirty-eight years old. She has never been to school and speaks no English. She knows little of life beyond Big Mountain. The law calling for partition and relocation encircles her life like a huge question mark punctuating a language she does not understand.

"I Am Used to This Place"

"What is it really, the problem for moving?" Roberta Blackgoat, neighbor and half-sister to Pauline Whitesinger, asked as she spun gray wool for the rug in the loom next to her. "Is it really no chance for us to stay?" Unlike most of the people of her generation on Big Mountain, Mrs. Blackgoat has had some schooling. She finished seventh grade at the Phoenix Indian School before coming home to stay. She spoke in English about the stock reduction program operated by the BIA to which she had sold seventy of her eight-four sheep. Reduction was imposed on all Navajos in the land dispute area to bring the stock population down to the carrying capacity of the range and—in the area partitioned to the Hopis—to protect the range for subsequent Hopi use. To encourage cooperation, the BIA paid 150 percent of the market value for the stock. They also sent out letters announcing that stock would be confiscated from those who would not sell their animals. Mrs. Blackgoat was angry about the loss of her sheep. "The money goes like cotton candy," she said. "If I have sheep, I have the money. That's where I keep the money safe. The sheep is my bank."

Mrs. Blackgoat receives $107 each month in Supplemental Security Income for herself and $66 for the support of her only dependent child, Vivian, a senior at Coconino High in Flagstaff. Her other five children are grown and live with their families away from Big Mountain. In late 1977, Cecilia was in training to be a rehabilitation counselor in Flagstaff. Bessie was also in Flagstaff, where her husband was a heavy equipment operator. Betty and her husband lived on-reservation at Kayenta, a small town near the Peabody mine, where he managed a trading post. Danny taught and did counseling at Coconino High, and Harry was a police sergeant at Tuba City. All the children return home frequently and help support their mother. "When they get paid, they bring me a pop," she laughed and flashed a smile that lit up the room. "That makes me proud." Mrs. Blackgoat had just returned from a shopping trip to Flagstaff with her daughter-in-law, and large grocery sacks filled the wood table in her one-room stone-block house.

As the visitors approached the sheep camp of Pauline Whitesinger, the late autumn sun was easing behind a ridge and lit the clouds in an orange glow. A commercial airliner scratched a thin white line in the darkening sky. Mrs. Whitesinger had just returned her flock to the corral. The bell hanging from a goat's neck clanged a tin sound. Cedar smoke drifted from the hogan's smoke hole. It was several months since the incident with the fence crew, and Mrs. Whitesinger had moved into an old log-and-mud hogan about a mile from her house.

A sturdily built woman with a round face, Mrs. Whitesinger said she was tired of speaking with reporters. In the time since she confronted the fence crew, Mrs. Whitesinger had been interviewed by Molly Ivins of the *New York Times* and Maggie Wilson of the *Arizona Republic*. Her husband had died several years previously, and her children were all away. Ruby was living in Provo, Utah. Philip and Paul were working at the Indian Health Service hospital at Tuba City, where Bonnie, the youngest, attended the BIA high school.

Mrs. Whitesinger moves with her sheep among several sheep camps within an area of several square miles, rotating her grazing to provide the best feed for her flock. Her hogan is about ten feet in diameter. Metal pans lie on the earth floor around the wood-burning stove, a Coleman lantern hangs from a nail above the sheepskin she uses as a bed, and a radio is next to her loom. The only steady source of contact with the world beyond Big Mountain, the radio brings her several hours of Navajo-language programs each day from stations in Holbrook and Flagstaff, where merchants do much of their business with Navajos and sell everything from pickups to hamburgers with Navajo-language advertising.

Most of all, Mrs. Whitesinger likes to listen to Harry Billie on

KDJI in Holbrook, whose high-octane, rapidfire Navajo assaults the microphone like an air hammer, baffling the tourists who pick him up on Interstate 40 and keeping thousands of his Navajo faithful in touch with what's happening on the reservation. On one early morning show in June 1978, the public service announcements went like this: the Indian Health Service Cancer Control Project was touring with a mobile clinic; the White Cone chapter was having a meeting; the rodeo movie *J. W. Coop* was showing at Indian Wells; Slim and Kay Tahe were putting on a Squaw Dance at their place near Toyei; the All-Indian Rodeo Cowboys Association was meeting to plan its season. The songs ran the musical gamut, from the Klagetoh Singers and their Navajo Songs About Love to the pop music of Jackson Browne to the country-western of Gary Stewart. Billie mixes in some English, throwing his words cheerfully into the microphone. "This is the Friday morning go-round show on KDJI from Holbrook, Arizona! We got sixty degrees under clear skies! Good morning, good morning, good morning to you! This song goes out to all my paleface friends! All Riiight! Ten Four!!"

Mrs. Whitesinger sat on a rock outside her hogan and scratched the dirt at her feet, as she explained why she could not accept relocation. "I think there is no way we can survive if we get moved to some other land away from ours," she said through interpretation. "We are just going to waste away. People tell me to move, but I've got no place to go. I am not moving anywhere, that is certain. If we uneducated people move out of here, we would probably just last two or three days."

Mrs. Whitesinger's fear of relocation is based on a clear understanding of who she is and of who she is not. She is a traditional Navajo, with more in common with the generations of Navajos before her, whose lives were defined by land and family and livestock, than with her own children. She is not one of the younger generation of Navajos who have been to school and learned to speak English and function according to the rules of Anglo society. She is firm in the conviction that it is too late for her to learn about the new world of her children. She shook her head from side to side, saying that a reporter once asked her why she liked living as she does. "Now that's a stupid question, don't you think? I like it here because I was born here and because I am used to this place." It was a statement without sentimentality, a simple statement of who Pauline Whitesinger is. For her there can be no other life, no other place, even if she can live here only with a few sheep left over after stock reduction, help from her children, and a welfare check from the federal government. Big Mountain is the middle of nowhere for someone from the outside world. But to Pauline Whitesinger, it is the center of everything. "This is where I will die of old age," she told the fence-crew foreman.

Writing in the *New York Times* after her visit to Big Mountain, Molly Ivins described the Navajo values that make Paul Fannin's assertions of "opportunity" for the relocatees simplistic and empty. "For many of the traditionalists, money has little or no value," Ivins wrote. "They live in a barter, not a cash economy. They don't want new houses. They want to keep their sheep and the hogans of their grandparents."[6]

There is another reason Mrs. Whitesinger is clinging to the land like the rugged plants that somehow draw sustenance from it. Her religion tells her she is a part of this land. But she is superstitious about talking of such things to an outsider. The outsider wouldn't understand anyway.

Gladys Reichard, an anthropologist who studied Navajo religion for many years, wrote that Navajo religion "must be seen as a design in harmony, a striving for rapport between man and every phase of nature, the earth and the waters under the earth, and the sky and the 'land beyond the sky,' and of course the earth and everything on and in it."[7] Nothing in her experience on Big Mountain had prepared Mrs. Whitesinger for the challenge to that harmony represented by the Navajo-Hopi Land Settlement Act.

2
The Navajos: The People, Their Land, and the Beginnings of the Land Dispute

The livestock that came with the Spanish conquistadores to the Southwest in the 1500s brought little change to the Pueblos, who used the animals as a supplement to their sophisticated agricultural system. But for the Navajos, stock, and especially sheep, were a blessing that changed the very foundation of life. In the four centuries since Coronado, sheep have become so central to the Navajo conception of life and of themselves that myth says the tribe has always had them. Traditional Navajos believe sheep are a gift of the Holy People, who expect the Navajos to nurture and protect them. In return for this care and observance of ritual, the Holy People will provide the rain to nourish the earth which feeds the sheep. So profound is the symbolic identification of sheep with well-being that during the Yei-Bi-Chei ceremony tips of sheep organs are fed to the patient to enhance his recovery.

During their long migration into the Southwest from Alaska,

the Navajos depended on wild plants and animals for their sustenance. Gradually, through contact with the Pueblos, they gained knowledge of agriculture, and some tended fields of corn, beans, and squash. The name "Navajo" probably derives from a Tewa Pueblo word meaning "large area of cultivated lands," but its exact origin is uncertain.[1] Most Navajos never took to the sedentary life of farming, however, and structured their lives around their sheep. Responding always to the needs of the flock, living in brush shelters that could be erected quickly, the Navajos moved continually for much of the year to find fresh grazing and new water. During the winter months they lived in huts fashioned from logs and mud, called hogans.

When the Americans conquered the Southwest in 1846, raiding was still an important part of Navajo life. Small groups of horsemen rode down upon Pueblos, Spanish villages, and Anglo settlements in New Mexico to steal stock and seize captives who could be used as slaves or sold in the active southwestern slave trade. Anthropologist Edward Spicer writes that killing, "except in some instances of revenge, was entirely incidental to acquiring goods and animals." The Navajos, in turn, were raided by New Mexican slave traders. Spicer reports that by 1860 "there were as many as five to six thousand Navajo slaves living with families in the New Mexican villages."[2]

Americans replaced Mexicans as the dominant power along the Rio Grande in 1846 and set out confidently to bring order to the huge area acquired by the 1848 Treaty of Guadalupe Hidalgo. Their peace-making efforts among the Navajo were frustrated because, contrary to the belief of the U.S. Army, the Navajos were not consolidated as a political or military entity. They were a tribe by virtue of common language and culture, and they called themselves "Diné," The People, distinct from all others. The Navajos were organized in autonomous bands of from ten to forty families under the leadership of a headman; treaties entered into by one band could not bind others. To the dismay of the Army and the New Mexican settlers, raiding continued.

New Mexico was in an uproar throughout the 1850s as settlers angrily demanded action from the Army. The conflict was aggravated by New Mexicans who sent their flocks farther and farther west, taking over Navajo grazing lands and presenting ever more convenient targets for raiding parties. In 1863 the new military

commander in New Mexico, Brig. Gen. James Carleton, prepared
to launch a sustained assault on the Navajos and Mescalero Apaches.
Carleton planned to drive the Indians from their lands and resettle
them on a reservation along the Pecos River in east-central New
Mexico. To supervise the reservation, Carleton would build a fort
at a location called Bosque Redondo, Spanish for "Circular Grove."
It would be named Fort Sumner, in honor of Carleton's predecessor, Gen. Edwin Vose Sumner. "Too long have they roamed lords
over this extensive and valuable tract of country," Carleton wrote
of the Indians.[3] "They are entitled to a portion of it for their maintenance but no more." Carleton also recognized that removal of the
Navajos would open up their land for development of its mineral
resources, which he believed to be extensive.[4]

The spearhead of Carleton's Indian removal policy was Kit
Carson, who had run away from his Missouri home in 1824 at the
age of fifteen and had achieved fame as a Rocky Mountain fur
trapper and guide for John C. Frémont's explorations of the West.
Carson was appointed Indian agent for New Mexico in 1854 and
left that post at the beginning of the Civil War to serve with the
Union forces of the First New Mexico Volunteer Infantry. While
the sons of immigrants clashed in waves of Blue and Gray far to the
east, Col. Kit Carson led seven hundred men in a very different
war.

By March of 1863, some four hundred Mescaleros were interned
at Bosque Redondo and Carson could turn his attention to the
much more numerous Navajos. With the help of Utes and Hopis,
Carson launched a brutal and unrelenting search-and-destroy campaign. His men crisscrossed Navajo country throughout the summer and fall, destroying crops, butchering sheep, putting the ax to
peach trees. Carleton's Indian policy was being applied with devastating effect. The Navajos could either surrender or starve.

Carleton's design was that the Navajos should give up their
sheepherding way of life and become farmers like the Pueblos. He
told Washington that the Army "can feed them cheaper than we
can fight them."[5] In a letter to Gen. Lorenzo Thomas, Carleton
described his aims as benevolent, even gentle. He said he intended to

> gather them together little by little, on to a reservation away
> from the haunts and hiding places of their country, and then

to be kind to them; there teach their children how to read and write; teach them the arts of peace; teach them the truths of Christianity. Soon they will acquire new habits, new ideas, new modes of life; the old Indians will die off, and carry with them all the latent longings for murdering and robbing; the young ones will take their places without these longings; and thus, little by little, they will become a happy and contented people, and Navajo wars will be remembered only as something that belongs entirely to the past.[6]

Carleton's soothing prose contrasts interestingly with a letter he received from Kit Carson, describing a group of Navajos who had surrendered at Fort Defiance and relating how thoroughly the Navajos were being humbled in the severest hour of their history:

Judging from the appearance of these captives, the generality of the Navajos are completely destitute. They are almost entirely naked, and had it not been for the unusual growth of the piñon berry this year, they must have been without any description of food. . . . The dread of being discovered by my Scouting parties which are continually in the field, prevents them from building fires for warmth, and this adds greatly to the horrors of their situation, when all the severity of winter in their mountains must be borne by them without protection.[7]

One by one, Navajo bands surrendered to Carson's soldiers. In March 1864, twenty-four hundred Navajos were taken on the "Long Walk" to Bosque Redondo. By the end of April, another thirty-five hundred had begun the trek. Some found sanctuary in the depths of the Grand Canyon, on top of Black Mesa, north of the San Juan River, and in other areas which the soldiers did not penetrate. But approximately eighty-five hundred Navajos were eventually relocated to the Bosque.

From the beginning, Carleton's reservation on the Pecos was a fiasco. Parasites ravaged the corn crop, while highly alkaline water struck down the captives with dysentery. Unable to obtain adequate logistical support, Carleton reduced already meager rations. Weak and dispirited in a hostile environment, Navajos, prodded by bayonets, went to work in the fields. Those who could escaped.

The Army finally recognized the futility of Carleton's experiment. "Would any sensible man select a spot for a reservation for 8,000 Indians where the water is scarcely bearable, where the soil is poor and cold, and where the muskite [mesquite] roots 12 miles distant are the only wood for the Indians to use?" the man who replaced Carleton wrote.[8] In May 1868, Gen. William Tecumseh Sherman came to the Bosque Redondo at the head of the Indian Peace Commission. When the Navajos turned aside Sherman's suggestion that they accept relocation to the Indian Territory south of Kansas, he agreed to a treaty that set aside a rectangular 3.5-million-acre reservation straddling the New Mexico–Arizona border. On the morning of June 1, a date now observed as a tribal holiday, twenty-nine Navajo headmen and former war chiefs signed the treaty with X marks, and the Navajos were soon on their way home in a long column escorted by Army troops.

"When we saw the top of the mountain from Albuquerque, we wondered if it was our mountain, and we felt like talking to the ground, we loved it so, and some of the old men and women cried with joy when they reached their homes," said Manuelito, one of the signers of the treaty.[9] The long Navajo nightmare, the Long Walk, was over. Tales of the humiliating subjugation and banishment have been told around hogan fires to each succeeding generation of Navajos, nourishing profound suspicion of white men and an even deeper attachment to the land bound by the Four Sacred Mountains.

Recovering from the Long Walk

Having failed in its attempts to make the Navajos a tribe of farmers, the government set out to help them reestablish themselves as sheep raisers. Thousands of sheep and goats were issued to the families that returned from the Long Walk, and Indian agents at Fort Defiance encouraged the Navajos to expand their flocks. It worked. Unlike the Sioux, whose confinement on reservations put an end to a way of life based on pursuit of the buffalo and forced them into dependence on Washington, the Navajos began six decades of relative prosperity. No longer fearing raids from enemies, they could concentrate on building an economy unique among American Indians.[10]

Trading posts were a key element in this economy's success. The first was established in 1871. Traders did business on a six-month credit cycle, allowing their customers to make purchases first against the spring wool crop and then against the fall crop of lambs. Weaving and silversmithing supplemented the income of many families, and such traders as Lorenzo Hubbell found off-reservation markets for Indian crafts.

"Flour, coffee, and sugar—in that order— were the staples most in demand and therefore most in supply at the old trading posts," Frank McNitt wrote in *The Indian Traders*. "Tobacco, by the plug or can, was greatly desired but considered more of a luxury than were yards of bright flannel, velveteen, or calico. Canned goods—fruits and vegetables—stocked the shelves in the early eighties, but the variety was limited and not too well regarded by the Indians for twenty or thirty years more."[11] By providing access to the manufactured goods of the off-reservation world, the trading posts enabled the Navajos to be more secure on the land with their sheep than ever before.

A trip to the trading post was an exciting expedition for everyone in the family—second only to the trips to ceremonial sings in social importance. The family gathered their wool or lambs, donned their best clothes and jewelry, and set out on a trip that often lasted overnight. Bargaining between trader and customer was done entirely in Navajo, and Navajos lingered for hours deciding what they would take in trade after the debts of the past six months had been paid. They enjoyed conversation with old friends, sized up a kerosene lantern, savored a can of tomatoes. "The scene . . . was in the extreme animated and picturesque, altho' the old den was so dark that upon first entering it was difficult to distinguish the mass of parti-colored blankets, men, squaws, and papooses pressed against the counter," Army Lt. John Bourke wrote. "The Navajos are keen at a bargain and as each unpacked his ponies and ripped open the blankets full of wool he had brought to market, he acted as if he knew its value and meant to get it."[12] Outside the children played with others who had come to trade, and those who had come from especially far away could find accommodations in the guest hogan next to the trading post. A family might finish its trip to the trading post by buying that kerosene lantern and maybe a new saddle before beginning its long ride home, certainly with the latest news and gossip, and possibly with credit remaining on the trader's books. In the sequestered world of the reservation, the trader was the only white man with whom many Navajos developed an acquaintance.

The 1882 Executive Order

In the 1870s and 1880s, while the Navajos were recovering from wounds inflicted at Bosque Redondo, events were unfolding that would set the stage for the Navajo-Hopi land dispute and the second Navajo Long Walk a century later. Although the 1868 treaty set aside some of the Navajo homeland as a reservation for the tribe, it also relinquished much of the best Navajo land in western New Mexico to the United States. The tribe's rapid population growth and the absence of marked boundaries were two factors in Navajo settlement outside the treaty reservation. There were others as well. "The Navajos at Fort Sumner had no concept of the geography of their own Navajo Country of the type necessary to understand or visualize the boundaries established by the Treaty of 1868," writes Robert Young, a scholar of Navajo history and the Navajo language. Young points out that Spanish was the intermediate language between the Army and the Navajos and that uneducated former Navajo slaves were used as interpreters. "As a result, the people merely understood that they were free, and they thronged back to the areas that they occupied before they were taken to Fort Sumner, neither knowing nor caring that such areas were outside the treaty boundaries."[13]

In response to the Navajo settlement pattern, and because most of the land near the reservation was of little interest to non-Indians, the reservation was expanded several times. The first additions were made in 1878, on the west and south sides of the reservation; and in 1880, additions were made on the eastern side.

In 1876, the Indian agent for the Hopi Agency at Keams Canyon wrote to the commissioner of Indian affairs, urging the creation of an exclusive Hopi reservation. The agent was concerned about the increasing presence of Mormon and Navajo settlers in close proximity to the Hopi mesas. Similar recommendations were made in 1878, 1880, and 1882 and, for the most part, were not acknowledged by officials in Washington. In these later years, a succession of Hopi agents expressed alarm that Navajos were encroaching upon Hopi farm lands and water supplies near the mesas.

Navajos had been living near the mesas at least intermittently since 1629, but it was only after the Long Walk that their population, the numbers of their stock, and the loss of lands in New Mexico demanded an expansion to the west. It has been estimated that over half the tribe were living outside the Treaty Reservation on December 16, 1882, the day President Chester A. Arthur signed an excutive order creating a 2,472,095-acre reservation "for the use and occupancy of the Moqui [Hopi] and such other Indians as the Secretary of the Interior may see fit to settle thereon." Three to six hundred Navajos and eighteen hundred Hopis were living within the boundaries of the 1882 Reservation at that time.

Although Arthur's executive order was preceded by reports of Navajo encroachment, the primary impetus for creation of the 1882 Reservation was the desire of Hopi agent J. H. Fleming to expel two Anglos, Sullivan and Merritt, whom Fleming believed to be meddlers in Hopi affairs. In October 1882, after Fleming advised Commissioner of Indian Affairs Hiram Price that he had expelled Sullivan from the Hopi villages, Price informed his agent that he could not legally expel anyone because no Hopi land had been withdrawn from the public domain. A month later Fleming advised Price that he was having more trouble with Sullivan and threatened to resign if a way could not be found to get rid of the troublemakers. On November 27, Commissioner Price directed Fleming to provide a description of boundaries for a reservation that would include the "Moqui villages and agency and [be] large enough to meet all needful purposes and no larger." The harassed Indian agent wasted no time, sending off his proposed boundaries a week later to Price, who drafted an executive order and sent it off to the Secretary of the Interior on December 13. Three days later President Arthur signed the order as drafted, giving Fleming the authority to evict Sullivan and Merritt, which he did immediately and with great satisfaction. On December 26, Fleming resigned.[14]

A century later, in consideration of the human and legal nightmares of the Navajo-Hopi land dispute—the anguish of relocation and the battles in the federal courts, Congress, and the Interior Department over ownership of the 1882 Reservation—the circumstances surrounding the executive order can only be seen as colossally unfortunate. In fewer than thirty days, Fleming's frantic determination to get rid of two troublemakers had stirred Washington to an action that has become the historic basis for removing several thousand Indians from their homes. In submitting his recommendations, Fleming showed a greater concern for geographic neatness than for the "needful purposes" of the Hopis. He described a rectangle, about seventy miles long and fifty-five miles wide, whose dimensions were one degree of latitude and one degree of longitude. Its eastern and western boundaries, respectively, were the 110th and 111th meridians; its southern boundary was halfway between the 35th and 36th parallels, and its northern boundary was exactly halfway between the 36th and 37th parallels. Certainly the executive order was prepared hastily. It also seems to have been prepared with little care.

It is doubtful that the Hopis and Navajos even knew of the hurried series of events in Washington at the end of 1882. On the reservation itself there were no discernible signs of change except for the absence of Sullivan and Merritt. The boundaries were not marked, and no effort was made to prevent or even discourage Navajo settlement of the lands within the reservation. Indeed, the order had made legal room for "other Indians" besides the Hopis. And so, for both tribes, President Arthur's order brought no immediate change.

The West was still in ferment in 1882, and the United States was still consolidating its claim to the vast frontier. Custer's debacle at the Little Big Horn was only six years in the past. Just five years previously Chief Joseph, whose Nez Perce had heroically resisted repeated takings of land promised to them by treaty, surrendered with memorable words: "I am tired. My heart is sick and sad. From where the sun now stands, I will fight no more forever." Geronimo, most feared of the Apache war leaders, who so vengefully defied the taking of his homeland, would give up the fight in 1886. Two years after that, a Paiute named Wovoka would have a vision that began the desperate cult of the Ghost Dance, which promised restoration of Indian land and the elimination of the white man. In 1890 the massacre at Wounded Knee, where the Seventh Cavalry had been sent in nervous response to Ghost Dance fervor, brought a brutal end to a tragic era.

As Indian America retreated, white America advanced. In 1880 only about five thousand people lived in Los Angeles. Then came the railroad. When President Arthur responded to Indian agent Fleming's exasperation with his executive order, the Atlantic and Pacific Railroad was laying track across northern Arizona in a line forty miles south of the executive order reservation. The *Prescott Miner* was confident that because of the railroad "commerce will open up anew, business revive, mining take a sudden start, immigration come in, money become plentiful, property advance in price, labor be in demand, towns spring up, our valleys and hills be settled, and general prosperity follow."[15] For white America it was an age of exuberant, inexorable expansion.

Forty Years of Federal Vacillation

Throughout the first four decades after establishment of the 1882 reservation, federal policy on rights to the reservation was characterized by a pattern of vacillation that hardened the positions of the Navajos and Hopis and compounded the difficulty of resolving their dispute. That vacillation was born of a conflict between two federal concerns: a desire to protect the Hopis from Navajo expansion, and a recognition that the 1882 reservation was far larger than the Hopis needed. Another factor may have been outright indifference in Washington to the struggle between two Indian tribes over a piece of desert in Arizona.

The federal pattern was set early, as illustrated by the series of events that began in 1888, when Herbert Welsh, corresponding secretary for the Indian Rights Association, visited the Hopis. He reported to the secretary of the interior that the Hopis had complained of the "continual intrusions and depredations of the Navajos, who steal their corn, their melons, their horses, and who in many cases have settled upon their reservation, and treat the [Hopi] lands as though they belonged to them, making use of the Moqui water springs and driving the lawful owners from them. . . ."[16]

Upon receiving the report, Interior Secretary William Vilas wrote to the secretary of war requesting that a company of troops be dispatched to the area with instructions to "remove all Navajo Indians found trespassing with their herds and flocks on the Moqui Reservation and to notify them that their depredations must cease and that they must keep within their own reservation." An army expedition requested by Secretary Vilas reached the 1882 reservation in December 1888. It took no action, however, because the commanding officer believed that forcible eviction during the rugged northern Arizona winter would have caused severe hardship. The troops left the area after warning the Navajos that their depredations must cease.

In 1890 Indian Commissioner T. J. Morgan took note of Hopi complaints against the Navajos and in the same correspondence remarked that "their reservation is much larger than they use or will ever need." Morgan went so far as to suggest that it would be "a great benefit" to the Hopis if a portion of the reservation were sold and wagons, horses, and plows given to the Hopis in return.[17]

The overriding concern of agents in the field was that the Navajos be kept at some reasonable distance from the Hopis. In 1891, Hopi agent George Parker and trader Thomas Keam decided that the Hopis would be protected if the Navajos were kept out of a circular area with a radius of sixteen miles from the central Hopi village of Mishongnovi. If enforced, this proposal would have had the effect of limiting the Hopis to some 519,000 acres of the 2.5-million-acre 1882 reservation. Nonetheless, the Indian Commissioner apparently acquiesced in the Parker-Keam arrangement, the circular boundary was marked by mounds and monuments, and the commissioner reported to the secretary of the interior that Navajo-Hopi conflicts "have been brought to a satisfactory conclusion."[18]

Of course, they had not been. Navajo expansion into the area immediately around the Hopi mesas continued unabated, and in 1900 Hopi agent Charles Burton reported angrily that the Navajos "have been allowed to encroach upon the Hopi reservation for years, taking possession of the best watering places, best farming, and best pasture land, and a great deal of trouble grows out of this. . . ."[19] Special agent Matthew Murphy reported eight years later that Navajos were living "within three miles of some of the [Hopi] villages."[20]

Despite repeated calls from their agents in Arizona to define a Navajo-Hopi boundary once and for all, government officials in Washington refused to intervene, largely because they feared that eviction of any Navajos would lead to violence. In 1914, a federal irrigation worker among the Hopis suggested that Navajos be removed from the land "immediately around the Hopi villages."[21] Three years later, however, Assistant Indian Commissioner E. B. Merritt acknowledged before a subcommittee of the Committee on Indian Affairs that government officials in Washington "have not seriously considered the question of excluding the Navajos from the area set aside primarily for the Hopi Indians."[22]

The correspondence of government agents to the Hopis in the early 1900s includes frequent expressions of somewhat grudging admiration for the Navajos and exasperation with the Hopis. Their policy had long been to get the Hopis to leave their mesa-top homes and move to open lands below, but this had been for the most part frustrated by Hopi tradition. Government agents were skeptical that the Hopis would use much of the 1882 reservation even if the Navajos were pushed back. Leo Crane, superintendent of the Hopi agency, expressed this sentiment when he responded to a proposal that 1,252,000 acres be reserved for exclusive Hopi use for a period of ten years, following which—if the Hopis had not made use of the land—the Navajos would be permitted in once again. Crane wrote that the Hopis "should not be permitted to eject an industrious (if disobedient) neighbor and then allow the land to waste and his sheep to decline in filthy mesa corrals while he indulges in snake dances, basket dances, clown dances, and the 10,000 other displays he uses as an excuse why he should not be on the range."[23]

Gradually, however, some Hopis began to respond to the government encouragement to move away from the mesas. Those who sought to move out, in the words of one government official, were "running up against the wall of the Navajos." The agent described the Navajos as "forceful and aggressive," the Hopis as "meek and quiet."[24] Another official complained in 1920 that Navajo pressure had confined the Hopis to less than 600 square miles (384,000 acres).[25]

Superintendent Edgar Miller expressed two contradictory sentiments on the land dispute in separate reports in early 1925. First Miller explained why he believed the Hopis were not interested in making extensive use of the 1882 reservation. "They will maintain their communities on these mesas when all of us are dead, unless they are driven off by force, for even those now having good ranches and property go back to the villages on the mesas and live there during the winter months," Miller wrote. "They are strictly a community people and their dances, religious customs, and ceremonials can not exist without their living as such. Neither can the Hopi exist without the dances and ceremonials, and this, to a large degree, explains why they have not prospered parallel to their neighbors, the Navajo."[26]

Later, in a tone of surprise, Miller took note of the new trend in Hopi land use, writing: "The Hopis are branching out far more than I anticipated, under our encouragement, and this brings more friction and trouble between them and the Navajos. Something will have to be done to protect them in doing this, and, at the same time, make the Navajos understand they must keep within proper limits of personal action and territory. It will be a delicate, important work, and only the most reliable disinterested persons should be put at it."[27]

Still, Washington took no action in the 1920s to restrict the Navajos to "proper limits." Responding to a call to action from U.S. Senator Ralph Cameron of Arizona, Commissioner Charles Burke wrote that the rights of the Navajos to the 1882 reservation "must be carefully considered," adding that a government attempt to evict Navajos would cause hardship and create friction.[28]

And so, as the 1920s ended, the Navajo-Hopi land dispute was not only unresolved, it was continuing to fester. While Washington twiddled its thumbs, the Navajos became more entrenched and the Hopis became more aggressive in their assertion of rights to the entire 1882 reservation. The decades of the 1930s and 1940s would be traumatic for the two tribes and for the government that stood uncertainly between them.

The Trauma of Stock Reduction

In the Navajo world view, physical or emotional sickness is the inevitable result of a loss of harmony with the spiritual forces that animate the universe. Traditionally, a Navajo who has become ill consults a shaman—star gazer, crystal gazer, or hand trembler—to learn how his natural balance has been upset. Perhaps he has unwittingly violated a taboo, or perhaps he has been witched. Once the problem is diagnosed, the appropriate ceremony or "sing" can be performed. Sings are dramatic reenactments of mythical journeys conducted by medicine men who have mastered the elaborate chants, sand paintings, religious paraphernalia, and medicines with which the ceremony is conducted within a rigid ritual framework. The longest sings last eight days and nine nights.

John Collier, commissioner of Indian affairs from 1933 to 1945 and a man of intense religious sensitivity, offers the following description of a sing in a book entitled *On the Gleaming Way:*

There has taken place a disharmony, some prevalence of the dark powers which are in the world. The sing restores harmony, goes back to the source of the light, brings the reign of light; and this not merely for the sick patient, but for all his family and friends, and not only through the medicine man's suggestion and prayer but through the union of happy emotion and confident willing on the part of every man, woman, and child who has joined in the ceremony. They have come from many miles away—twenty, thirty, fifty miles. A Navajo sing is a communal healing, and the patient throws the healing back to all who are assisting him, in a profound process of therapeutic suggestion and self-suggestion which reaches to the obscure, central depths of the body and soul.[29]

When he took office during the Roosevelt administration, Collier was troubled by a disharmony that threatened to shred the fabric of Navajo life. The number of sheep, goats, and horses had gotten so out of balance with the land that fed them that millions of acres of the reservation had been seriously damaged by erosion. Navajo livestock had increased from about twenty thousand sheep units in 1868 to well over a million in 1928. (A sheep unit is the measure of the forage consumed by one sheep; a cow equals four sheep units, and a horse equals five.) The population of the tribe had swollen from about fifteen thousand in 1868 to some forty thousand during the same period and was increasing at a rate unmatched by any population group in the country. The reservation had been expanded several times from its 1868 boundaries, but most of the additional acreage was arid and poorly vegetated.

A survey completed in 1935 showed that the reservation range could support only about 560,000 sheep units and was suffering terribly from overgrazing.[30] As plants were eaten to the roots, the soil lost its ability to retain water, and a cycle of severe erosion began. Moisture that had once been absorbed into the earth now gushed from the highlands in torrents, ripping gullies in the valleys below and spreading a network of fingerlike erosion scars out from a central wash. Windstorms whipped denuded areas into sand dunes. Engineers warned that far-off Boulder Dam was being filled by sediment from Navajo country.

"The range must be saved, or the Navajos must disperse into the white world,"[31] Collier wrote later, expressing the urgency of the early 1930s. Taking advantage of federal appropriations for work projects during the first years of the New Deal, Collier launched his "Great Program" to adjust stock to the carrying capacity of the range. In November 1933, he presented his plan to the twelve-man Navajo Tribal Council. Established by the secretary of the interior ten years earlier to approve oil leases, the council would be called upon repeatedly in the coming years to risk the wrath of their people by endorsing drastic livestock reduction.

To encourage cooperation from the council, Collier promised that the government would supply funds for dams, wells, roads, and schools on the reservation. Income earned by Navajos employed on these projects would offset the loss of income from stock, he said, reduction would lead to an improved range and greater productivity from the animals the Navajos retained, and scientific breeding techniques would further enhance livestock quality. Over the objections of a third of its members, the council passed a resolution pledging to support "the wise men who urge this step."[32]

Armed with the council's endorsement, Collier impetuously pushed his program ahead. It was flawed by a requirement that every flock be reduced by 10 percent, regardless of its size. Such a cut was immensely more painful to the struggling owner of 50 sheep than to one whose flock numbered 100. A more basic weakness of the program was that it proceeded from a rationale incomprehensible to most Navajos. The technicians who sounded the warnings of impending ecological disaster were equipped with reports and data of the highest scientific validity and went forth in the zealous certainty that they were acting in the best interests of the people. But the concepts of "sheep units" and "range carrying capacity" were beyond the ken of a people whose language and values ordered the world in ways far different from the ways of the white man and who were emotionally and spiritually bound to their stock. The agents of Washington, of a government that for sixty years had encouraged the Navajos to increase their flocks, met with suspicion, bewilderment, and resistance. "In my long life of social effort and struggle, I have not experienced among any other Indian group, or any group whatsoever, an anxiety-ridden and anguished hostility even approaching to that which the Navajos were undergoing," Collier wrote in his memoirs.[33] Some of those who resisted were jailed.

Anguish was particularly acute among Navajo women, whose

role in society is largely defined by their duties to tend the sheep and maintain the homestead. Anthropologist Gladys Reichard put it this way: "The Navajo, particularly the women, are 'sheep-minded.' From the first white crack of dawn to the time when the curtain of darkness descends they must consider the sheep. Yes, and even beyond."[34] Sheep were the primary support for three-quarters of the Navajo families in the 1930s, providing food, clothing, and credit at the trading post.[35] Mothers and grandmothers saw themselves being disenfranchised by a program whose only compensation went to the men in the form of wage work. Sheep, not dollars, were the Navajo standard of wealth. The Navajos had never dealt in a cash economy, and to them dollars were an ephemeral concept.

Collier confronted a chastened and weary tribal council at Fort Defiance in 1934, when he said ominously that further reduction was necessary. The council agreed, but only after Collier promised to exempt families who owned fewer than 100 sheep. Goats became the major target of this second phase of stock reduction, and the government intended to supply the new reservation schools with the animals it purchased. Difficulties in transporting the animals resulted in a new insult to Navajo sensibilities, however, when the government agents, unable to arrange transportation, shot and left to rot goats remaining after families had butchered all they could use.[36] Some thirty-five hundred goats were destroyed in one grim episode that made the Navajos shudder at what they perceived as willfully malicious waste of life. Navajo respect for living things is such that before a medicine man picks a plant, he offers a prayer explaining the need for the plant's medicinal qualities. The slaughter of goats was regarded as gross barbarism. "You wouldn't approve if we asked you for five dollars and you gave it to us and we struck a match and burned it up in front of you," a tribal leader complained.[37]

Many Navajos regarded John Collier, the symbol of the reduction program, as another white man who felt no respect for Indians. The opposite was true. Collier was no typical commissioner of Indian affairs. He was upset by Washington's heavy-handed paternalism toward Indians, and he had been careful to consult the tribal council before proceeding with stock reduction. Nonetheless, some Navajos accused him of coercion and hypocrisy. "We Indians don't think it is right for Collier to tell us we should govern

ourselves and then tell us how to do it," the Houck chapter wrote
in 1936. "Why does he want to fool us that way and make us
believe we are governing our country, when he makes us do what
he wants?"[38] The Manuelito chapter also condemned Collier and
stock reduction: "John Collier says the Indian don't understand
him; but it looks like John Collier don't understand the Navajos."[39]
Tribal Councilman Howard Gorman said years later Collier was
hated because he "ruined something precious in the lives of the
people."[40]

Collier's reaction to overgrazing was in some ways heavy-
handed and authoritarian. He saw the problem clearly, but in his
concern for quick remedial action he did not take into account
Navajo attitudes and the absence of economic alternatives on the
reservation. It is nonetheless unfortunate that even today Navajos
think of John Collier as a cruel man. During his tenure as Indian
commissioner, Collier displayed a respect for Indians never before
seen in an Indian Service remarkable for its arrogance. Collier
thought twentieth-century America had much to learn from Indian
cultures, as his biographer, Kenneth Philp, wrote:

> Sensing the universal significance of tribal life, Collier ques-
> tioned the wisdom of the government's assimilation policy
> which tried to turn the Indian into a white man. He raised the
> pregnant hypothesis that tribal institutions should be preserved
> and studied because they contain the lost attributes of com-
> munal experience, the beauties of art, a passion for the earth,
> reverence for the human personality, and the profound values
> of comparative religion.[41]

In his dealings with the Navajos, Collier acted hastily, without
knowing the consequences of his actions, but never with ill will.

A Game of Wait and Hope

Washington remained convinced that the Navajo range must
be saved if the tribe were not to become wards of the government,
but after 1937 the stock reduction program proceeded with planning more careful than that which flawed the initial effort. Navajo
and Hopi lands were divided into eighteen grazing districts, and
grazing permits were issued which allowed a specific number of
sheep units to the holder, no more than a certain number of which

could be in horses. By this time a new tribal council had been formed, and it worked militantly against government controls. One tribal leader denounced range management as a "communistic plan," and the tribe stood united against further reduction.[42]

Today there are still thousands of Navajos who have had no formal education, who have not been exposed to scientific concepts, and whose ideas about sheep and rain and the land have been shaped in a world that posits a unique set of natural laws, described as follows by anthropologist David Aberle:

> Supernaturals gave sheep to the Navajos for their livelihood. When the Navajos increase their flocks, the supernaturals see that the Navajos care for their gifts and bring rain. But when they use them improvidently or give them away, the supernaturals respond by failing to bring rain. Hence reduction brings drouth and damages the range.[43]

The continuing strength of this thinking was demonstrated in a book published in 1974 by the Navajo Community College that gathers the remembrances of Navajos who experienced stock reduction in the 1930s and 1940s. "Before stock reduction it rained all the time," Ernest Nelson said with angry conviction.[44] "There was a lot of livestock everywhere, and it rained and rained. Then when John Collier put a blockage on the livestock, the rain ceased altogether." Curly Mustache said that before reduction, livestock flourished and "the rainfalls were never shy."[45]

During the drouth of 1974, several dozen middle-aged and elderly Navajos in the 1882 reservation were asked if they thought there were too many sheep for the range to support. Without exception the people answered no, that all would be well if the rains came. When they were asked why the rains were not coming, the most common response was a glance skyward and the word "Chidi-naat'a'í," "car that flies"—the white man's airplane, dozens of which leave vapor crisscrosses over the reservation each day on flights to and from the West Coast. "The clouds are here, but those airplanes chase them away," a woman said through interpretation. "All they do is stir up a lot of dry wind." Some of the people responded that the turmoil of the land dispute had disrupted the natural order, and still others believed abusive drinking or inattention to traditional religious life was to blame. Younger Navajos increasingly accept range management principles as valid, but throughout the reservation the Navajo elderly shake their heads in firm and sincere disbelief of such secular concepts. In the oil-rich Utah portion of the reservation, they claim that the smell from oil wells is the cause of the drouth.

The feelings of thousands of traditional Navajos represent a force to be reckoned with in tribal government and elections. Soon after initiating their campaigns, candidates for the chairmanship routinely pledge that they will do nothing to reduce livestock. The *Navajo Times* reported in 1966 that when incumbent chairman Raymond Nakai addressed a campaign rally, he said that "he personally did not mind if certain individuals had more sheep than they had sheep permits to cover, but that he did not want to be informed of sheep in excess of permits . . . that people could just herd them over the hill where they would not be seen."[46] Chairman Peter MacDonald communicated the same message more delicately in 1977 when he said, "You cannot just say to a livestock owner who gets most of his earnings [from stock] and maybe provides for another family or two that he has to get rid of his stock."[47]

And so, while the Navajo range continues to suffer from overgrazing, tribal leaders play a game of wait and hope—waiting for new generations who will accept stock controls and be able to work in the cash economy, and hoping for economic growth to ease the burden on the land. Criticism of Navajos for clinging to their sheep can rightfully be no more severe than criticism of the rest of America for clinging to automobiles. Navajos, especially the elderly, have feelings for sheep far richer than the love of Americans for machines whose thirst for petroleum is eroding the nation's economy even as the machines allow the economy to keep functioning. Navajos pray for rain to nourish their flocks, and suburbanites hope technology will step in when the oil runs out. Both groups hope for a magic solution while their situations grow steadily worse.

The First Navajos Are Expelled

For the first two decades of the twentieth century, government officials had been frustrated by Hopi refusal to make use of lands beyond the mesas. But as the 1930s began, they were becoming alarmed at the rate of Hopi movement into portions of the 1882 reservation long settled by Navajos. "I had the impression that the Navajo was crowding in on the Hopi," A. G. Hutton wrote after a visit to the reservation in 1930. "However, I could not find evidence to support this impression, but instead the Hopi is crowding into territory that has been used entirely by the Navajos in the past, and it appears to me that in making any decision in the matter that the rights of the Navajo should be given careful consideration."[48]

Another government official, H. H. Fiske, expressed similar sentiments in a 1930 report, noting that the government attempt to get the Hopis to move out of the villages was "resulting in an increased effort on their parts to establish a foothold and rights at various watering places, to which the rights of the Navajos have long been established."

From the perspective of the 1980s, after the Hopis have convinced Congress that Navajos should be evicted from nearly two-thirds of the 1882 reservation, the most interesting portion of Fiske's report is his commentary on the Hopi talent at public relations:

> The Hopi, by reason of living within one of the most spectacular parts of the country, which is in the direct path of the tourist, and by reason of retaining sufficient of his ancient customs to vividly illustrate a bygone age; and by reason of his picturesque community life, has a tremendous appeal to the traveling public. He is approachable and recognizes the possible advantages to result from enlisting the sympathetic intervention of outside influences. The traveler listens, is duly impressed, and accepts as conclusive the statements thus prepared for his consumption. He has neither time nor interest to investigate them, but acting upon his unchallenged information he enlists his activities in their behalf. The Navajo does not have these Hopi characteristics. He is somewhat nomadic, self-reliant, neither seeking nor desiring sympathy. He is somewhat unapproachable, and quite unresponsive to the advances of the curious. Hence, he is branded by the Hopi as an aggressor, seizing his every opportunity to encroach upon the Hopi, and true to his Navajo characteristics he makes no effort to deny or to counterbalance the outside bathos which is being cleverly capitalized by the Hopi.[49]

In delegations and letters to Washington, Hopi leaders pressed for the eviction of Navajos from the entire 1882 reservation. This demand was expressly rejected, but officials in the nation's capital began for the first time to look seriously at the suggestion that the

2.5-million-acre reservation be partitioned between the two tribes, and the first of a series of studies anticipating partition was begun. In early 1931, Indian Commissioner C. J. Rhoads and Secretary of the Interior Ray Lyman Wilbur joined in a letter agreeing that "there should be set aside and fenced for the exclusive use of the Hopis a reasonable area of land." They said they were "disposed to accept" a plan to set aside 438,000 acres, including the Hopi villages and surrounding lands, for the Hopis, but directed that further field studies be undertaken to prepare for partition "when the time comes."[50]

The first direct move toward partition was made in 1936 as part of the program establishing grazing districts throughout Navajo and Hopi lands. District 6 was established as an exclusive Hopi grazing area, and the balance of the 1882 reservation was divided into districts where only Navajos would be granted grazing permits. As first proposed by John Collier in 1936, District 6 would have contained 499,248 acres centered on the Hopi mesas. Collier initially sought to bring the Navajos and Hopis together to negotiate boundaries for the district, but when the Hopis refused to participate in such discussions, Collier told them the boundaries would be established anyway.[51]

In November 1939, C. E. Rachford, an associate forester with the U.S. Forest Service, was named to head a commission to conduct a further field investigation. Submitting his report four months later, Rachford said that more than four thousand Navajos and nearly three thousand Hopis were then living in the 1882 reservation. He said Navajo hostility and aggressiveness had forced the Hopis into an area entirely too small for a reasonable expansion of their increasing population. Rachford's recommendation that District 6 be expanded to 520,727 acres was accepted and implemented.

The Hopis objected strongly to being limited to one-fifth of the 1882 reservation. Stock reduction was hard not only on the Navajos, but also on Hopi stockmen, who resented their confinement in District 6. They labeled the Navajos as trespassers and asserted rights to all the lands between the San Francisco Peaks near Flagstaff on the west and the Chuska Mountains along the Arizona–New Mexico border to the east. Based on aboriginal use for hunting, gathering, and religious shrines, the claim included the entire 1882 reservation and several million acres beyond, which had been granted to the Navajos by a 1934 act of Congress. Collier rejected the claim and proceeded with his districting plan. He told the Hopis their restriction to District 6 would not compromise their rights to the rest of the 1882 reservation. This had to be a half-hearted assurance at best, however, because Collier's districting plan recognized Navajo settlement of the bulk of the reservation as an accomplished fact.

Despite his statement to the Hopis, Collier intended that the grazing districts would effect a partition of Navajo and Hopi interests in the 1882 reservation. In 1940 he sought the approval of the interior secretary for his plan, an action that would have formalized the division of the land, but Nathan R. Margold, the Interior Department's solicitor, blocked his path. Margold said the secretary could not approve the division for a number of reasons, citing a 1918 law that required statutory authority for such an action, and the rights acquired by the Hopis with the issuance of the 1882 order and the adoption of the Hopi Constitution in 1936.

In 1941, Collier submitted to the Hopi Tribal Council a new proposal, according to which District 6 would be expanded once more, this time to 528,823 acres. The council rejected the plan. Collier then ordered yet another study of the boundary problem by Willard Centerwall, a Forest Service employee from Tucson, whose report recommended that District 6 be expanded to 641,797 acres. A significant development at this point was that the Hopi Tribal Council endorsed the Centerwall proposal. But then, on the recommendation of government agents in Arizona, the Centerwall proposal was reduced by 10,000 acres, and the district boundaries were defined once and for all to include 631,194 acres.

Throughout this period of District 6 expansion, government officials were working without the aid of a survey and thus computed acreage figures from maps. Such computations were inevitably inexact. In 1965 the Bureau of Indian Affairs finally completed a survey that showed that the final boundaries adopted for District 6 in 1943 actually defined an area of 650,013 acres, or nearly 20,000 acres more than the figure originally reckoned. Approximately one hundred Navajo families were living within these final boundaries and were forced to relocate to land outside the district. Many suffered what were later acknowledged to be "severe personal hardships." Some of those families face relocation a second time because of the 1974 land dispute legislation, which has resulted in the expansion of the Hopi Reservation to 1,561,054 acres.

A New Beginning, or the Beginning of the End

With the range districting plan in place, the federal government began to turn its attention to the economic conditions of the Navajo Reservation. At the end of World War II, several thousand Navajo veterans and workers in war-related industries returned home with new skills and a taste for the wage economy. The tribe had grown to 61,000 by 1947 and was increasing at a rate of about 2 percent annually. Navajo grazing lands continued to deteriorate; the secretary of the interior estimated in 1948 that the reservation could support 35,000 Navajos at most in the traditional economy. The need for a broader-based economy was apparent.

The Navajo and Hopi Rehabilitation Act of 1950 was intended to address these economic conditions as well as to join the two tribes in a common effort at development. The act provided for range conservation programs; natural resource, agricultural, and business development; and housing, school, hospital, and road construction. While the act resulted in tremendous improvements on both reservations, both reservations remained economically depressed. Today, thirty years later, the sternest challenge to the Navajos and Hopis is to develop modern economies that can support their people. If the people cannot find work, the dispersal feared by John Collier will be inevitable. Navajo and Hopi young people want to stay on the reservation, but their material expectations have risen far above those of their grandparents. They want modern housing, automobiles, refrigerators, and televisions. Peter MacDonald expressed the economic reality well when he said, "We are either at the point of a new beginning or simply the beginning of the end."[53]

There is plenty of statistical evidence to buttress the argument that the Navajo Reservation is a sort of Third World developing nation right here in the United States. Perhaps the most alarming evidence is demographic: the on-reservation Navajo population increased at a rate of from 2 to 3 percent annually during the 1960s and 1970s. In 1978, 142,000 Navajos lived on the reservation; by the end of the century, the population could reach well over 300,000. Seventy-one percent of the population is now under thirty. The statistics on education are not encouraging either, despite considerable improvement since the 1940s. The median level of schooling for Navajo adults is 5.7 years. According to the 1970 census, only 3,846 of the 11,964 Navajos from ages twenty-five to thirty-four had completed high school, and only 1,073 had any college. Dropout rates from high school and college remain alarmingly high.[54]

Undereducation, lack of job skills, and difficulties with English contribute to an unemployment rate of 31 percent of the Navajo work force. Many of those classified as employed work only part-time or seasonally. Approximately 65 percent of the Navajos had incomes below the poverty level in 1969.[55]

In the past several years the economic outlook has improved. The federal Comprehensive Education and Training Act (CETA) has provided work for thousands, the Economic Development Administration has extended millions of dollars in grants to the tribe for public works projects, and the Department of Housing and Urban Development has provided considerable support to the tribe's own housing authority. But these programs do not reflect vitality in the Navajo economy. They show, rather, the tribe's dependence on federal dollars. There is little of what economists call infrastructure upon which the tribe can generate its own wealth. The tribe's economic development division has difficulty attracting industry because the reservation is far from large trade centers, has an underskilled labor pool, and lacks managerial talent. Without government jobs, a large-scale exodus of the young would have begun long ago. Fully two-thirds of the jobs on the reservation are in state, tribal, and federal agencies. The Bureau of Indian Affairs alone employs some fifty-five hundred Navajos, most of whom work in schools.

The tribe's greatest hope for the future may lie under the land, in the mineral wealth that has allowed the tribal government to develop its own considerable bureaucracy since the 1920s, when oil was discovered in the Utah portion of the reservation. Oil and gas production will be insignificant by 1985 if no new wells are discovered, but the reservation's strippable coal reserves are huge, and the Navajos also own some of the richest uranium deposits in the world.

If the Navajos are to build an economic future, they must buy at least part of it with minerals. They are determined to receive greater royalties from energy companies than they are now receiving under coal leases arranged by their own general counsel and the BIA in the 1950s and 1960s with subsequent approval by the tribal council. MacDonald finds the leases outrageous, complaining, "The unconscionable conduct of the federal government, the states, and industry in the exploitation of our natural resources is a national disgrace."[56]

With their own minerals department and environmental protection commission, the Navajos are now far more sophisticated than they were in the days when they signed away their mineral wealth for a fraction of its value. On another front, the Navajo Tax Commission has developed possessory interest and business activities taxes that will bring millions each year to the tribal treasury if the federal courts uphold the right of the tribe to impose the taxes.

Minerals will help the tribe capitalize its future, but they will not secure it. A class of entrepreneurs, merchants, salesmen, and managers will be needed to develop businesses that can keep Navajo dollars working on the reservation. As things now stand, well over half of each dollar taken home by Navajo wage-earners is diverted to the off-reservation economy in the first round of spending, contributing to the prosperity of border towns that provide goods and services not available on the reservation.[57]

Few Navajos are businessmen. "There is a pervasive cultural resistance to competitiveness on the part of individuals which has stifled entrepreneurship," a document published by the tribe's economic planners notes. "It is felt that one man gains at another's expense."[58] Attitudes and values thus compound the difficulties of developing the reservation economy.

Another problem is that every foot of reservation land is jealously guarded as part of some family's customary use area. Customary use is as close as the Navajos come to individual ownership of land, which is held in common by the tribe. Anyone seeking a business site lease must run a bureaucratic gauntlet that includes the local chapter, tribal government, BIA, and the Indian Health Service. The process, which often drags on for years, was lamented by the U.S. Commission on Civil Rights. "Starting a business on the Navajo reservation involves endurance; the process is time consuming and seems designed to confuse, if not discourage the prospective entrepreneur," the commission observed in a report.[59]

Peter MacDonald has said repeatedly that the tribal government will do all it can to promote small businesses and encourage industrial development. But his visionary public pronouncements have not been followed by the vigorous administrative commitment that is necessary if the reservation is to be more than just a place Navajos visit on vacation from jobs elsewhere. In at least one community where he has encountered political opposition, MacDonald has actually blocked plans for development.

MacDonald—he took the name as a small boy from the song "Old MacDonald Had a Farm" because his teachers could not pronounce his Navajo name—is a complex, enigmatic man. A Marine veteran of World War II, an engineering graduate of the University of Oklahoma, he worked for six years as an engineer in California before returning to the reservation to administer a federally funded poverty program. He professes his determination to preserve traditional Navajo values, yet he is a conservative and a member of the Republican Party. He wears impeccably tailored three-piece suits, drives a Lincoln Continental, plays golf, and enjoys staying at the finest hotels. In public appearances he is charismatic and eloquent, yet those who know him best say he is prone to fits of brooding introversion. MacDonald deeply resents the stereotyping of Indians and any slight from the non-Indian world. When President Carter held an energy conference at Camp David in 1979, MacDonald fired off a letter admonishing him for not inviting a single representative of the Indian tribes whose lands hold much of the nation's energy resources. Before that, MacDonald took the lead in organizing the twenty-four-member Council of Energy Resource Tribes, proclaiming that it would make sure Indians received the greatest possible return from their minerals.

On the reservation, MacDonald and the tribe's general counsel, Phoenix attorney George Vlassis, are often criticized for running the tribal government as if it were their own private corporation. The critics say MacDonald has manipulated the tribal council through his control of appointments to prestigious committees. They charge that MacDonald has thwarted the administrative review power of the tribal courts by extending the probationary period for tribal judges from two years to an indefinite period, during which judges may be removed at MacDonald's discretion. MacDonald's opponents are particularly upset at what they charge is a cynical attempt to squash dissent. In 1979, after a Navajo attorney in the tribe's legal department warned that a new pensions system would be a strain on the tribal treasury, he was fired by George Vlassis for what Vlassis called "immaturity." More than twenty tribal employees received termination notices in 1979, as

MacDonald and Vlassis put a clamp on political opposition.[60] In that same year the *Navajo Times*, a weekly paper owned and operated by the tribe, was instructed to play down controversial stories and play up the administration.

MacDonald's opponents charge that he has isolated himself inside a small ring of advisers selected for their loyalty to him rather than for their administrative ability. They say that even the tribe's Environmental Protection Commission is little more than a public relations ploy because MacDonald has ignored the commission's attempts to have a say in the tribe's policies for energy development while he pursues a course of rapid development of Navajo coal and uranium. Opposition to MacDonald has for the most part been ineffectual, however, and in 1978 he easily won election to his third four-year term.

The Land Dispute Goes to Court

Despite the attempt of the Navajo and Hopi Rehabilitation Act to merge the destinies of the two tribes, they remained antagonistically split by their fight over the 1882 Reservation. In 1958, Congress passed legislation that authorized the two tribes to enter into a lawsuit in federal court to determine their respective rights to the 2.5-million-acre tract. The act was endorsed by both tribal councils on the advice of their attorneys, and Norman Littell, general counsel for the Navajos at that time, was so confident of victory that he magnanimously urged the tribal council to request that Congress provide for payment of Hopi legal expenses.

In 1960, in a month-long trial before a special three-judge federal court in Prescott, Arizona, the Hopis, the plaintiffs in the lawsuit, claimed that the entire 1882 Reservation should be recognized as belonging exclusively to them. The Navajos replied that the Hopis had rights to only about one-fifth of the 1882 Reservation and sought a decree quieting Navajo title to the remainder of the land.

The intertribal court fight excited attention throughout Arizona, especially among those who believed that the disputed lands held a mineral bonanza. While the court was still hearing testimony, the *Arizona Star* reported:

This is Indian country—a land made famous by Zane Grey, Hollywood movies, and color photographs; a land that holds the traveler enthralled with the vast, lonely distances, the buttes and mesas and the Navajo with their sheep and Hopi with their pueblos.

This picturesque surface covers a rich treasure house below ground.

Eons ago a geological god of plenty spread here in profusion beds of anthracite coal, uranium, pools of petroleum and pockets of natural gas.

Geophysical surveys by major oil and uranium companies have indicated that the disputed land caps one of the last great store houses of natural resources in the U.S.

These companies are now awaiting the outcome of the trial, ready to tithe the victor millions of dollars for the privilege of looking for the hidden minerals.

The tribe who holds the land stands to gain millions through leases, bonuses, and royalties.[61]

Two years later, after examining the mountains of records submitted by both tribes, the court reached its decision in the pivotal case of *Healing v. Jones* (named after the chairmen of the Hopi and Navajo tribes, respectively). The court found that the Navajos and Hopis had joint and equal rights to the 1882 reservation outside District 6, which it said would remain exclusively Hopi.

The *Healing* court made its determination of joint and equal rights for the two tribes despite its finding that the actions of various secretaries of the interior—beginning in 1931 when Secretary Wilbur joined Indian Commissioner Rhoads in a letter approving the proposal that the reservation be divided between the two tribes—had implicitly settled the Navajos there. It found that Hopi rights to the entire 1882 reservation had never been lawfully terminated by the government or abandoned by the Hopis. "The failure of the Hopis, prior to the settlement of the Navajos, to use a substantially larger part of the 1882 reservation than is embraced within District 6, was not the result of a free choice on their part," the court wrote. "It was due to fear of the encircling Navajos and inability to cope with Navajo pressure."[62]

In another key ruling, the court said it had no authority to partition land in which both tribes had an interest. That, it said, was a legislative matter that only Congress could address.

And so, instead of resolving the Navajo-Hopi land dispute, the *Healing* decision became the legal foundation for many more years of struggle and controversy between the two tribes. As a practical matter, joint use was not possible because thousands of Navajos were settled throughout the area, most of them eking out a subsistence with their flocks. For the next twelve years the Hopis would argue that the only appropriate congressional response to the *Healing* decision, which the Supreme Court summarily affirmed after reviewing the records in 1963, was to partition the Joint Use Area equally and relocate several thousand Navajos. With more help from the federal courts and in alliance with several Arizona congressmen, they finally got what they wanted.

3
The Hopis: Confrontation on the Mesas

More than 500 years before Western civilization took tentative root in the rocky soil of New England, the Hopi Indians sang to the corn they planted in sandy fields on a high desert in what became the state of Arizona. Not concerned with seeking newer worlds, they invested their genius in religious ceremonialism which yearned only to sustain life in a stern environment. Above all they sought to bring rain. When they failed, crops failed and Hopis starved. This was a land to which the Americans could bring their cities only by erecting dams to make waterworks of rivers.

When white Americans encountered the Hopis in the second half of the nineteenth century, having just wrested a vast new territory from the Mexicans, representatives of Washington joined Christian missionaries in proclaiming a new order. Their jarring presence touched off a debate on the mesas that continues a century later, when Hopis can buy TV dinners and eight-track tapes in village stores.

During the years of the Vietnam War, the Hopis began to see a different type of American. Disaffected with the science that they said sapped their spirituality, fearing that technology was about to conjure the Apocalypse, some American young hailed the Hopis and urged them not to be seduced by convenience. They were drawn to a system religiously far more intense and materially far simpler than their own. In the Hopi way they saw an antidote to their spiritual poverty. "Hopi," they learned, means "People of Peace."

The flow of dissenters from America began shortly after Frank Waters published his *Book of the Hopi* in 1963. Billed by its publishers as "the first revelation of the Hopi historical and religious world view of life,"[1] the book became part of the 1960s counter culture, and the Hopis became Native American gurus.

Some Hopis received the newcomers hospitably. After decades of misunderstanding from government agents and missionaries, they were pleased to find recognition. A few of the traditionalists accepted invitations to speak at religious conferences in New York, San Francisco, and Stockholm, where they warned that the West had severed heart from head. They became militants in the cause of blocking the entry of the twentieth century into their villages. But back home matters were not so simple. The tribal council, established by the government in the 1930s to coordinate relations with Washington, petitioned the BIA to remove the "hippies." A decade later, Wayne Sekaquaptewa, publisher of the Hopi newspaper *Qua Toqti* ("The Eagle's Cry"), spoke contemptuously of whites "who want to keep us in our 'primitive' state and display us to the world as some primeval culture out of the past." His brother, Tribal Chairman Abbott Sekaquaptewa, said the outsiders would be less enthusiastic if they knew the discomforts of an outhouse in subzero weather.

For centuries religion bound the Hopis like the strands that wrapped their prayer sticks. They believed that the universe was governed by rules of reciprocity, which held that the actions of one affected the throbbing unity of the All. Each Hopi was expected to observe his duty in the social and religious systems. Deviation, they believed, meant disaster. The Americans carried a different message to the Hopis. They said nature could be restrained and the individual could achieve material and spiritual salvation apart from the group. Wayne Sekaquaptewa celebrated the freedom offered by America, the idea that happiness should be pursued. He disdained the "scare tactics" of Hopi elders. "It is hardly impressive," he wrote in 1974, "to walk up to an $8.00 an hour construction worker and tell him that if he doesn't change his waywardness, it won't rain on his fields."[2]

Like the Navajos, the Hopis have been enveloped by a society of 220 million people and a mass culture of infinite distractions. Hopi teen-agers spend nine months of the year at BIA boarding schools in Arizona, Nevada, or California, learning in the classroom that rain is a matter of storm fronts and pressure systems and in their free time learning whatever young Americans learn at disco dances and Pizza Huts. Their parents can step back into their homes after the Snake Dance and flip on the "Gong Show," "Charlie's Angels," or "The Price is Right." Traditional leaders have sought to sequester a few villages by forbidding modern utilities, but the tribal council continues to seek government help for sewer and electrical lines, highways, and housing projects. Even in Old Oraibi, the oldest community in North America, television antennas punctuate the horizon like exclamation points above homes where the tube is plugged into the car battery. There are government work projects or welfare checks for those who need them and paved roads to Winslow and Flagstaff and on to Phoenix and Los Angeles, where many Hopis now live and work.

It is all quite bewildering, as the list of "leading problems" among the Hopis indicates. Alcoholism is the most prevalent sickness, traffic accidents the primary cause of death, and boredom the number-one complaint of teen-agers home for the summer. Even Wayne Sekaquaptewa, who died in mid 1979 after a long illness, felt some ambivalence. "It is our distinct feeling that we Hopis, most of us that is, have embarked upon the Bahana's trail, but that we are not altogether sure that is where we want to go," he wrote in his weekly column.[3] The Bahana is the white man, America— frozen food, hospitals, monthly payments, and paychecks.

Building the Tribal Council

Implicit in all aspects of Hopi life, the debate over Hopi purposes focuses most sharply on attempts to organize the tribe politically. Until 1936 there was no Hopi "Tribe." For the hundreds of years the Hopis lived on the mesas, they shared religion, language, and agriculture without having any central political authority, any formal union of the villages. The different villages were neighbors; they were not a nation. Each functioned as an autonomous unit under the direction of the kikmongwi, the chief, and his advisers. The leadership structure was theocratic and hereditary. Anthropologist Mischa Titiev wrote in 1944 that "between pueblo and pueblo there is an attitude of jealousy, suspicion, and subdued hostility. . . ."[4]

In the 1930s, when John Collier was the commissioner of Indian affairs, government agencies were for the first time sensitive to this decentralization. Government anthropologist Oliver La Farge, assigned the task of writing a constitution to summon into being a tribal council, a secular mechanism by which the Hopis as a tribe could work with Washington, wrote of the irreconcilability of the Hopi way and constitutional government:

> The Hopis are going to organize, first because John Collier and a number of other people decided to put through a new law, the [Indian] Reorganization Act. These Indians didn't think this up. We did. . . . We came among these people, they didn't ask us, and as a result, they are our wards. It's not any inherent lack of capacity, it's the cold fact of cultural adjustment. . . . I said all the right things—"this is your decision, it is up to you"—but my manner was paternal and authoritarian. . . . We bring to these Indians a question which their experience cannot comprehend, a question which includes a world-view and a grasp of that utterly alien, mind-wracking concept, Anglo-Saxon rule by majority vote, with everything that follows in the train of that.[5]

The Hopi constitution declares that the tribe is "a union of self-governing villages, sharing common interests and working for the common welfare of all."[6] The constitution does not require that every village participate in the tribal council, however. It provides that until a village decides to elect representatives, "It shall be considered as being under the traditional organization, and the kikmongwi of such village shall be recognized as its leader."[7]

The Hopi Chairman and the Quest for Survival

Despite the summons to work together, the Hopis have remained antagonistically split. An anticouncil faction still scorns the council as an illegitimate artifice superimposed by Washington to speed their assimilation into American society and alienate them from the land so that energy companies can take Hopi mineral resources. "It seems it is a great struggle now between those people who want to follow their own way of life and those who have broken away from the life pattern and accepted the policies of the white man," kikmongwi Dan Katchongva told a three-man panel sent to the reservation by the commissioner of Indian affairs in 1955 as the council struggled to establish itself. "Things have become so confused because we can never get together in that way. Many would like for the Hopis to be all under one leader or one great central authority. But our life is set up in such a way that each village has its own village leader, and each one takes care of its own life."[8]

The great strength of the council is that it has become a source of employment among a people whose material expectations can no longer be met by agriculture. In 1977 the council supervised the expenditure of about seven million dollars and directed a bureaucracy of four hundred persons. Dozens of Hopis work for the Bureau of Indian Affairs and the Indian Health Service in an economy where federal dollars are by far the most significant influence.

The leader of the procouncil faction is Chairman Abbott Sekaquaptewa, who says his critics are inspired more by jealousy than by concern for traditional values. "As long as the tribal council is able to bring about programs, there is going to be jealousy," he said in an interview at tribal headquarters in New Oraibi. "This puts the council in the position of having made certain accomplishments on behalf of the people that will tend to make people support the council."

Sekaquaptewa is accustomed to derision. In the 1930s, after his parents bought diapers and a gas-powered washing machine and began canning peaches, they were accused of wanting to become Bahanas and were hounded from the village of Hotevilla. As a result of their parents' progressive philosophy, neither Abbott nor his brothers received the priesthood initiation, a traditional prerequisite for leadership. Sekaquaptewa has maintained a passion for the land, however. On the crutches he has needed ever since childhood arthritis crippled his legs, he works the corn fields of the family and helps supervise the family ranch.

Intense, articulate, and determined, Sekaquaptewa has no patience with opponents of the council. "If they are looking for survival, the way to survive is to adapt to life as it is today and to learn its ways so you can cope with it," he said. "There is no way in the world we can escape modern society, even if we build a stone wall around the reservation."

Most Hopis are ambivalent about the council. They are hungry for jobs, but also instinctively respectful of the traditional leaders. One man spoke bitterly in 1978 of council attempts to "run over our elders." Part of his anger may have stemmed from his inability to find work with the tribe. He suspected that he had been blacklisted in New Oraibi because his father-in-law was one of the council's most persistent critics.

The anticouncil faction is hampered by ideological rigidity and a tradition that prevents the emergence of a single powerful leader. In recent years, some traditionalists have cautiously supported the council. Some voted for the first time in 1978 to help elect Stanley Honanie vice-chairman. A soft-spoken graduate of Northern Arizona University, a holder of the Hopi priesthood, Honanie is representative of the Hopi young who are trying to reconcile America and the mesas. Relations between Honanie and Sekaquaptewa are strained and sometimes hostile.

A Clan Chief Fights the Civic Center Project

Karl Johnson, former coach of the Oraibi Lobos basketball team, was excited when construction of the Hopi Civic Center began in 1977. "The idea of a gym has been a dream of ours for a long time, when we played in the snow and sleet," he told a reporter for *Qua Toqti*. Winifred Sahu of the Hopi Alcoholism Program was also pleased. "This is a changing world, and many people say they drink because they get bored," she said.[9]

Herbert Hamana, head of the Sand Clan at Old Oraibi, felt differently. Eighty-three years old, he had never played basketball and had never been driven to alcohol by boredom. He spent most of his time tending a corn field and weaving sash belts worn by ceremonial dancers. In the spring of 1978 Hamana stood before the tribal council and told the story of the long-ago time when the Sand Clan migrated to Old Oraibi and received permission from the kikmongwi to farm the land where the civic center was being constructed. In return for use of the land, the Sand Clan obligated itself to perform the Awaquol ceremony in the fall so that the following year's harvest would be bountiful, he said.

Hamana demanded an end to construction. "Who is wrong?" he demanded in Hopi. "I, who want to keep my land for my clan and my kikmongwi, or you who act on your own authority? This is my land, I have earned it. It is my right, my authority."

Two years previously, when the federal Economic Development Administration awarded the tribe a million dollar grant for the civic center, it set down a guideline that the facility be centrally located. Tribal officials sought the permission of Shungopavi village to locate the civic center nearby, just west of the Hopi Cultural Center. Village leaders turned them down with thinking explained to a non-Indian reporter by Stanley Honanie: "Would you want Dodger Stadium located next to your church?" As the village where the ceremonial calendar and religious societies are most intact, Shungopavi is indeed a Hopi church. Then, without seeking the permission of Herbert Hamana, tribal officials began construction on Sand Clan land that was not under cultivation.

The council had sought the EDA grant because it wanted to boost recreational opportunities on the reservation, where facilities for sports and entertainment were noticeable mostly by their absence. The building that housed the basketball court was so inadequate that the only room for spectators was in two rows of folding metal chairs set tightly between the court and the walls. Out of appreciation for their fans, players not in the game watched from a perch on the stage. Compared to the old building, the civic center would resemble the Astrodome. It would house a gym with 2,500 seats, men's and women's locker rooms, a stage, showers and sauna, kitchen, and facilities for movies.

Hopis other than Herbert Hamana were troubled by the elaborate newness forming on the brown earth a few miles east of Old Oraibi. There was talk in village plazas that the civic center would be a source of aggravation. Vice-chairman Honanie feared that the activities to be held there—games, dances, fairs, movies—would provide new occasions for drinking and subsequent traffic accidents. He said it would be wise to wait another ten years before going ahead with the project. "By then maybe we'll be ready," he said. "Look at the civic center at Tuba City. They have a lot of trouble over there." But at thirty-two, Honanie was still active in the men's basketball league and admitted he had grown weary of sitting on the stage.

Hamana had to fight the civic center under rules he did not understand. With a lawyer whom friends found for him in the off-reservation town of Holbrook, he first sought injunctive relief in the tribal court, complaining that a civic center on Sand Clan land would "bring about more disharmony among the villages and families of the Hopi people and will disrupt the religious ceremonies and the villages and clans of Oraibi and other villages." When wind gusts from the west blew down a section of the walls of the rising civic center, Hamana appeared to be the beneficiary of supernatural assistance. Wayne Sekaquaptewa could only shake his head. In an editorial headlined "Superstition Can Dominate Your Life," he lamented the sentiment that an authority higher than the tribal court had ruled on the case. "We Hopis are a superstitious people," he wrote. "There were already people saying that the project was jinxed. This incident is only going to reinforce those ideas."[10]

Sekaquaptewa had reasons of his own to be concerned about a jinx. In addition to publishing *Qua Toqti*, he was principal owner of the construction company that had the civic center contract. His majority interest qualified the company for minority preference, while his non-Indian partners directed the work. They were well over half finished when the tribal council refused to pay cost overruns estimated at $180,000. Chairman Abbott Sekaquaptewa, Wayne's brother and ideological ally, wanted no gossip about a deal. Construction was halted for eight months before the council finally brought in subcontractors to finish the job. By this time, the lengthy proceedings in tribal court had worn Herbert Hamana out.

On both sides of the tribal council debate, the fundamental question is Hopi survival. The anticouncil faction wants to preserve, as nearly intact as possible, the values that shaped Hopi life for centuries when time moved in the cycle of the religious year. The procouncil faction holds the view that if Hopi society resists change it will become brittle and eventually crumble. Against a background of ideological conflict and personal antagonisms, the Hopi Council still has a long way to go before it can claim a mandate. Three villages continue to abstain from participation on the council, and turnout for tribal elections is habitually weak.

But the council's ability to bring money and jobs to the reservation makes it likely to prevail, winning the minds if not the hearts of most Hopis. Time on the mesas is moving in the linear course of Western man, eroding the past in a rush lamented by writer Charles Lummis at the beginning of the twentieth century:

> . . . old cultural values and skills and institutions are destroyed and the Indian traditionalists or Old Guard can only lament the decay or death of a way of life that seemed to them richer, more religious, more in accord with the nature of the universe than the Christian-democratic-technological society which has now imposed itself.[11]

Westernization

In 1886, nine years before Herbert Hamana was born, the commissioner of Indian affairs said his mission was to "assist in the great work of redeeming these benighted children of nature from the darkness of their superstition and ignorance."[12] President Theodore Roosevelt said a few years later that the aim of federal Indian policy "should be their ultimate absorption into the body of our people."[13] In 1979, while the world pondered the revolution by which Iranians under the banner of the Ayatollah Khomeini reclaimed their country from the Westernization of the Shah, a writer for the *New Yorker* magazine took stock of the ideology of Western civilization. "Until our time, the people of Western Europe had scarcely any doubt that theirs was mankind's highest civilization and that they had a mission of converting others which was part of man's enlightenment and progress," William Pfaff wrote. "The native peoples of Asia, Africa, and the Americas were expected to acknowledge Western truth as against native error. The issue thus posed for them was one of cultural as well as religious apostasy and conversion."[14]

"What a Religious System!"

Christianity, education, and the allotment of tribal lands into individually owned plots were the truths that government agents and missionaries who came to the Hopis at the end of the nineteenth century sought to substitute for "native error." Allotment failed entirely. Christianity and education have survived their collision with Hopi ways, at first because they were encased in a steel will that no resistance could crack. When Hopi women hid their children among rocks along mesa edges to keep them out of school, government men furiously stormed the villages and seized the children. Charles Lummis complained that Hopi children were being educated "by assault and battery."[15]

The missionaries built their churches despite Hopi protests. The most persistent preacher of Christianity was the Mennonite Heinrich Voth, who fled persecution in his native Germany and moved first to Russia, then to the United States. In 1893 Voth came to Oraibi, where he earned the name "Kihikaimta," "One who digs among the ruins," because of his fascination with archaeology. Voth was intrigued by Hopi religion. With camera and notebook he pushed his way past indignant Hopi priests into the underground ceremonial chambers called kivas. The publications of his meticulous observations survive, but the church he built was destroyed by lightning, which Hopis still regard as retribution for Voth's intrusions and his display of ritual objects at the Field Museum of Natural History in Chicago. Religious leaders were dismayed when they saw pictures of the museum exhibits published in books.

Voth was enthralled by his studies. "What a pantheon, what a religious system, what a rich language, what traditions, what organization!" he exclaimed. He was disturbed, nonetheless, that the Hopis had no concept of a saving God, of a personal savior. "And yet, how utterly little to satisfy the longings of the soul, to give peace to the heart for this life and hope for eternity." He yearned to "tell them of the God of love which their pantheon with its hundreds of deities does not have, and of His Son Jesus Christ who died for their sins to save them and give them eternal life."[16]

Many Hopis have become faithful members of the half-dozen Christian denominations that have missions on the reservation. Others continue to find greater relevance in Hopi tradition, as Dan Talayesva relates in his autobiography, *Sun Chief:*

> I decided to set myself against Christianity once and for all. I could see that the old people were right when they insisted that Jesus Christ might do for modern whites in a good climate, but that the Hopi gods had brought success in the desert since the world began.[17]

Talayesva writes that among clowns in the ceremonial dances:

> It was considered a good trick to put on spectacles and a long tailcoat, fold a piece of cardboard to represent a Bible and hymnal, and stride pompously into the plaza to sing hymns and preach a sermon on hell fire. The Christians who did not like this could stay away, for then we could have a better time and probably get more rain.[18]

Hopi Dances: A Life and Death Matter

Two of the most compellingly spiritual events any visitor to Arizona can witness take place 150 miles apart. One happens every evening; sunset at the Grand Canyon, when the massive gorge swells soundlessly in a crescendo of color and shape and then is muffled by the night. The other happens only once each year, when the Hopi corn must have one final blessing of rain to withstand the August sun. It is the Snake Dance, where pairs of Snake priests move slowly around the village plaza, one clamping a rattlesnake or bull snake in his mouth just behind its head, his partner soothing the reptile with the strokes of a feather.

If all is well as the dance ends, fertile and bulging clouds approach the mesas, the sanction of Hopi religion, the affirmation of Hopi life, the assurance of survival through another winter, which will be only half over when the Soyal priests begin the prayers that guide the sun northward to warm the fields for planting. In December the kachinas, the spirits that animate the Hopi universe, return to the villages from their home in the San Francisco Peaks. The Hopis believe that when they put on the kachina masks, the kachina enters them and they become part man, part kachina—messengers of prayer for the well-being of all life everywhere. The kachina dances are the culmination of weeks of spiritual discipline that is especially rigorous for the kikmongwi. "One of the duties of the village chief is that he concentrates on . . . the physical, emotional, mental, and spiritual welfare of the pueblo, including its nonhuman partners, and even all mankind with greater intensity and tranquility than does any member of the group," anthropologist Laura Thompson wrote. She described the office of kikmongwi as "fraught with heavy moral obligation,"[19] and she observed that the Hopis seek to exercise some measure of control over their environment by living carefully, by "regulating their behavior, emotions, and thoughts in a prescribed manner."[20]

Until the advent of federal programs and a limited wage economy, the most self-evident truth of Hopi existence was that the rains must come. It was an awesome and terrifying truth, and it produced a tension that sought expression in Hopi religion. The eerie, droning Hopi chants, haunting and resonant from some deep well of yearning, are part of the Hopi attempt to synchronize their energies with the energies of the universe. In their own way they are as precise and controlled as the equations that raise dams on the Colorado River. "Indeed, the orthodox Hopi believe not only that man can positively affect the functioning of the world of nature, but in the measure that he fails to do so, its harmonious functioning will be destroyed," Thompson wrote. "The movements of the sun, the coming of rain, the growth of crops, the reproduction of animals and of human beings depend, to a certain extent, on man's correct and active participation in the rhythmic life process."[21]

This compulsiveness of Hopi religion had two effects that bear directly on their dispute with the Navajos. Both effects stem from the fact that the Hopis felt constrained to remain within their communities on the mesas. First, the Hopis were subject to epidemics; two smallpox epidemics in the nineteenth century cut their population significantly. Second, the Hopis were unable to build their farms or graze their sheep far from the mesas. Indian agent Leo Crane was infuriated by Hopi tradition. "They have been known to be four days preparing for a dance, two days dancing, and two days recovering from the effects of it," Crane wrote in 1914. "Their dances are innumerable. In the meantime, stock, fields, fences, work of all kinds necessary to his improvement, are allowed to go to the dogs. This is the sort of man who complains that he is being driven to the wall by an energetic, crafty, hustling neighbor."[22]

Crane's view of Navajo hardiness was not unmixed, however. Four years later he wrote that the Navajos, because they lived in scattered groups, "may encroach, rob, kill cattle, etc, and then [have] 3,000 square miles of the most inhospitable country in which to hide away." Crane added that the Navajos "have never respected anything save one thing—the uniform of the United States Cavalry."[23]

The "Friendlies" and the "Hostiles"

Within Hopi society, the rigid demands of tradition left little room for innovation. Observance of societal demands was enforced by gossip, witchcraft, banishment, and even violence. In 1700, after the village of Awatovi welcomed back Spanish priests expelled twenty years earlier in the Pueblo revolt against Spanish domination, it was sacked and its people were killed by furious neighboring villages. Two centuries later the debate over American domination led to a traumatic schism at Oraibi.

Loloma, Oraibi's kikmongwi, led a delegation to Washington in 1890 to learn about the new white men who had come to the mesas. What they saw there overwhelmed them. "When they were near to Washington as their destination, they noticed that the population became more and more," a Hopi recalled in 1955. "And when they got closer to where they should be, they noticed two roads. There was one road where the vehicles were running back and forth up above and one road on the ground so that many people were moving. And like when you disturb an ant hill, that is the way he described the people. So he realized there was almost no alternative for him to take, and he made up his mind that the only thing they could do was make a treaty and make friends with the people in Washington."[24]

Other Hopis had different ideas. Led by Youkeoma, they resisted the Americans and demanded to be left alone. In late 1890 troops from Fort Defiance seized 104 Oraibi youngsters and carried them off to school. The following year villagers tore up the survey stakes by which their land was being plotted for individual allotment. The Americans brought out Gatling guns to remind the Hopis who was boss and called the people "friendlies" or "hostiles" according to their attitudes.

The inter-Hopi feud climaxed in 1906, when Tawaquaptewa was kikmongwi and leader of the friendlies. Youkeoma scratched a line in the dirt, challenging Tawaquaptewa's forces to push him and his men over. Youkeoma lost the symbolic "Push War" and took his followers five miles to the west, where they established a new village called Hotevilla. Youkeoma was arrested repeatedly for his defiance. Tawaquaptewa was ordered to school at Riverside, California, to be indoctrinated in behavior appropriate to a chief of Hopis under American rule. He returned home in 1910, bitter and disillusioned, to find that the population of his village had dwindled further with the departure of Mennonite converts to the settlement of frame houses at the foot of Third Mesa known as New Oraibi and by the founding of the village of Bakabi by yet another splinter group. Tawaquaptewa died in 1960 without clearly designating his successor as kikmongwi. For years his children quarreled as to who was the rightful chief.[25]

The Hopi Publisher

Wayne Sekaquaptewa felt none of the prevalent confusion about how to go about being a Hopi today. He believed the Hopis must make a clean break with the past, and he viewed the traditionalists as a tired remnant of a world view no longer relevant to life on the mesas.[26] Sekaquaptewa appealed constantly to his readers, the young most especially, to accept "the reality that our religion and our philosophy can no longer cope with the present run-away world."[27] *Qua Toqti*'s cartoons ridicule the traditionalists, news articles make no attempt to conceal their bias, and Sekaquaptewa himself had a habit of quoting unnamed sources who felt nothing but scorn for opponents of the tribal council. The only part of the paper that makes any attempt at balance is the Letters to the Editor section, which in 1974 ran an angry letter from Herbert Talahaftewa and Otis Polilema of Shungopavi. "Your attempts to discredit the traditional people through the use of your paper has [sic] caused disruptions, arguments, and hatred among the village people," they wrote.[28]

In his newspaper columns Sekaquaptewa tended to come across as intolerant and perhaps a bit mean, but in person he was often warm and disarmingly candid. He said in 1978 that the paper had lost $140,000 in its first five years, but he shrugged off the loss without complaint; it could be absorbed easily by other businesses. In addition to *Qua Toqti*, Sekaquaptewa owned the Hopi Crafts business; Southwest Excursions, which shuttled tourists around in vans; and Pueblo Builders, the only construction outfit on the reservation until it closed down shortly after his death. Until mid 1979, he also owned part of the business that operates the motel-restaurant-museum complex at the Hopi Cultural Center.

Sekaquaptewa was also president of the local Mormon Church, which claims to have more Hopi members than any other Christian denomination. Hopi Mormons tend to be enthusiastic advocates of social change and economic individualism, and their president believed his secular and religious activities had a common aim. "Everything I do in my life I do as a missionary," he said. "I tell the people what they must do to be able to survive and function in today's world." As he talked, his breath was labored by the stomach cancer he had been fighting for years. "Someone has to advance the process of enlightening the Hopi people. I am one of the tools." He was indifferent to the criticism of the traditionalists. "It doesn't bother me. I maintain there's a type of work on the reservation which was given to me—to help make the Hopi aware of his predicament and to help him out of it." It was a difficult task. Sekaquaptewa remarked editorially in 1977 that "trying to stir up the Hopi public to take an interest in public matters is like trying to push a donkey through the needle's eye."[29]

Sekaquaptewa regarded his entrepreneurial success as proof of the Mormon doctrine that promises earthly blessings to members of the priesthood. Part of his mission, he felt, was to bring those blessings to his people, and he reported with pride that he employed nearly 100 Hopis. That made him the third-largest employer on the reservation, behind the federal and tribal bureaucracies. "The Book of Mormon says be self-sufficient," he pointed out. "Only when the Hopi is at the point of self-sufficiency is he going to stop and consider what you tell him. Then you bring out the doctrine and you tell him, 'Brother, do you know your history?' "

Sekaquaptewa said the Book of Mormon, which relates that American Indians are the descendants of a Hebrew named Lehi whom God called from Jerusalem just before it was destroyed by the Babylonians in 600 B.C., is the true account of Hopi history. He said the account of Lehi's voyage to America directly parallels Hopi oral history of the clan migrations. As an example of the parallels, he cited the account that Lehi's people traveled across the ocean in boats made of reeds, and he pointed out that Hopi legend relates that the Hopis emerged into the present world by climbing from the previous world in the hollow center of reeds. "We are descended from the Hebrews, and our people were priesthood holders and performed rituals in the temples," he said.

According to the Book of Mormon, Indians are properly called Lamanites, after Lehi's son Laman, and their dark skin is a punishment from God. The first book of Nephi relates, "after they had dwindled in unbelief, they became a dark, and loathesome, and a filthy people, full of idleness and all manner of abominations."[30] The second book of Nephi offers hope of white skin for Lamanites who accept the Church: "And the gospel of Jesus shall be declared among them . . . and their scales of darkness shall begin to fall from their eyes; and many generations shall not pass away among them, save they shall be a white and delightsome people."[31]

The teaching that dark skin is a curse is embarrassing to some Indian Mormons. George Lee, a Navajo and a member of the Mormon Council of Seventy, told the *Los Angeles Times* his people "get upset" at the teaching. "The Indian people who belong to the church really don't want to have their skin color change; they like being brown," Lee said.[32] Sekaquaptewa preferred to view as a metaphor the teaching that Indians who convert to Mormonism will become white. "It means we will acquire the higher values and ethics of the more enlightened people and perhaps even surpass them," he said. But Church President Spencer W. Kimball affirmed the teaching as literal truth to the *Los Angeles Times*. He said photographs of Indian children on placement with Mormon families in Utah show that their skins do indeed become lighter in a Mormon setting. Kimball attributed the change to the care, education, and music lessons the children receive on the placement program. "When you go down on the reservation and see these hundreds of thousands of Indians living in the dirt without culture or refinement of any kind, you can hardly believe it," he said. "Then you see these boys and girls playing the flute, the piano. All these things bring about a normal culture."[33] Non-Mormon Indians tend to become angry at the mention of Mormon doctrine; they point out that children on placement in Utah spend less time in the sun than when they are at home on the reservation.

Born in 1923, Sekaquaptewa was trained as an electronics technician in the Air Force and later worked as a troubleshooter for Phoenix radio station KOY. For five of his nineteen years in Phoenix, Sekaquaptewa lived under the station's transmitting tower, whose electronic emissions he believed may have been responsible for his cancer. After divorcing his Chinese wife, whom he had met in China after World War II, he returned to the reservation. There he started a crafts business and married an Anglo woman from Texas who worked as a dormitory counselor at the BIA boarding school in Tuba City. In 1972, Wayne and Susan Sekaquaptewa learned that he had cancer. Seven years later, after a courageous struggle with his sickness, he was dead.

Wayne Sekaquaptewa's newspaper was in the forefront of the Hopi effort in the land dispute with the Navajos. News of the tribe's drive in Congress for partition legislation dominated the paper in 1973 and 1974, and his editorials condemned the Hopis who sided with the Navajos. He made persistent efforts to stir animosity between the two tribes. In 1973, after a Navajo had won the annual race sponsored by the Oraibi Trading Post, Sekaquaptewa berated Hopi manhood in *Qua Toqti*, informing Hopi men that they should be embarrassed by the victory of one of those "unmentionable tribesmen."[34] In early 1979, when the paper ran a picture of Hopis carrying supplies to Navajos stranded by mud after weeks of miserable weather, the caption reminded Hopis of the "enemy Navajo and the 100-year-war."[35] So many of his readers expressed indignation at the caption that a week later Sekaquaptewa ran an apology.

Many Hopis were furious at Sekaquaptewa for his harshness and his cavalier rejection of the traditionalists. Vice-chairman Stanley Honanie said in 1978 that Sekaquaptewa's attitude "burns me up." Even Abbott Sekaquaptewa said he felt "a great sense of loss, both for us and the world at large" at the dwindling of the Hopi priesthood. Fewer and fewer young Hopis are willing to undergo the rigorous mental and physical discipline of the initiation process.

Wallace Youvella, a thirty-year-old artist from First Mesa, said the kachina dances have become "just a side show, just something we do." Youvella said some dancers drink liquor before they enter the village plazas. "The dances are supposed to be done with a feeling of humility," he said. "We don't have that anymore." Youvella said that although he feels the need to pray, to put himself in the presence of a higher power, he finds no spiritual fulfillment in Hopi religion. Asked how he would try to meet his spiritual needs, he responded, "I'm not a Christian yet, but I probably will be soon. Still, when those dances are going on, I may not be there, but my heart is with those guys that are still really trying."

Youvella's mixed feelings, his sense of hurt and even of anger at the loss of something good in Hopi life, his uncertainty about how to replace it, carry over to the tribal council. "I'm a progressive," he said, "but in a way I'm still traditionalist. I feel that as long as our elders are here the council should consider them. Now the council says they're the voice of the people. But I would say they're a group of their own, they're a political machine. I'm for progress—for new schools, new gas stations, for improvements in the villages—but progress has to work from the past."

4

Navajo-Hopi Relations: The Push for Partition

Trying to describe how Navajos and Hopis get along is no easier than trying to describe how non-Indians in the Southwest get along with Indians in general. In the eighteenth and nineteenth centuries there was a great deal of conflict. More recently the relationship has been characterized by great deal of cooperation and goodwill. Still, at base lies the vague tension inevitable between people of contrasting histories, languages, and life-styles. There is another historical parallel that cannot be overlooked. Just as non-Indians poured into the West in the confidence that it was their manifest destiny to make more intensive use of the land than the Indians had, so the Navajos spread their swelling numbers out beyond the Hopi mesas with their sheep camps, filling the vacuum created by the traditional Hopi insistence on staying close to their villages. In their presentations to the federal courts and congressional committees that reviewed the land dispute, representatives of the two tribes greatly oversimplified the character of their relationships. The Hopis argued that the Navajos were their implacable foes bent on Hopi destruction. The Navajos maintained that they could hardly be better neighbors. The reality is more complex —and more interesting.

Until the middle of the eighteenth century, when an expanding population and pressure from New Mexicans forced the Navajos westward, there was little contact between the two tribes. Some of the isolated Navajo bands were desperately poor desert wanderers who did not hesitate to steal from Hopi fields. In 1851 the annual report of the commissioner of Indian affairs told of a delegation of Hopis who traveled to Santa Fe to meet with Indian agent James Calhoun: "They complained that the Navajos had continued to rob them until they were exceedingly poor. . . . The Navajos having exhausted, or nearly so, the supplies of the Moquies [Hopis], are now at peace with them, and will remain so until the Moquies increase their stores to such an extent that shall awaken their cupidity."[1] Eight years later two Army officers on a military exploration of Navajo country reported, "It is a well settled fact from the best information that the Navajo Indians live a great deal upon the Moquies, and what they don't sponge they rob."[2] The Navajos eventually moved right to the edge of the mesas, occupying the side canyons that had water and running their stock over Hopi fields.

While some of the Navajos were thieves who drove the Hopis to distraction, many enjoyed warm relations with their neighbors. Gradually there developed a tense symbiosis between the Navajo sheep raisers and the Hopi farmers. The Navajos rode into the Hopi villages in wagons filled with freshly butchered mutton and traded for corn, fresh fruit, and the Hopi specialty—the parchment-thin, brittle, and delicious piki bread. Trading and socializing went on in high spirits for days at a time. Maybe the Hopis had sash belts or baskets that caught a Navajo eye. In the fall the Hopis returned the visits, loading up their wagons with peaches and corn and making the round of Navajo sheep camps for more trade. Navajo medicine man Frank Mitchell says in his autobiography that his grandmother moved near the mesas to be able to trade with the Hopis.[3]

Indian agent John Bowman explained the duality of Navajo-Hopi relations in 1884. "Quite frequently trifling quarrels arise between members of these two tribes," Bowman wrote in his annual report. "These are usually caused by careless herding of the young Navajos, who allow their herds to overrun these outlying Hopi gardens. The Navajos are almost invariably the aggressors. These are the most serious difficulties these two tribes have had for years. . . . The best of good feeling generally exists between these tribes; they constantly mingle together at festivals, dances, feasts &c."[4]

In the late winter of 1979, as he ate lunch at his mobile home at Moencopi, Jesse Seyestewa talked about the contacts his family had with the Navajos when he was a child. "We'd let them know ahead of time when we needed mutton, and they'd come around at dance time and spend a couple of days." But the Hopis always remained wary of the Navajos, Seyestewa explained. "My parents used to tell us the Navajo is like a coyote. He steals anything he can get his hands on. My father told me—I hate to say it—he said they're born to be stealers. He said the white man and the Navajo are just alike."

The comparison between the Navajo and the white man comes up frequently in discussions with Hopis, who say both groups are aggressive and domineering. There is even a Hopi legend that accounts for the aggressiveness in the Navajo character. When mankind's previous existence came to an end with the abandonment of the underworld, all the groups of men were gathered together, the legend goes. Ten ears of corn of various sizes were laid on the ground, and representatives of the groups were instructed to choose the ear that would determine how they would live. The longest ear represented wealth and the pleasures of the flesh, but held no promise of stability. The shortest ear was the symbol of long survival in a humble life. The Navajos quickly took the longest ear, while the Hopis waited until all other groups had chosen before taking up the shortest ear. The short ear of corn is used even today in religious ceremonies to symbolize Hopi life.

Differences in character and temperament do color the Navajo-Hopi land dispute, but the dispute is fundamentally the result of competition of the two tribes for a limited range. In his autobiography *Big Falling Snow*, Hopi-Tewa Albert Yava describes Hopi attempts to move away from the mesas as a risky business. "If a Hopi went out there to build a house or set up a sheep camp, the Navajos did whatever they could to discourage him and make him go back where he came from. I knew a number of people who had that experience. . . . When there were ceremonial activities in the villages, those people came home to participate, leaving their places unattended. When they got back afterwards they found that their houses had been knocked down and their property destroyed. This was the way the Navajos tried to prevent the Hopis from using the land."[5] Even today Hopis who want to show their hostility toward the Navajos refer to them by the name Tusavuhta, meaning "to pound," because, as the Hopis explain it, Navajos sometimes killed their enemies by pounding their heads with rocks.

The best and the worst of Navajo-Hopi relations can be seen in the experiences of two Hopi families, the Nahas and the Navasies.

Neil and Myrtle Naha became close friends with the Navajo families near their ranch at Teesto, in the southern portion of what became the Joint Use Area. One of their daughters married a Navajo, and they pointed out that intermarriage has long been common. "We were just like one family," Mrs. Naha said in 1979. "We'd visit each other, they used to babysit our children, we looked after each other. In no way did they hurt us the way Abbott [Sekaquaptewa] has been saying." Mr. Naha said he was upset that Navajo families, including his friends the Miller Attakais and the Tom Bahes were being forced by the JUA partition to move out. "We don't have any anger with the Navajos," he said. "We feel for them because they been there all these years. They really feel bad about it. They're always talking about it." The Attakais and Bahes have already been forced by the government to move once, in 1943 when District 6 was expanded. There was room for them at that time just south of the District 6 line. Now they don't know where they can go.

A few miles northeast of Teesto, in the Jeddito Valley, the Navajo population was increasing rapidly in the 1920s and 1930s, and the family of young Melvina Navasie was being caught in a squeeze. When Melvina was a child and herded her family's sheep, Navajos on horseback used whips to chase her away from grazing land they wanted for their own. They made life miserable for the Hopi family, trampling their crops and vandalizing their home. The most grievous insult came in the early 1950s, when Navajo youths hung Melvina's father by his feet in a hogan. He died a month later from hemorrhaging. But Melvina's family stayed on at Jeddito.

Now the Navasies are eager to see the Navajos relocated. "We want them out because we know that the Navajo harrassment will always be there as long as the Navajo remains around us," Mrs. Navasie told a Senate committee in 1978. Their land at Jeddito has been partitioned to the Navajos, and the Navasies have plans to move a short distance to the Hopi partition area, from which Navajos are to be relocated. "We have waited all our lives to live in peace and for the Hopi people to get back some of their lands we have lost to the Navajo people," Mrs. Navasie said.

In most instances, Navajo-Hopi relationships have been less sharply defined. When Walter Albert moved to Sand Springs around 1920, Navajos rode up on horseback and demanded that he go back to his village, where they said Hopis belonged. Mr. Albert stayed on at Sand Springs, however, and gradually won the acceptance and affection of his Navajo neighbors. He remains there today. Mr. Albert also has a home in Moencopi village, where he talked about the old days as his children watched a movie on the color TV next to a wall that held nearly a dozen kachina dolls. He spoke more comfortably in Hopi than in English, letting his son Roy interpret for the visitor. Mr. Albert said he learned to speak Navajo at Sand Springs, sang with his neighbors at their Squaw Dances, and enjoyed the big get-togethers they had each year at branding time. He said he lived at Sand Springs primarily during the summer, and when he returned to the village to do carpentry or masonry on government construction projects, he hired a Navajo to tend his herd. Still, he added, some Navajos were not so friendly and rustled his stock from time to time.

Roy offered an explanation for the ambivalence of Hopi feeling toward the Navajos. "We're entirely different cultures," Roy said. "In Hopi society the man does most of the work. He is responsible for growing the food. But with the Navajos, the woman took care of the sheep, while the man was a raider, a stealer. The Navajos were my father's best friends, but still he couldn't trust them. There's a saying in Hopi: When you shake hands with a Navajo, be careful, because his other hand might be reaching for your pocket. We got along pretty good, I suppose, but it's hard for us to feel bad that they have to move out." Roy said he resented the failure of the government to make a final definition of land rights between the two tribes a long time ago. He gave an example of how this failure has damaged his friendships with Navajos in recent years. "If you don't mention the dispute with them, it's okay. But nowadays a Hopi doesn't go out to a Squaw Dance unless he wants to commit suicide." Drinking is commonplace as fry bread at Squaw Dances nowadays, and hostility quickly finds its way to the surface.

How the Hopi public feels about the land dispute is difficult to measure. Opinion polls haven't made it to the mesas yet, and there remains a strong reluctance on the part of many to become involved in political squabbles. Certainly the votes that have elected Abbott Sekaquaptewa to two consecutive four-year terms as tribal chairman must be seen as an endorsement of his hard line. But most Hopis don't vote. Participation in tribal elections is chronically poor because of indifference or outright hostility to the tribal council. In the 1973 elections, while the land dispute was flaring in Congress, 861 Hopis went to the polls. In the three villages of Shungopavi, Hotevilla, and Bakabi, with a combined population of nearly 2,000, only 86 votes were recorded.

An outsider traveling the mesas in 1978 and 1979 got varied reactions to the land dispute. A member of a road construction crew who flagged him to a halt on Highway 264 said, "I don't know much about that. I guess it's just the council that wants that." At the Keams Canyon Cafe a Hopi waitress said, "I don't pay any attention to it." And a teacher from Moencopi said he "couldn't care less" about the land dispute. There were plenty of voices on the other side. A Hopi teacher at the BIA boarding school at Tuba City said she thinks the Navajos should be moved "back where they belong." And another Moencopi resident said the Navajos are getting what they deserve.

"The Average Hopi Isn't Going to Benefit Very Much"

In the light of the Hopi claim before Congress that Navajos in the JUA threatened them with cultural extinction, it is important to note that the first serious Hopi attempt to make use of range land well beyond the mesas began in the 1920s, when an emergent group of economic individualists, breaking the centuries-old pattern of Hopi life, recognized cattle raising as an attractive alternative to the traditional farming economy. The land close to the villages was taken up by clan holdings, but areas farther out were not subject to traditional claims. The hearty few who made the effort to move there were confronted by Navajos already in the area who frequently harassed them back to the mesas. In a number of instances, however, the Hopis persevered and held their ground. It must be emphasized that only a few Hopis tried to move from the mesas, that the great majority of the people stayed in the agricultural economy, and that the Navajo threat to Hopi farming lands was checked with the establishment and subsequent enlargement of District 6. The Navajos now living in the JUA represent no threat to the Hopi culture. Instead, they are a hindrance only to what might be called a new Hopi elite, most of whom are relatively affluent and who want to expand their cattle holdings. Albert Yava speaks of this new Hopi elite in *Big Falling Snow:* "We used to have groupings by clans and families and kiva lodges, and now we have to add a grouping by wealth. The well-off Hopi has special interests. If he owns a lot of cattle for example, that land we have been contesting with the Navajos is much more important to him than to a poor family in Shipaulovi. The average Hopi isn't going to benefit very much from the land settlement."[6] Myrtle Naha said the same thing more succinctly. "Who's going to live out there?" she asked. "The people in the villages don't want to move away from the mesas."

The Hopi family that will gain the most from partition of the JUA is one of the least traditional, most affluent families in the tribe—the family of Abbott and Wayne Sekaquaptewa. They are a remarkably talented and grimly determined family with a fascinating history. The father of Abbott and Wayne Sekaquaptewa was one of the Hopi children dragged off to school by government agents at the beginning of the twentieth century. At school in Phoenix and Riverside, California, Emory Sekaquaptewa, Sr., learned the machinist's trade. He took to the new ways eagerly, working at a BIA school in Idaho before returning home to Hotevilla around 1918. "Everyone was expected to forget what they learned off the reservation and come back to being a Hopi again," his son Wayne said sixty years later. But Emory had different ideas. He made his first overt break from tradition by refusing initiation into the priesthood. Then, as we have seen, he and his wife Helen incurred the wrath of their neighbors by taking on Bahana ways. The Sekaquaptewas were mocked for trying to become Bahanas, their children were beaten up, they became pariahs.

Emory's family had a farm on clan land twelve miles southwest of Hotevilla, near the border of what became the enlarged District 6. When the harassment in the villages became intolerable in 1935, the family moved to the farm, growing corn and grazing sheep and cattle. To communicate with his neighbors, Emory learned to speak Navajo. In a book she wrote with the mother of Congressman Morris Udall, however, Mrs. Sekaquaptewa recalls the difficulty her family had with some of the Navajos in the area:

The wagon road that the Navajos traveled going to Oraibi to trade passed right by our garden, and many times they stopped and helped themselves to the melons, fruits, and vegetables. If they traveled on horseback, their trail passed right in front of our house, and nothing was safe. We sometimes went into the village for a few days and on our return we would find the door broken in, food taken, and things generally scattered about.[7]

Emory and Helen Sekaquaptewa raised extraordinary children. Abbott and Wayne are not the only ones to have achieved distinction. Emory, Jr., was the first Arizona Indian to attend West Point. Health problems forced him to resign during the first year, but he went on to earn a law degree and is now a member of the faculty at the University of Arizona. Eugene is a Marine veteran of the Iwo Jima invasion.

Abbott was born in 1929, six years after Wayne. He spent most of his adolescent years laid up in Phoenix with severe arthritis that still cripples his legs. Intense, curious, he read incessantly. Years later, after he was appointed by the governor of Arizona to a state board which required its members to have high school diplomas, Abbott went down to the State Education Department and in one day earned his high school equivalency diploma. An article in the *New York Times* in 1979 described him as "a stern, crippled man, whose life contains no humor, little joy, and a fierce devotion to what he perceives as his people's interest."[8] Lacking the priesthood initiation that is traditionally a prerequisite for a leadership position, marked by a physical handicap and membership in a controversial family, self-conscious about his lack of formal education, Abbott Sekaquaptewa is a man determined to prove himself. He worked in a number of mid-level positions with the tribal council before serving three one-year terms as chairman in the early 1960s. When he selected the number 13 as his personal brand at the family ranch, he made a grim statement of his defiant approach to life. He has led the Hopi fight to have Navajos expelled from the JUA. Anthropologist Richard Clemmer describes Sekaquaptewa as a man who "burns with a commitment to Hopi ethnicity and a passion for unremitting vengeance against the Navajo."[9]

Those closest to Abbott Sekaquaptewa say he has made the
land dispute his life. They say he frequently puts aside other tribal
issues to concentrate single-mindedly on assuring that the victory
his tribe won over the Navajos in 1974 does not slip away. During
an interview at his Oraibi office in 1978, he spoke seethingly about
"having our noses rubbed into the dirt by the Navajos," being
"robbed blind," and "100 years of indignity." He said the Navajos
were not the only ones to suffer from stock reduction in the 1930s,
that his family were forced to sell all but a few of their animals. But
if he has intensely angry feelings about the Navajos, he also has
intensely fond feelings for the land. "Man, I'd like to see this land
bloom the way the elders said it used to when the grass grew
knee-high and the sunflowers bloomed in the valley and made the
whole land bright yellow, and the hummingbirds and butterflies
flew in the cornfields. That is life. That was happiness."

Sekaquaptewa acknowledged that partition of the JUA is turning over to the Hopis large areas no Hopi ever attempted to settle
because of their distance from the mesas, for example, Big Mountain. He insisted, nonetheless, that the Hopis used the entire JUA
before the Navajos came. "They say the Hopis weren't using the
land," he said ("they" being the Navajos). "The point is: by what
standards? Why should the Hopis have to be judged according to
the standards of the Navajos or the white man? We were using that
land. But we have a different way of using it—gathering wood,
hunting, visiting shrines. There were antelope in this area before
the Navajo moved in. And the one and only reason why there are
no antelope here is the same reason the eagles are going—because
the Navajos have moved in." He countered a question about his
feelings for Navajo relocatees by referring to the Hopis who were
intimidated from the land by the Navajos. "It is time someone else
did a little giving," he said. "The hardship is not limited to contemporary Navajo citizens. We know more about hardship in this
whole case than they do."

It is clear that Abbott Sekaquaptewa and his family know a
great deal about hardship. But it is also clear that the Sekaquaptewa
family is anything but typical of the Hopi Tribe and that their
determination in the land dispute is a major factor in the expulsion
of many Navajos who never harmed the Hopis, who simply made
their homes on land the Hopis used only periodically.

The Troublesome Concept of Joint Use

In 1978, Glenn Emmons, commissioner of Indian affairs in the Eisenhower administration, recalled that he had "just groaned" when he heard in 1962 that a Joint Use Area had been established. Emmons said the 1958 legislation authorizing a lawsuit between the Navajos and the Hopis had been intended to bring about a final definition of ownership of the disputed land. Far from resolving the land dispute, however, the court had merely redefined it with a troublesome equation for ownership of three-quarters of the 1882 reservation: Hopi equals Navajo. "It will now be for the two tribes and government officials to determine whether with these basic issues resolved, the area outside District 6 can and should be fairly administered as a joint reservation," the court decreed.

The task of acting on the Healing decision fell in 1963 to Indian Commissioner Philleo Nash, who recalled in 1977 that the Joint Use Area quickly became known in the BIA as the "No Hope Area." When Nash called representatives of the two tribes together at Scottsdale's Valley Ho Hotel on August 6, 1963, he said he was "not approaching the question of joint use or joint administration in any kind of pessimistic attitude." He might have added that he wasn't really optimistic either.

The negotiations went nowhere fast. The Navajos insisted that they be allowed to buy out the Hopi interest and suggested that the Hopis use the money to buy public land in Arizona. They said they could not accept the relocation of several thousand of their people which would be required by equal partition of the JUA. The Hopis were just as firm in their refusal to sell and their demand for a timetable for Hopi use of half the JUA. Navajo counsel Norman Littell expressed the futility of the negotiations when he said, "What has evolved is a clear picture of the irresistible force meeting the immovable body." Armed with a court ruling that they owned half the land, the Hopis were the irresistible force. Settled in great numbers throughout the JUA, the Navajos were the immovable body.

Philleo Nash might have been tempted to use the cliché about being caught between a rock and a hard place to describe his indelicate position. A federal court had dropped an extraordinarily sensitive controversy in his lap and had almost blithely suggested that he get together with the two disputants to decide what to do about it. Nash dismissed the Hopi recommendation that separate grazing districts be established for Navajos and Hopis, with authority over the districts to be vested in the respective tribes. This would be "a form of partition," Nash said, and the BIA had no authority to partition. Abbott Sekaquaptewa had another idea. Why not set up a single grazing district the tribes could share equally? That would have had the same practical effect as partition, because it would have pushed thousands of Navajos off the range, Nash recognized. The idea "will require some study," he responded lamely.[11]

The commissioner's headaches were not limited to the partition issue. Hopi counsel John Boyden demanded action to stop Navajos from overgrazing the JUA range, announcing indignantly that the carrying capacity there was declining drastically. "We feel that it is imperative and to the best interests of both tribes that immediate stock reduction be had," Boyden said. He insisted that the Hopis had "a right to ask the government to protect our property."[12]

A federal court would hold in 1974 that Navajo use of the entire 1882 reservation had been "expediently sanctioned by government indifference." A review of official government correspondence and the series of events preceding the establishment and enlargement of District 6 appears to justify the conclusion that the court was only partially correct. Certainly it would be unfair to accuse Philleo Nash, Indian commissioner from 1961 to 1966, of bureaucratic languor. By the time the courts turned the dispute over to Nash, he had only a choice between two unpleasant alternatives. He could force the Navajos to give up half the range, by imposing stock reduction even more drastic than that attempted by John Collier, or he could maintain the status quo, waiting for the courts and Congress to devise a precise formula for use of the JUA. If he chose the first alternative, he would be confronted with the economic and cultural demoralization of several thousand already impoverished Navajos. If he chose the second, he would be neglecting his responsibility to protect Indian lands and the judicially recognized rights of the Hopis.

Nash's vacillation at the conference table with the two tribes is understandable. He admitted that Interior "has taken a very lenient attitude towards overuse on the Navajo land because of the human factor," then went on to hedge awkwardly in response to

Boyden's demand for protection of the JUA range. First Nash promised he would move "as rapidly as possible" to stop overgrazing. A few minutes later he backed off that position, saying he did not want to "leave the impression with the Hopis that we are going to have a crackdown, because we are not." He later moved to neutral ground with the weak pledge that Interior would move to stop overgrazing with "deliberate speed."[13] As events developed, Interior would not take a strong stand on the issue of Hopi rights in the JUA until 1972, when a man named Harrison Loesch was the assistant secretary for Land Management.

The Hopi Energy Connection Foreshadowed

Desire to get at the mineral wealth of the 1882 reservation had long made the land dispute a matter of interest beyond the two reservations. The *Healing* court found that wherever mineral wealth was discovered in the JUA the two tribes would have to negotiate with energy companies for its development and share equally in its profits—even if the JUA were partitioned. In the post-*Healing* talks with the Navajos, Boyden said the Hopis might not allow mineral development unless there were movement toward Hopi control of half the JUA, and he hinted broadly that the Hopis would welcome oil company pressure on Interior to partition the land. If the Hopis did not link subsurface development with surface control, "then the matter of partition is of no interest at all for the oil companies," he said. "But if partition was holding up the oil development, the oil companies would be awfully interested in getting the legislation. It is just practical."[14]

Oil Leases in District 6

For years before the early 1960s there had been speculation that the 1882 reservation, and District 6 most especially, held great reservoirs of crude oil. An editorial writer for the *Arizona Republic* gushed optimism in 1948: "Interest in the mineral wealth that lies under the ground in Arizona is intensified by a geologist's report that the Hopi Reservation in Arizona 'contains the largest oil fields in the country.' " He posed a provocative question: "Is oil to repeat for the Arizona Hopi the tale of fabulous wealth it brought to the Osage of Oklahoma?"[15]

Abbott Sekaquaptewa certainly hoped so. And now that the tribe held exclusive ownership of District 6, he opened the doors to eager oil companies. At a meeting in Keams Canyon in September 1964 to open sealed bids from companies seeking the opportunity to drill, Sekaquaptewa said income from oil leases would be "the first step toward economic development and the eventual independence of the tribe." Representatives of twelve oil companies listened anxiously as the bids on fifty-six tracts were announced.[16] The right to explore for oil went to the highest bidder for each tract, and the top fifty-six bids brought a quick $984,256.31 to a tribal treasury that had never before held such an amount. By the end of October, total lease income had swollen to $2.2 million, and the tribe was finally able to pay John Boyden for his years of work on the land dispute. Boyden submitted a bill of $780,000 for the work that had culminated in the *Healing* decision. But he would receive even more. In a moment of euphoric generosity, a tribal councilman said he thought Boyden had done so much for the tribe that he should be a millionaire. The rest of the council agreed and voted to pay Boyden $220,000 more than he had asked.

The highest bid for a single tract was $95,748.56 at Keams Canyon. The second highest bid for the same tract was $2,802.12, prompting one oil man to explain, "You play your cards as you see them, and you don't look back."[17] The oil companies would need all the stiff-upper-lip spirit they could muster after drilling dozens of dry wells in District 6. Their geologists had been deceived by the twists and folds in rock formations, which usually indicate oil and natural gas traps below. All the wells came up dry, and the leases were abandoned.

A Coal Lease on Black Mesa

Although the dream of fabulous oil wealth was not realized, there never was any doubt about the vastness of JUA coal deposits. In 1966, the Peabody Coal Company signed a thirty-five-year lease with the Navajo and Hopi tribal councils, allowing it to mine a large part of Black Mesa, a thirty-three-hundred-square-mile "island in the sky" in the northern JUA. The coal would be used to fire two electrical generating stations far from the mine. With water drawn from deep below the mesa, it would be flushed through a pipeline 273 miles to the Mohave generating station, located on the Nevada side of the Colorado River and operated by Southern

California Edison. It would also be transported to the so-called Navajo plant at Page, Arizona, by a 78-mile railroad constructed specifically for that purpose. Operated by the Salt River Project of Arizona, the Navajo plant was constructed after Representative Wayne Aspinall, powerful chairman of the House Interior Committee, persuaded (some said "forced") the Navajos to sign away rights to 34,100 acre feet in the Upper Colorado River Basin. The Navajos, according to historian Alvin Josephy, Jr., "were eager for the new income and job opportunities that the Salt River Project negotiators promised them. But the Navajo eagerness did them in. Somehow, in a classic repeat of business dealings between Indians and whites, they failed to realize that they held very good cards in their hand, and neither the Department of the Interior—which should have protected them but instead participated in the poker game against them—nor their tribal attorneys guided them in playing their chips to their own best advantage."[18] The coal lease and water deal were made during the administration of Navajo Chairman Raymond Nakai. In 1974, when Peter MacDonald was chairman, a lawyer hired by the tribe called the waiver of water rights "a miserable deal for the Navajo Tribe."[19]

The Hopis Move on Two Fronts

The post-*Healing* negotiations begun by Philleo Nash in 1963 reached their low point eight years later, when John Boyden led a Hopi delegation to Window Rock for a meeting with the Navajo Tribal Council. The Navajo position was laid out for all to see by Carl Todacheenie, a councilman from Shiprock, a town in the New Mexico portion of the reservation and far removed from the JUA:

> The only way the Navajo people are going to move, we know, is they have to have another Bataan March. The United States government will have to do that, and I don't think they're about to do it. And we, as leaders of the Navajo people, cannot say "move back," because that land is theirs by occupancy. The same as the United States acquired all of the lands here in the United States, we're following their example. If they can do it, we have done it already. We're settled out there, and we're not going to advise our people to move out regardless who says. They probably got to chop off our heads. That's the only way we're going to move out of there.

Todacheenie's statement was the most forceful expression yet of Navajo solidarity against partition and of the tribe's conviction that the federal government would not take the drastic step of evicting Navajos from the JUA. To the Hopis, it was another demonstration of Navajo arrogance. They were determined to achieve partition and removal of the Navajos, and they were convinced that the *Healing* decision would ultimately win them half the disputed land if they persisted. "The wheels of justice grind slow but exceedingly fine," John Boyden often told frustrated tribal leaders. As early as 1963, after Philleo Nash told the Hopis he would not remove Navajos from the JUA, Boyden had gone to Congress with partition legislation. But the bill sponsored by Colorado's Wayne Aspinall got nowhere. Seven years later, the tenacious Hopi general counsel prevailed upon Arizona Congressman Sam Steiger, whose district included much of the JUA, to sponsor another partition bill. The Steiger Bill was part of a two-pronged Hopi offensive, because at the same time Boyden sought help in the federal courts.

In early 1970, Boyden petitioned the district court in Tucson for a writ of assistance to enforce Hopi rights as cotenants of the JUA. He claimed the Navajos had denied the Hopis joint use and that the United States had failed to act on the *Healing* decree. Judge James Walsh, one of the three federal judges who heard the Healing case, denied the petition with a one-sentence explanation that the 1958 act "left to Congress rather than the courts the question of tribal control over lands in which the Navajos and the Hopis were found to have a joint and undivided interest." The judge was taking the position that Congress had tied his hands. But the Ninth Circuit Court of Appeals in San Francisco disagreed, citing a principle established by the Supreme Court that the power to render a judgment implicitly includes the power to enforce it.

The issue of Judge Walsh's authority to issue a writ of assistance was a tightly technical legal question. But when Judge Ben Duniway wrote the appeals court's opinion, he digressed from legalese to make an interesting commentary on the land dispute. Rejecting the Navajo argument that widespread Navajo settlement of the JUA made it impossible to grant the Hopis use of half the land, he wrote, "Obviously, where the tract of land is large and the population is sparse, these [arguments] are straw men."

This statement demands attention. For the appeals court action was legal dynamite that exploded in the center of the land dispute logjam, sending out shock waves that helped to trigger the

Navajo and Hopi Land Settlement Act of 1974. The federal court was moving the land dispute toward resolution by making "straw men" of one of the starkest facts of life on the Navajo Reservation: the land was already filled beyond its capacity to support the livestock economy. Navajos outside the disputed lands were struggling to eke out a subsistence living and could hardly make room for relocatees from the JUA. One has to ask if Philleo Nash, who spoke of the "No Hope Area," knew more about this melancholy situation than Judge Duniway, who spoke of "straw men."

The Ninth Circuit court was attempting to move the land dispute off dead center, to give the *Healing* decision some practical meaning. In this it was powerfully successful. The court wanted Judge Walsh to act, but what action it anticipated was far from clear, as this passage from Judge Duniway's opinion shows:

> A district judge is not a creature without imagination. He can hear testimony from the parties and the United States as to what the actual situation is, and can tailor the relief to be afforded to the facts that confront him, always bearing in mind that the objective is to achieve what the court has decreed, the exercise by the Hopi and the Navajo of their "joint, undivided, and equal interest."

The Navajos appealed the ruling to the Supreme Court, arguing that to allow the Hopis use of half the JUA would damage "several thousand Indians, their families, their homes, their livelihood, and their historic and emotional attachment to the land." The Supreme Court affirmed the decision of the Ninth Circuit, however, and the case moved back to Judge Walsh's Tucson courtroom in the summer of 1972, when the Hopis were ready with hard evidence on damage done to the JUA range by Navajo overgrazing.

Under Boyden's questioning, range expert Barry Freeman testified that a 1964 BIA survey established that the carrying capacity of the JUA was 22,036 sheep units. A 1968 livestock enumeration counted 88,484 sheep units there, he said, indicating an overstocking rate of 400 percent. Freeman catalogued the depressing toll of overgrazing. Eighty percent of the JUA range was producing zero to25 percent of its potential, and 20 percent of the range was producing 25 to 50 percent of its potential, he said. Freeman explained that as overgrazing continues, the quality of forage declines, as desirable species of vegetation are replaced by species poorer in palatability, nutritional value, and rate of development. He said the JUA range had probably lost carrying capacity since 1964 and concluded that "without remedial treatment in terms of reduced livestock numbers, the introduction of range management practices, and very good, judicious livestock management, this area can only continue to deteriorate."

For the Navajos, there was no refuting Freeman's testimony. The land was indeed dying. It was being smothered by Navajo stock. They responded in the only way they could. The land might be saved if the court ordered stock reduction, they said, but a people would be destroyed. Dr. Otto Bendheim, chief consultant in psychiatry for the Indian Health Service, described what the stock reduction program of the 1930s had done to the Navajo psyche. Bendheim said stock reduction had "rekindled, reinforced a preexisting suspicion and hostility of white people, for the white government, the Bureau of Indian Affairs—all the way up to the government in Washington, representing the entire white culture by which the Navajos were surrounded." This antagonism sometimes resulted in violence, Bendheim continued, but more generally manifested itself in "withdrawal by the Navajos from the dominant culture and [their] being reinforced in their preexisting ideas that white people are exploitive, are not understanding, and hostile to the Navajos."

Bendheim talked gravely about other consequences of stock reduction—alienation from that which had long defined "Navajo," and subsequent self-rejection and self-destruction:

> As well as they were able to live in a traditional way, engage in what they knew best—animal husbandry, particularly sheep herding, deriving their livelihood from the meat of sheep, the wool of sheep, making artifacts . . . they were to that extent self-reliant, independent, and were living in their traditional culture. But when the sheep supply became insufficient for this purpose, they had to look for other means of making a livelihood. Many of them, very large numbers, reverted to handouts, welfare by the government. Others had to leave the reservation and become nomadic, fringe inhabitants of the fringe cities, such as Gallup, Flagstaff, Phoenix, Los Angeles, Denver, Salt Lake City, Albuquerque, where hundreds of Navajos lived, many of them in the gutters, many of them unfortunately given to alcoholism, some of them to prostitu-

tion. This, I believe, was a direct effect of their discontinuation of their traditional pattern of functioning.

The Ninth Circuit had made another round of stock reduction inevitable when it ordered Judge Walsh to fashion a remedy. Still, counsel for the Navajo, George Vlassis, sought to convince the court that stock reduction would be an excessively harsh, even brutal remedy. He maintained that the vantage point of a courtroom deprived Judge Walsh of the firsthand experience of life in the JUA necessary to make a fair decision, and he asked that the court appoint a special master to hold hearings and document the circumstances of the Navajos before reporting back to the court with a recommended course of action. "Decisions made which affect people who live substantially below the edge of poverty as defined by the mainstream of society must be made with great deliberation and due regard for the grit and determination that these people are required to have to survive from day to day," Vlassis said.

John Boyden was in no mood for further deliberation and said it was high time some regard was shown to the Hopis. "The inconvenience of people who are destroying somebody else's land seems to be the only obstacle to giving justice at this time," he said. Boyden mocked Navajo claims of hardship with a statement that may have been intended to remind Judge Walsh of Judge Duniway's "straw men" remark. "They have no trouble moving forward," Boyden said. "The time they have difficulty is moving back to their own country."

Ever since it established grazing districts in the 1882 Reservation, the Bureau of Indian Affairs had recognized that Navajo settlement there was an accomplished fact and that attempts to remove Navajos would involve far more than inconvenience. Essentially, the Bureau was recognizing the human rights of people who subsist on the land. The decisions of the federal courts were guided by the logic of property rights. The *Healing* court found that the Hopis had as much right to use the land as the Navajos. Nearly a decade later the Ninth Circuit ruled that Judge Walsh had the power to enforce that right. Judge Walsh did just that in the fall of 1972. He found that since the *Healing* decision, Hopi use of the JUA for grazing "has been less than 1 percent because of the harassment, verbal abuse, and threats of the Navajos," and that the Navajos "continue to overgraze, misuse, and damage the lawful interest of the Hopi Tribe awarded by this court." The Bureau of Indian Affairs, he found, "still continues to procrastinate, vacillate, and refuse to deliver to the Hopi Indians or to assist the Hopi Tribe in obtaining their one-half undivided interest in the surface of said Joint Use Area."

Judge Walsh ordered specific steps to assist the Hopis. He directed that Navajo stock be reduced to half the carrying capacity of the JUA range within one year, when Navajo grazing permits in the area were to be cancelled and new permits would be issued—half to the Navajos and half to the Hopis. According to BIA figures, the 1,150 Navajo families in the JUA owned 5,000 horses, 8,000 cattle, and 63,000 sheep and goats—the equivalent of 120,000 sheep units— on land capable of supporting only 22,036 sheep units. Because the Navajos were entitled to only half the carrying capacity, their stock had to be reduced by 90 percent. The average family would be allowed 9.5 sheep units. The other major directive in Judge Walsh's order was a prohibition on any new Navajo construction in the JUA. Ever since the *Healing* decision the BIA had denied the Navajos in the JUA any funds for schools, housing, or public works projects. Judge Walsh's order had the effect of making their circumstances even more difficult.

Navajo officials did little to encourage their people to comply with the order, maintaining that was the responsibility of the BIA. So John Boyden went back to court once again, this time asking Judge Walsh to find the Navajos in contempt. Judge Walsh spoke impatiently from the bench, announcing his determination to carry out the legal process begun in *Healing*. "There has to be a day of reckoning." he said. "Either that decree means something or it doesn't. And if it has to be done by the court's directing the United States to go out there and do it involuntarily and at all costs, it will be done."

In January 1974, as the House Interior Committee studied legislation to partition the JUA, Judge Walsh denied a Navajo motion for more time to reduce their stock. Four months later, he found Peter MacDonald in contempt for not observing the stock reduction order and fixed a fine of $250 for each day Navajo stock remained above half the carrying capacity. The contempt order was the first blow in a one-two combination that staggered the Navajos on May 29, 1974. For at the same time Judge Walsh was finding the Navajos in contempt, the House of Representatives,

2,000 miles away, was passing legislation to partition the JUA equally between the two tribes and evict several thousand Navajos.

The Hopis Go to Bat for the Power Companies

During the time John Boyden was preparing his strategy for the courts and Congress, Hopi Chairman Clarence Hamilton, the predecessor to Abbott Sekaquaptewa, was winning sympathy for the Hopi land dispute cause among some very powerful economic forces. Hamilton played a fascinating role in what the *Wall Street Journal* said might be "the most significant environmental struggle of the decade," the showdown between energy companies and environmentalists over plans to develop a massive electrical grid in the open-sky country of the Southwest.[20]

In 1971, six huge coal-fired electrical generating plants were either being operated, constructed, or planned by a consortium of twenty-three power companies known as Western Energy Supply and Transmission (WEST) Associates. Two of those plants were the Mohave and Navajo stations. Most of their electricity was to be supplied to the rapidly expanding markets of Phoenix, Tucson, Las Vegas, and Los Angeles through transmission lines hundreds of miles long. Environmentalists warned that pollutants from the electrical plants would mar the skies over six national parks, including the Grand Canyon, twenty-eight national monuments, the national recreation areas at Lake Mead and Lake Powell, and the Navajo and Hopi reservations.

"So the stage seems set for the old familiar ecology shootout," the *Wall Street Journal* reported a bit facetiously. "Over here, in the black hat, industry, greedy, rapacious, insensitive as stone to anything but the bottom line on the income statement. Over there in the white hats, the conservationists, bent on heading off the black hat before he shoots up the town."[21] When the Senate Interior Committee held a series of hearings on national policy regarding energy and the environment, an executive with the Salt River Project, the Arizona agency that manages the electrical plant at Page, framed the problem more literally: "Sooner or later, everyone is going to have to realize that we have to pay some environmental price to live in the way we've grown accustomed to live. Maybe this is where and when we learn what the price, the tradeoff, is going to be."[22]

Black Mesa, the energy source for two of the plants in the WEST system and an area sacred to both Navajos and Hopis, became the symbol of environmentalists' determination to limit the tradeoff and preserve the pristine beauty of the Southwest. Several environmentalist groups joined forces with sixty-two Hopi traditionalists who filed suit in federal court seeking an order to halt the strip mining of Black Mesa. The traditionalists had an urgent sense of purpose. Believing that man's disrespect for the sacredness of the earth put the entire world at risk, they spoke of Hopi prophecies that warned:

> There would be a change in the pattern of life as we near the end of the life cycle of this world, such that many of us would seek the materialistic world, trying to enjoy all the good things it has to offer before destroying ourselves. Those gifted with the knowledge of the sacred instructions will then live very cautiously, for they will remember and have faith in these instructions, and it will be on their hands that the fate of the world will rest.

It was their responsiblity to live carefully so as to delay for as long as possible the inevitable destruction of the world by fire, the traditionalists believed. In a statement accompanying their lawsuit, they expressed alarm at the technology of the white man:

> We, the Hopi leaders, have watched as the white man has destroyed his land, his water, and his air. The white man has made it harder for us to maintain our traditional ways and religious life. Now for the first time we have decided to intervene in the white man's court to prevent the final devastation. We should not have had to go this far. Our words have not been heeded. We can no longer watch as our sacred lands are wrested from our control and as our spiritual center disintegrates. We cannot allow our spiritual homelands to be taken from us. The hour is already late.

Although it emerged from a centuries-old prophetic tradition, the suit itself was a tightly reasoned challenge to the right of the Hopi Tribal Council to approve a lease on behalf of the Hopi people. The lawyer for the traditionalists, Robert Pelcyger of the

Native American Rights Fund, noted that because some Hopi villages had decided not to send representatives to the council, only eleven of the eighteen council seats had been filled, and "of these, only six or seven were properly certified," according to procedures specified in the Hopi Constitution. Therefore, Pelcyger argued, the council lacked a legal quorum, and the secretary of the interior's action in approving the lease was "arbitrary, capricious, an abuse of discretion."

The case collapsed before the court considered the issues it raised. The court ruled that in order for the case to proceed, the traditionalists must join the tribal council as defendant along with the secretary of the interior. But since the council was recognized by the federal government as a sovereign governing body, it was immune from suit.

Lawyer Pelcyger was frustrated and angry by this legalistic Catch 22. "It is as if the American courts were powerless to grant relief to American citizens when the federal government ignores the Bill of Rights," Pelcyger wrote in his appeal to the Supreme Court. The court rejected the argument and refused to hear the appeal.

In approving the Black Mesa lease Interior Secretary Stewart Udall had hailed it as a boon for an economically depressed area. Udall said the strip mine on Black Mesa and related electrical generating projects would mean "new jobs, large tax benefits, and tremendous economic advantage, not only in royalties and jobs for the two Indian tribes, but for the entire Southwest."

Udall's Department of the Interior also had a stake in western energy development. Through its Bureau of Reclamation, Interior owns 25 percent of the Navajo plant and has plans to use its portion of the plant's output to pump water from the Colorado River to the Central Arizona Project, which will meet part of the state's growing water demand. Alvin Josephy reported that the "planning, testing, negotiations, and lease and contract signings" associated with the Black Mesa coal development program "were carried out so quietly that they provide a classroom example of how serious has become the lack of accountability by government agencies working hand-in-glove with industry in the United States today." He criticized the failure of government agencies to allow for public review or to assess the environmental impacts of planned energy development. "The atmosphere and environment, fundamental to the quality and future of life of a huge part of the Southwest, encompassing thousands of square miles in many states, was literally appropriated by the members of the power consortium," Josephy wrote in a 1971 article in *Audubon Magazine*.[23]

Public interest in the "ecology shootout" was spurred by the report that the only man-made object visible in a photograph taken by the Gemini 12 satellite at an altitude of 170 miles was the plume from the Four Corners plant, a member of the WEST system on Navajo land in northwestern New Mexico. When New Mexico state officials called for a moratorium on power plant development because of the attendant environmental problems, Interior Secretary Rogers Morton responded by naming a study group to make a "comprehensive examination" of WEST plans. A year later, in July 1972, the *Washington Post* reported[24] that the Environmental Protection Agency had "charged the Interior Department with giving superficial attention to potential damage to the environment."[25] As the publicity mounted, the Los Angeles City Council voted not to take part in the Page power plant unless environmental standards were strengthened.[26]

Clarence Hamilton came forward to defend the power plants. Addressing the Arizona Advisory Commission on the Environment, the Hopi chairman said, "In a real sense, we consider ourselves fortunate to have these power plants developed in the areas around our reservation. Income from the sale to these plants can be of great benefit in improving the economy of my people. Without the power plants we would have no market for our coal and our economy would suffer."[27] Al Wiman, a reporter from Los Angeles television station KABC, learned that the speech had been written by the Hopis' Salt Lake City public relations firm, David W. Evans, and Associates, who also represented WEST. When David Evans, a member of the firm, learned that Wiman was planning to reveal his findings in person to the Arizona Advisory Committee on the Environment, he traveled to Los Angeles in an attempt to dissuade Wiman from making the trip. Wiman went anyway.[28]

Peter MacDonald, meanwhile, was not sounding nearly as friendly to the energy companies. Shortly after he was elected tribal chairman, he said he would try to renegotiate the Navajo portion of the contract with Peabody. He told the Senate Interior Committee that if the power plants "pollute our homelands, we will do everything within our power to alter that situation . . . My father gave me clean air and clean water, and I will give the same to my son. We will not turn our land into another Los Angeles, and we won't let anyone else do it." MacDonald announced that the tribe was establishing an environmental authority to monitor the mines and plants, and said, "If they cause us any harm or damage, we will do everything or anything that is necessary to stop that harm."[29]

In a 1974 article for the *Washington Post*, free-lance writer Mark Panitch put the energy controversy in the context of the Navajo-Hopi land dispute:

> The relationship between the Hopi council and the power companies became almost symbiotic. On the one hand, Hamilton speeches written by Evans would be distributed through the public relations machinery of 23 major Western utilities. On the other hand, these utilities would tell their customers, often through local media contacts, that the Hopis were "good Indians" who wouldn't shut off the juice that ran their air conditioners.
>
> Because of the efforts by representatives of the Hopi to present that tribe's viewpoint, the Hopi rapidly took on the aura of the underdog who just wanted to help his white brother. Some of the Navajo, on the other hand, were saying threatening things about closing down polluting power plants and requiring expensive reclamation of strip-mined lands.

Panitch added an interesting detail about the relationship between Peabody Coal and the Interior Department. He said that when citizens wrote to the department for information on Black Mesa, "they were sent a brochure prepared and published by the Peabody Coal Company."[30]

Hopi defense of strip-mining and coal-fired power plants was the first demonstration of the Hopi ability, in concert with their public relations allies from Salt Lake City, to win favorable attention in the Southwest. It was also a demonstration of how meticulously John Boyden had planned his strategy to win passage of legislation to partition the JUA and relocate Navajos. At the post-*Healing* discussions in Scottsdale, Boyden had spoken of attempting

to win help from the oil companies, but in the 1970s it was coal
interests who had the most at stake in the land of the Navajo-Hopi
land dispute. Two facts demonstrate the extent of the land dispute's importance to coal interests. First, the Joint Use Area contained huge reserves of recoverable coal. And second, even though
the Navajos and the Hopis will share equally in mineral development anywhere in the JUA, the tribe that controls the surface
controls access to the subsurface by its authority to grant rights-
of-way.

In 1977, when the Joint Use Area was partitioned between the
two tribes, much of the coal-rich land was turned over to the Hopi
Tribe.

5

Congress, Round One

Passage of the Navajo-Hopi Land Settlement Act was fundamentally a victory of Hopi property rights over Navajo human
rights. Only a few members of Congress paid any attention to the
squabble between two Indian tribes over dusty rangeland off in a
corner of Arizona. They had other things to worry about in those
days of Watergate and energy shortages. But in the end, most
endorsed the reasoning expressed by Florida's James Haley: "There
is only one major issue. That is whether the Hopi Tribe should be
forced by legislation to sell to the Navajo Tribe a portion of the
Hopi lands."[1] They rejected the thinking articulated by South
Dakota's James Abourezk: "The status quo is preferable to all that
damn refugee trouble."[2]

Ever since the *Healing* court established the Joint Use Area,
the Hopis had been trying to get the Navajos off half the land. BIA
officials held the status quo because they recognized the implications of partition and relocation. Dee Brown, author of *Bury My
Heart at Wounded Knee*, said uprooting the Navajos "would rank
among the biggest forced relocations of a single group of Indians in
American history. It would certainly be the largest since the end of
the Indian wars."[3]

The Hopis were persistent and resourceful. They kept knocking
on doors in Congress and in the Interior Department, and they
developed a public relations campaign to overcome the fear that
relocation would result in violence and national disgrace. Indeed,

91

they turned the tables on this fear, arguing that relocation was the only way to *avoid* violence. Evans and Associates, their Salt Lake City public relations firm, cranked out news releases warning that unless Congress acted, Hopis and Navajos would be at each others' throats in a war that would shame the federal government.

For years, Navajo stock had been straying across the boundary between the JUA and the exclusively Hopi District 6. In some cases Navajos took their sheep to watering places on Hopi land. In 1970, the Hopi Tribal Council passed an ordinance declaring Navajo stock on Hopi land to be in trespass and subject to impoundment. The stated purpose of the ordinance was to protect the Hopi range. A second purpose, apparently, was to provoke the Navajos.

The Hopis hired a non-Indian named Elmer Randolph to enforce the ordinance. A feisty former rodeo cowboy who liked to throw his weight around, Randolph earned a reputation as a bully for his rough handling of Navajos. A particularly nasty incident began when Randolph ordered a ninety-seven-year-old Navajo named Tsinijinnie Yazzie to get off his horse and submit to arrest for trespassing with his sheep. Yazzie did not understand English and remained mounted, so Randolph jerked him off the horse, injuring him seriously. Randolph jailed Yazzie on charges of trespassing and resisting arrest. The Navajos were furious, and attorney Robert Hilgendorf, who worked with a legal services organization on the Navajo Reservation, said the Hopis were obviously harassing the Navajos. "I can't help but notice that Hopi police, particularly the non-Indian rangers, delight in making trouble for the Navajos," Hilgendorf said.[4]

Randolph and the other Hopi rangers were especially active in early 1972, just before the House Subcommittee on Indian Affairs held hearings on the Steiger Bill. An angry Peter MacDonald claimed Hopis had fired on Navajos on several occasions and said he feared the Navajos would "get their fill of this and take things in their own hands."[5] That, of course, was just what the Hopis wanted. "A routine problem of livestock trespassing on a neighbor's pasture has been expanded to depict an unreal situation of Hopi people living in terror of Navajos," he said.[6]

Frustrated at losing their stock, Navajos at Coal Mine Mesa built a fence to keep their stock out of District 6. The fence bordered the ranch of the Sekaquaptewa family, who pointed out that a fence that would keep Navajo stock in the JUA would keep Hopi stock out of the JUA. When the Sekaquaptewas tore the fence down, they brought along a television crew from Phoenix. Then they called on Arizona Governor Jack Williams to send in the National Guard.[7]

As they released stories to the southwestern press warning of the Navajo peril, Evans and Associates worked hand in hand with the Hopi rangers. Free-lance writer Mark Panitch wrote in his 1974 article for the *Washington Post* that the Evans firm "virtually stage managed a range war on the borders of the Hopi reservation." Panitch had covered the "range war" while he worked on the staff of the *Arizona Star* (Tucson).

For state editors weary of school board meetings and other peaceful discussions of public issues, the story of war on the reservation made great copy. "During 1971–1972 few newspapers escaped having a Sunday feature on the 'range war' about to break out between the two tribes," Panitch continued. "Photos of burned corrals and shot up stock tanks and wells were printed, although such incidents were not widespread. . . . By calling Evans and Associates, a TV crew could arrange a roundup of trespassing Navajo stock. Occasionally, when a roundup was in progress, Southwestern newsmen would be telephoned and notified of the event."[8]

At the subcommittee hearings, Sam Steiger also had a part in the melodrama. Speaking in his gravest tones, Steiger told his colleagues that the JUA range was about to be set aflame by the passions of two seething foes. "There is nothing funny about the violence that has already transpired—livestock mutilations, corral burnings, fence destruction, water tank burnings, and at least one shooting incident," Steiger said. And then he pleaded for congressional action to restore order to the troubled Arizona range. "If we permit ourselves to be seduced into some kind of legal procrastination and someone is killed, I am sure we would then assume the responsibility that is patently ours," he said. "Let us not wait for that kind of catalyst."[9]

Sam Steiger, Cowboy Conservative

Throughout its history the land dispute has been a tangle of conflicting emotions, perceptions, and personalities. Sam Steiger is one of its most interesting figures. As a young man, he left Manhattan for the open sky country of the West and earned a bachelor's degree in animal husbandry from Colorado A. and M.

Drafted into the Army in 1950, he rose to the rank of first lieutenant in thirteen months during the Korean War and won a Purple Heart and Bronze Star for rescuing five men from a burning tank. Back at his adopted Arizona home, he bought a ranch and dealt in horses and cattle. Then one of his friends bet Steiger five dollars he didn't have the nerve to run for the state Senate. The friend should have known better.

The incumbent from Yavapai County, a Democratic veteran of six terms, was so confident of reelection that he took a trip to Europe while Steiger was out shaking every hand that wasn't steering a pickup or a horse. Steiger won the election in 1960 and took off on a rough-and-tumble career that took him to the U.S. House of Representatives six years later. Never known for tact or restraint, Steiger turned heads in Washington as a freshman congressman by appearing on the nationally syndicated Joe Pyne talk show, where he said some of his colleagues came to work drunk and weren't smart enough to push a wheelbarrow.

In a city of self-conscious style, Steiger was a breath of fresh air, even when he came to Capitol Hill in cowboy boots caked with dung from his Virginia ranch. In his book *O Congress,* Michigan Representative (now U.S. Senator) Don Riegle fondly recalls Steiger's reaction to a speech on the House floor urging support for the nation's wheat farmers. As Riegle tells it, Steiger stood at the rear of the chamber in his cowboy boots making "loud clucking noises just like a mother hen."[10] Others found Steiger less than endearing, particularly those who wanted tight regulations on strip-mining and the use of federal lands. "If there is any member of the House Interior Committee whose name causes conservationists to become apoplectic, it is Sam Steiger," a liberal group of Congress-watchers reported in 1975. "Steiger seems to derive a certain pleasure from being exuberantly tactless," they added.[11]

All his political life, Steiger baffled those who knew of his New York beginnings. He couldn't claim the pioneer heritage of Barry Goldwater, but he practiced the same brand of Arizona conservatism. He blasted the federal bureaucracy, supported a controversial proposal for a dam in the Grand Canyon, and opposed legislation to regulate strip-mining and control land use. During his 1976 campaign for the Senate, Steiger outraged the state by shooting two burros which, he said, had charged him. Shortly after the incident a Coconino County official jokingly asked Steiger if he had shot any other burros lately. "Nope," came the puckish reply, "I got a freezer full." Steiger was outrageous, but no one could deny that he had a good sense of humor.

If politics is "the slow public application of reason to the governing of mass emotion," it can be said that Steiger failed the political process in the land dispute.[12] He was a central part of the Hopi campaign that exaggerated the dispute in order to arouse public emotion and Congress against the Navajos. He mocked Navajo claims that relocation would be cruel and insisted that the provisions of his bill for relocation assistance were "excessively generous." Steiger may have sincerely believed in partition and relocation as the best way to resolve the land dispute, but his methods in proselytizing others to his belief are suspect. "I thought the Hopis should get the land which the courts said they had a right to," he said in a 1977 interview, "and I didn't see any sense in getting involved if I wasn't going to play to win."[13]

Interior Takes a Hard Line

Graham Holmes, director of the Navajo Area office of the Bureau of Indian Affairs from 1966 to 1971, was a lawyer at BIA headquarters in Washington in 1972 and attended a meeting at which Indian Commissioner Louis Bruce and Assistant Interior Secretary for Land Management Harrison Loesch prepared for the House hearing on the land dispute. Holmes said Bruce had not wanted to support the Steiger Bill but Loesch, Bruce's superior, announced that Interior would come out in support of the legislation. "Loesch pointed a finger at him and said, 'You will support the Department's position,'" Holmes recalled in 1978. When the two officials appeared together at the hearings, Loesch did most of the talking. He acknowledged that "the human dislocations are very troublesome," and that "it is hard to really take a hard line," but he favored partition because it would put the Hopis in possession of half the JUA and relieve the pressure on the badly overgrazed range.[14]

The issue of Navajo overgrazing supplemented the central Hopi argument that they were legally entitled to half the JUA. Steiger, Congressman James Haley of Florida, and Loesch reasoned that the range would have to be protected even if there were no land dispute. And they believed stock reduction would force the Navajos off the land even if Congress did not order partition. The Navajos would have improved their position before Congress had they expressed a willingness to reduce their stock to the carrying capacity of the range. But as we have seen, Navajo politicians have never been willing to address the overgrazing issue. The Hopi claim to half the carrying capacity of the JUA compounded their problems. Committee counsel Louis Sigler asked Peter MacDonald if the Navajos would be willing to reduce their stock to half the JUA carrying capacity.

"If a new place is provided for them, yes," MacDonald replied. Sigler said testily, "That is an if. What if there is no new place?" MacDonald snapped, "Then I throw the question back to the U.S. government. Then why tinker with it, because it is a dead end? If we are going to solve the problem that is there, then we have to be open-minded about it and see what we can do, rather than just ask the people to drop their means of existence and not make any provisions or overtures in the way of easing the pain that is going to be experienced. . . ." MacDonald called the Steiger Bill "madness" and "a monstrosity."[15]

The principal Hopi spokesmen were John Boyden and Abbott Sekaquaptewa, the architects of Hopi land dispute strategy. Boyden had seen the 1958 bill that authorized the *Healing* suit through Congress, had argued the Hopi case before the court, and had written the Steiger Bill. In early 1972 he was preparing to ask Judge Walsh for the writ of assistance that would demand Navajo stock reduction. Ironically, Boyden had tried to become the Navajos' general counsel in 1947, before he was hired by the Hopis. The land dispute might have been a different story if the Navajos had hired him instead of Norman Littell. "We're not here asking for sympathy," Boyden told the subcommittee. "We are just asking for simple justice that the Supreme Court of the United States has said is ours in this area."[16] Sekaquaptewa, who was preparing to run for the Hopi chairmanship against incumbent Clarence Hamilton, said the continuing Navajo possession of the entire JUA constituted "a violation of human dignity and the stripping away of a people's birthright unequaled anywhere." He insisted that Navajo intrusions into District 6 threatened the Hopis with "systematic elimination as a people."[17] Simple justice and survival—these were the Hopi themes before Congress. They were much more positive than the Navajo plea, which might be summarized as, "We are in a difficult position. We have nothing but our land and our livestock. Please do not take them from us." The Hopis were demanding justice; the Navajos were asking for mercy.

Near the end of the hearings, the subcommittee heard from a member of the Hopi traditionalist faction. Mina Lansa, kikmongwi of Old Oraibi, supported the Navajos in the land dispute because she believed the real purpose of the Steiger Bill was to enable the Hopi Tribal Council to open up the land around the mesas to energy development. She had been raised with prophetic warnings of white men who would speak with "a sweet tongue," expressing friendship to the Hopis so that they could steal the land. She regarded Steiger, the tribal council, and mining companies as far more dangerous than the Navajos, whose presence she saw as providing a buffer zone around the Hopis. Mrs. Lansa told the subcommittee that the tribal council "are not telling us anything they work on in their council hall." She accused the council of distorting the land dispute. "The council of people, Clarence Hamilton and others, say all the Hopis are supporting this bill through newspapers and publicizing to the world that both Hopi and Navajo are going to fight each other," she said. "These things are not true, and it makes us very ashamed to hear and see that some of our young people who claim to represent us created much publicity in this way while in this capital lately."[18] This expression of a radically different Hopi position made no apparent impression on the members of the subcommittee.

The Chairman and the Senator

When the House of Representatives passed the Steiger Bill by voice vote at the end of July, Peter MacDonald was desperate. His own political future, along with the future of several thousand of the most traditional members of his tribe, was at stake. MacDonald thought he knew a way to block the bill in the Senate, however, and he gambled.

When the Navajo chairman was working as an electrical engineer in Southern California in 1964, he had worked on Barry Goldwater's presidential campaign. He was a Goldwater conservative—a most unusual orientation for an Indian leader and a delight to a Republican Party that in the summer of 1972 was proclaiming a "new majority" for Richard Nixon. MacDonald was to be a member of the Arizona delegation to the Republican National Convention, and Barry Goldwater had helped arrange for him to be one of the speakers who would place Nixon's name before the convention. And then, abruptly, MacDonald fell from Republican grace. His name was stricken from the list of nominating speakers, and he became an enemy of Barry Goldwater. How did this happen?

Having passed the House, the Steiger Bill was referred to the Senate Subcommittee on Indian Affairs. The chairman of the sub-committee was George McGovern, Democratic candidate for president. MacDonald flew to Washington to meet with McGovern, who expressed his distaste for relocation and said he thought Congress should give the two tribes until the end of the year to negotiate a settlement of their dispute. "If there has been no satisfactory agreement reached before next January, I will propose comprehensive new legislation designed to resolve the problem in such a way that no family is needlessly removed from its home land," McGovern wrote afterward to the Navajo chairman. "Any such legislation must provide for maximum utilization of the joint use land in question and must be fully deliberated in both houses of Congress after all the facts are known."[19]

MacDonald was relieved—and thankful. He told the *Washington Post* that unless Republicans supported the Navajos in the land dispute he might "have to support George McGovern." The story ran on August 5, two weeks before the Republican convention.[20]

Before MacDonald's statement to the *Post*, Barry Goldwater had remained steadfastly neutral in the land dispute. He was genuinely fond of both tribes and wanted to offend neither. As a young man, Goldwater had traveled widely on the Navajo and Hopi reservations, taking photographs that won critical acclaim and were prized by collectors. He owned a trading post at Navajo Mountain that burned in 1951. Although Goldwater did not visit the reservations often after the fire, he maintained his interest in both tribes and could be counted on to help them obtain federal funds for schools and hospitals. The senator enjoyed entertaining friends in Washington with stories about his Indian friends. He even regarded himself as something of an Indian expert. During his presidential campaign he traveled in a plane named Yei Bi Kin (Navajo for "House of the Holy People") and in a train named Baa Hozhnilne (Navajo for "To Win Them Over"). His house on Camelback Mountain in Phoenix is named Be Nun I Kin (Navajo for "House on the Hill"). The senator's magnificent collection of kachina dolls symbolized his sentimental attachment to the Hopis.

Peter MacDonald's statement that he might support George McGovern offended and angered Barry Goldwater, who felt betrayed by a man he had regarded as his friend. In a judgment supported by several others involved in the Navajo-Hopi dispute, Wayne Sekaquaptewa traced Goldwater's advocacy of the Hopi position to MacDonald's playing of the McGovern card. "He was sitting on the fence before that," Sekaquaptewa said. The senator and the chairman have been feuding ever since, with tragic consequences for the Navajos of the Joint Use Area.

A Charge of Racial Discrimination

The Navajos thought the Steiger Bill was dead for 1972 when George McGovern said his subcommittee would not move on it. But Henry Jackson, chairman of the full Senate Interior Committee, felt the Senate had an obligation to act on the bill since the House had passed it, and he scheduled hearings on the land dispute. At the hearings John Boyden once again cried out for justice for the oppressed. He said the land dispute was more than just a squabble between two Indian tribes. "This is a problem to determine whether, under the constitution of the United States, a minority within a minority can have the opportunity to have its rights after they have been adjudicated by the highest court in the land."[21]

The Navajo case was presented by Richard Schifter, a member of the Washington law firm that represented the Navajos in the land dispute. Although Schifter became involved in the land dispute much later than Boyden, he developed convictions as intense as those of the Hopi general counsel. Schifter was convinced that relocation would be a disaster, and he thought the Steiger Bill smacked of racism. He asked the committee to consider two acts of Congress which had settled Indian claims to lands occupied by whites. Both of them, the Pueblo Lands Act of 1924 and the Alaska Native Claims Act of 1971, had authorized possession of the land for the non-Indians and monetary compensation for the Indians. Like Boyden, Schifter put the Navajo-Hopi land dispute in a large frame. "Could it be, may I ask, that where the settlers are white, we pay off the original owners in cash; but where the settlers are

Indian, we find expulsion and removal an acceptable alternative? Can such a racially discriminatory approach be considered as meeting the constitutional requirement of due process?"[22]

Schifter also argued that there were established principles of federal Indian law that the *Healing* court had ignored but that Congress should heed. Asserting that the *Healing* court had erred in finding that ownership of the Joint Use Area was equal, he referred the committee to several decisions of the Indian Claims Commission, which was established by Congress in 1946 to compensate Indians for land taken from them. The decisions cited by Schifter had directly addressed the question of how joint tribal rights to land should be partitioned and had found that ordinary principles of property law should not apply. A passage from the case of *Blackfeet and Gros Ventre Tribes v. the United States* illustrates Schifter's point:

> To do this [apply ordinary property law principles] would be contrary to reason since a subsistence use of the land necessarily implies use in proportion to numbers. . . . we think the proper and just manner of dividing tribal interests in a given area is by population.[23]

An application of this principle of Indian law, Schifter concluded, would entitle the Navajos to nearly all of the 1882 Reservation outside of District 6. In the end, Congress would ignore Schifter. The 1974 act would apply Anglo concepts of legal title to the JUA, but it would go contrary to the custom of allowing settlers to remain on Indian lands while compensating the tribe whose land had been settled. The Navajo plea that the Hopis should be compensated would be ignored, and the Navajo settlers on Hopi land would be ordered to relocate.

Red Power

Security was tight in Winslow on March 7, 1973, as Senators James Abourezk of South Dakota and Paul Fannin of Arizona arrived for a day of land dispute hearings. Over the previous several months, the politics of Red Power had become the politics of confrontation in a series of violent incidents stretching from Washington to New Mexico, and state officials feared an attempt to kidnap one of the senators.

Five days before Richard Nixon's landslide victory over George McGovern in November 1972, several hundred Indians had come to Washington on what they called the Trail of Broken Treaties. Their planned program for the week—a round of issues workshops, spiritual services, and meetings with government officials—terminated suddenly in the armed occupation of the Bureau of Indian Affairs headquarters four blocks from the White House. Renaming the building the American Indian Embassy, the militants vowed to fight to the death if police moved in to expel them. A week later, after the government promised to establish a task force to listen to Indian grievances, they vacated the building, leaving behind damage estimated at $200,000.[24]

For seven hours of a night in late January 1973, six members of the American Indian Movement (AIM) occupied the Indian Health Service hospital in Gallup, New Mexico, at the western edge of the state, just a few miles from the Navajo Reservation. They said their action was intended to demonstrate the dissatisfaction of Indians with the health care the government was obligated by treaty to provide.

On February 27, eight days before the Winslow hearing, armed militants, including Dennis Banks and Russell Means, who had led the takeover of the BIA in Washington, seized the South Dakota hamlet of Wounded Knee, site of the infamous massacre of Sioux by the Seventh Cavalry in 1890. They demanded a Senate investigation of Washington's treatment of the Sioux and the dismissal of Oglala Sioux Chairman Richard Wilson, whom they charged with nepotism, protection of bootleggers, and deployment of a goon squad to harass political opponents. Wilson labeled the militants "renegades," "vagrants," and "intruders" and said he had 800 to 900 supporters ready to go into Wounded Knee to clear them out.[25] Journalists from around the world converged upon Wounded Knee as federal marshals surrounded the hamlet. The occupation lasted more than two months and became a symbol of the surging Red Power movement.

The indignation of two young Navajos resulted in tragedy on the streets of Gallup the first day of March. Larry Casuse, president of the Indian students' organization at the University of New Mexico, and fellow student Robert Nakaidinae abducted mayor Emmett Garcia from Gallup's city hall. They were furious that the governor had appointed Garcia to the Board of Regents of the university. They hated Garcia because he owned a third of the Navajo Inn, a package liquor store near Window Rock just a few hundred yards from the reservation line, across which the purchase or possession of alcohol is prohibited by tribal law.

The Navajo Inn was a grim showcase for the problem of alcohol abuse among the Navajos. Casuse called it a place "where numerous alcoholics are born." Writing in the *New Yorker*, Calvin Trillin described the Navajo Inn as "a small cinder block building surrounded by open space and on some paydays by so many passed out Navajos that it takes on the appearance of a bunker in a recently contested battlefield."[26] Sometimes people passed out from the liquor and froze in the night. Sometimes they staggered onto the darkness of Highway 264 to be mowed down by passing vehicles. The inn was destroyed in 1977 when the Pittsburgh and Midway Coal Company bought it and the surrounding land to build an access road to its strip mine.

Garcia worked to obtain funding for an alcoholism treatment center in Gallup. But as far as Casuse and Nakaidinae were concerned, this made the mayor a hypocrite who expressed false concern for the misery that filled his pockets. Casuse had spent his entire life in the confused margin between two worlds. His Navajo father had met his Austrian mother while in the army. The young man's abduction of Garcia was an affirmation of his Indianness and a statement of his rage at the degradation of his people. Holding a gun to Garcia's head, he and Nakaidinae marched him to a sporting goods store on Route 66, where Casuse was killed in an exchange of gunfire with Gallup police.

Senate Hearings in Winslow

Six days after the bloodshed in Gallup, Senators Abourezk and Fannin came to Winslow shielded by bodyguards. Dozens of state and local police made themselves conspicuous to ensure that the violence in Gallup would not move the 130 miles west on Interstate 40 to Winslow. The hearings were peaceful. Most of the people who filled the Civic Center were Navajos from the JUA who were not involved in Indian militancy.

The Navajos presented their arguments in the morning; the Hopis responded in the afternoon. One of the topics was the Hopi impoundment program, which the Navajos called "pure harassment to gain publicity for the Hopi chairman." Navajo Peterson Zah said Clarence Hamilton "has so little support for these tactics from his own people that he must use hired Anglos to carry out such policies."[27] Peter MacDonald said the problem of Navajo trespass and Hopi impoundment could be solved with a fence around District 6. He said the Navajos had offered to build a fence along the border but had been blocked by the Hopis. Abbott Sekaquaptewa rebutted sharply. "Now that we are doing something to prevent Navajo takeover of our exclusive Hopi lands, we are accused of creating incidents for publicity purposes," he said. "Are we to stand by and do nothing while they take over the last vestiges of our homeland?"[28]

One of the Navajos expelled from District 6 told of the "loneliness, sickness, and heartaches" of losing his home.[29] Hopi vice-chairman Logan Koopee countered with a litany of names of Hopis he said had "died of a broken heart" because of the Navajo settlement of the JUA. "In simple terms this bill would prevent any further loss of Hopi land," Koopee said. "It would return to us at least a modest measure of economic security and opportunity."[30]

Peter MacDonald hammered away at the divisions within the Hopi Tribe, claiming most Hopis did not support the tribal government's efforts to have Navajos evicted from half the JUA. "There is just a small group of Hopi leaders who want to build a Hopi empire at the expense of thousands of Navajos who earn a meager living off the land which they consider their own," MacDonald said, as he proposed a Navajo buy-out of the Hopi interest.[31] Sekaquaptewa countered with the claim that the *Healing* decision had been "a compromise of Hopi land rights." He said the Hopis would accept no settlement short of equal partition. "We cannot compromise what is already a compromise," Sekaquaptewa said. "It is immoral to even think of doing so."[32]

A member of the Senate Interior Committee staff stayed in Arizona after the senators left. Bill Chandler spent several days talking with Navajos and Hopis, then wrote a report of his findings and impressions. "I tried to examine the other side of the Steiger proposal," Chandler said in a 1977 interview. "I tried to look at some of the problems of the bill, to examine the assertion that relocation was something we could live with, that it was workable and ought to be done." Chandler said he concluded in his report that relocation would be "fraught with enormous if not insurmountable difficulties."

Goldwater Speaks Out for the Hopis

Senator Abourezk made it clear in Winslow that despite the gulf between Navajo and Hopi positions he wanted the two sides to continue negotiations. In April and May, Navajo and Hopi representatives met in Salt Lake City and Phoenix. The Navajos offered two plans. The first called once again for the Hopis to accept compensation for their JUA interest. In the second plan, the Navajos offered to turn over to the Hopis part of the southern JUA and proposed that the Hopis use the land as a corridor from District 6 to new lands they might buy south of the JUA border with federal assistance. For the first time, then, the Navajos showed a willingness to accept limited relocation in order to achieve a settlement that would leave the bulk of the disputed lands in Navajo hands.

The Hopis were not interested. After the meeting in Phoenix, Abbott Sekaquaptewa said they could see "no reason to continue this exercise in rehashing what has already been settled . . . as far as we are concerned, we cannot further undignify ourselves by participating in these so-called negotiations."[33] While the Navajos cast about desperately for an alternative to the Steiger Bill, the Hopis shut off negotiations in the growing confidence that the Steiger Bill would become law.

By the time the House held its 1973 hearings on the land dispute, the Steiger Bill had been joined by two other proposals. Arizona's John Conlan and New Mexico's Manuel Lujan sponsored the Navajo buy-out alternative, and Lloyd Meeds of Washington, chairman of the Indian subcommittee, introduced legislation for mandatory arbitration. John Boyden told the subcommittee that failure of Congress to put the Hopis in possession of half the JUA "would constitute one of the most unfair and unconscionable acts ever perpetrated by the United States upon its Indian wards."[34] Peter MacDonald also lobbed a rhetorical bomb. He said forced relocation would be "a tragedy of international proportions," and he warned that the government "will have to send the Blue Coats again" to quash Navajo resistance to relocation. "It is inconceivable that in the second half of the twentieth century the tragedies of frontier times could be knowingly repeated—the forced eviction of Indian people, the long marches, the Trail of Tears," he said.[35]

By this time, subcommittee members who had not declared themselves for one of the three bills probably wished they could throw up their hands and walk away. They were baffled by the land dispute. Both sides spoke so passionately. The Joint Use Area was terra incognita, an unchartered land inhabited by people they could not presume to understand. And then Barry Goldwater came over to show them the way out of their confusion. With all the confident certainty of a John Wayne character in a movie of the Old West, Arizona's most distinguished political figure said he understood the land dispute and knew how to settle it once and for all. The issue really wasn't so complicated, Goldwater believed. The Hopis were right and the Navajos were wrong.

Delighted to have such a formidable ally, Sam Steiger introduced Goldwater as "a longtime friend of Arizona Indians." He said Goldwater "not only knows the people, he knows the land. He knows it in a way I think very few non-Indians know it." Lloyd Meeds of Washington state was also gracious, telling Goldwater, "You've obviously had an abiding interest in Indian affairs."[36]

Goldwater spoke proudly of Arizona's Indian heritage. "We have fifteen tribes in Arizona," he said. "They occupy nineteen reservations, which constitute almost 30 percent of the total land area of my state. And we have, in fact, more Indians in Arizona than any other state, when you think of full-blooded Indians retaining their language, their customs, and most important of all, their religion and culture."

In their lobbying efforts against the Steiger Bill, Navajo officials met congressmen and aides who were incredulous that relocation would be difficult for a tribe whose lands totaled nearly 16 million acres. The Navajos argued that they had received most of the land only because it was poor and no one else wanted it. They said Navajos lived far apart because they had to, and they explained that every foot of the reservation was part of some family's customary use area. When Senator Goldwater explained his previous silence on the land dispute, he mocked this stark fact of Navajo life. "I have not supported the Steiger approach mostly because it involved money," he said. "And I do not think we have to pay money to relocate Indians, when in the case of the Navajo they have 16 million acres." Senator Goldwater said the Navajos had "literally tens of thousands of acres that are not being used." The Navajos were incredulous at the announcement that there were open lands on their reservation. It was not the last time Goldwater would make a mistake in interpreting the land dispute to Congress.

Goldwater went on to say his argument on behalf of the Hopis was "a very simple one" and said he did not think the Navajos had "any right encroaching upon the Hopi Reservation." He illustrated his reasoning. "I do not know what the Navajos would say if the Hopis started moving around Window Rock and setting up their nice little pueblos over there—or even what would happen if some of the Hopis showed up at Kayenta, which they would not do, of course, and put on one of their ceremonials. In other words, if you move onto my land, I would raise hell with you, and I would get you off, unless you wanted to buy, which does not happen in this case."[37] The Navajos, of course, wanted very much to buy.

That Senator Goldwater had reduced the land dispute to a seriously oversimplified formula was beyond the ability of most congressmen to grasp. Important to them was that a senator of national reputation, a former candidate for president, an Arizonan reputed to know his state's Indians well, had agreed in principle with the Steiger Bill. Goldwater had not spoken specifically of relocation, but clearly he was willing to accept it. For conservative congressmen, especially, that was good enough. Steiger Bill stock rose fifty points immediately.

Anthropologist David Aberle gave the Navajo response. Aberle's observations on Navajo life had been formed through years of field work on the reservation, but they had none of Goldwater's immediate credibility. Goldwater was a senator, Aberle a professor. "I would like to comment that it has been said this morning that there is lots of unused land on the Navajo Reservation," he said. "I think it is important to keep in mind that the Navajo Reservation is a paradox. It is an area of low population density which is severely overcrowded and has been for decades. The kind of free land that has been talked about simply does not exist."

Aberle asked the subcommittee to consider that the Navajos of the JUA are "an undereducated population, far from the job market, with a per capita income of around $600 per annum, compared to about $831 for the entire Navajo population and $3,484 for the entire United States." He argued forcefully against relocation:

> I cannot see any outcome of the planned relocation but a mess in which Murphy's Law operates. Anything that can go wrong will go wrong. Navajos in the disputed territory and outside are partially dependent on welfare. But they are not

demoralized, and they try to make a living. I think that the
result of [relocation] may be generations of indigence, instead
of a population of remarkable people whom I have come to
admire. . . . [The sheep herd] provides the herder with a significant economic role in the family, with an opportunity for
valuable work and with a corresponding feeling of pride, worth,
and independence. For that reason, the Navajos are, on the
whole, far less demoralized than many other Indian groups in
the country.

The herd may not be the sole source of family income. It
may be supplemented by some wage income of a younger
family member and some welfare payments. But the herd
remains the family's mainstay, both economically and psychologically. It gives the family the stability on which it rests and
which enables it to raise a generation of reasonably well-
adjusted people who, with the benefit of the security of their
home life and an adequate education, may be able to make an
adjustment to the complex prevailing culture.

Remove the sheepherder to a place where he cannot man-
age stock, remove the herd, and you have removed the foundation and security on which the family rested. Demoralization
and social disorganization are the inevitable consequences,
and the younger people, no longer the beneficiaries of a stable
home life, become just another addition to the problems of
maladjustment and alienation in our society.[38]

Aberle's statement identified the dilemma of traditional Navajo
life, the moral issue that made the land dispute much more than a
fight for land. A culturally and physically isolated group of American Indians were clinging to a way of life in which the bonds to
land, family, and livestock anchored everyone against the turbulence of cultural transition. The young were accommodating themselves to the economic reality that the livestock economy had become
archaic, had worn out the land. The young were getting educated,
learning job skills, moving into the wage economy, frequently leaving the reservation to find work. But the elderly could not remake
their lives, shove aside centuries of history, and move away with
the ease of non-Indians moving to retirement communities in southern Arizona. They were tied to the land, and they were terrified
that Congress might make them leave. They could not transfer

their way of life to other reservation lands, because those lands were already overcommitted, and a move to the confusing world of town was out of the question. With instinctive stubbornness, they were saying they would not leave because they could not survive anywhere else. "I do not want to be misunderstood," Aberle said. "I am not here to defy the law. I do not believe the Navajo will view themselves as defying the law if they merely stay in their homes. They will view the order to leave as defying the principles of order that are the essence of their own lives and beings."[39] He urged Congress to make alternative lands available for the expansion of the Hopi cattle industry.

Congress did not take Aberle's advice. It opted for partition, the active, "bite-the-bullet" alternative to settle the problems of Hopi land rights and Navajo overgrazing. We have already said that partition was a victory of property rights over human rights. It was also a victory of economic imperatives over a traditional tribal culture.

John Boyden's Strategy

Senator Goldwater's statement that there was no need for the government to help Navajos relocate probably surprised John Boyden. It certainly pleased him. The resourceful Hopi general counsel drafted a bill for Goldwater's sponsorship that would have required the Navajos to get out without a dime of assistance for new homes. Arizona's other senator, Paul Fannin, joined in as cosponsor. In a press conference announcing his sponsorship, Fannin railed against Navajo overgrazing. "We not only have violence between Indians," he said. "The Joint Use Area is dying."[40]

Next to the Goldwater-Fannin Bill, the Steiger Bill seemed downright kind—which was precisely Boyden's intent. Boyden continued his deft tactical maneuvering at the end of 1973 by persuading Utah Democratic Representative Wayne Owens to sponsor a substitute for the Steiger Bill. The Owens Bill proposed that the JUA be partitioned by the federal court in Arizona rather than by Congress directly. Boyden's strategy in switching sponsors was as simple as it was shrewd, and it had the full support of Steiger, who pledged to continue his fight for partition. Boyden succeeded in creating a coalition between Steiger, a conservative Republican, and Owens, a liberal Democrat. Between the two congressmen,

Boyden was convinced, there would be enough votes for partition of the JUA.

Sam Steiger was an easterner who had gone west to become a cowboy. Wayne Owens was a westerner with the urbane sophistication of the Northeast. He had been an officer in Robert Kennedy's presidential campaign; then he went to Washington to work on the staff of Senator Edward Kennedy. In 1972 Owens won his congressional campaign against four-term incumbent Sherman Lloyd by making a much-publicized 689-mile walk across Utah's huge Second Congressional District. En route he attacked Lloyd for an environmental record that had earned Lloyd a spot on Environmental Action's Dirty Dozen, a distinction also held by Sam Steiger. All things considered, Owens and Steiger made an unlikely pair.

Just before the 1973 Christmas recess, the House Subcommittee on Indian Affairs turned back Lloyd Meed's proposal for forced arbitration by an eight to six vote. They then endorsed the Owens Bill and sent it on to the full Interior Committee. Subcommittee consideration of the Owens Bill featured an interesting exchange between Steiger and New Mexico's Manuel Lujan.

Lujan noted that in previous land controversies, where Indian tribes had rights to land occupied by non-Indians, Congress had ordered financial compensation for the Indians. He suggested that it would be inconsistent for Congress to direct the relocation of Navajos from the JUA. Steiger shot from the hip in response. "I would simply tell the gentleman that the distinction between that situation and this one is that in those instances, we are dealing with non-Indians occupying and believing they have a right in the lands. Here we are dealing with two tribes. That is the distinction."[41] He did not elaborate.

Near the end of 1973 Abbott Sekaquaptewa was elected chairman of the Hopi Tribe, and shortly after assuming office he won an appropriation from the tribal council for a full-scale lobbying effort in Washington. The Hopis had all the momentum. They were prepared for a climactic final push.

The Navajos Make a Deal With the AFL-CIO

After clearing the Indian Affairs Subcommittee, the Owens Bill needed endorsements from the Interior Committee and the full House before it could begin working its way through the Senate. The Navajos put another obstacle in the bill's path in early 1974 when they enlisted the aide of one of the most powerful organizations in Washington, the AFL-CIO.

The labor movement had never got a foothold in Arizona, where Barry Goldwater personified the state's hostility toward unions. Goldwater was particularly upset that the AFL-CIO's political wing, the Committee on Political Education (COPE), disbursed millions of dollars and thousands of workers nationwide to the campaigns of select candidates. He claimed that such activity concentrated enormous power in the hands of a few labor leaders. "Unions exist, presumably to confer economic advantages on their members, not to perform political services for them," he wrote in *The Conscience of a Conservative*. "Unions should therefore be forbidden to engage in any kind of political activity."[42]

Richard Schifter, Washington attorney for the Navajos, told Peter MacDonald that the tribe could derive two benefits if it relaxed its own long-standing opposition to organized labor. First, he said, if the unions were allowed to organize on the reservation, they could provide training programs for Navajo workers. And second, a Navajo alliance with labor could be helpful in making sure that the tribe's position on the land dispute would be heard in Washington. The deal Schifter recommended was struck. In a related element of the partnership, COPE helped the tribe with a massive voter registration drive in 1974 aimed at defeating the Republicans who had been the traditional enemies of labor and who had more recently become adversaries of the Navajos in the fight over the JUA.[43]

Two Views of Partition

Sam Steiger cried foul in the weeks before the Interior Committee met to discuss the land dispute, claiming labor should not be involved in the land dispute. Like the subcommittee, the full committee would choose between the Owens Bill for partition and the Meeds Bill for forced arbitration. Lobbying on both sides was intense.

In a 1977 interview, Meeds explained how his visit to the JUA had convinced him that he should oppose partition. He said he met a number of Navajos, including one angry young man just back from Vietnam, who swore they would not leave their homes. "I was pretty much for the Hopi position until I visited the disputed area," Meeds said. "That trip showed me the tenacity of a people whose ancestors were born and raised in a particular area and have developed very close ties to the land. I saw that we were talking about land where people were living as opposed to just raising cattle, which is what the Hopis wanted the land for. There are alternatives to raising cattle, but not too many alternatives for people who are living on the land." Meeds said the Hopi position was very strong legally, then added, "Still, I think that if other members had been out there, they would have come back feeling the same way I felt. You've got to do more than just look at the pages of a legal decision. The legal theory is that people should live on land they own. But we were involved in some stark human facts, not some cold legal theory. The fact was that these people had lived their lives there."

Ohio Republican Ralph Regula took an opposing view. Regula had never visited the JUA and had never heard of the Hopis before the land dispute came to Congress. Still, as one who had been raised on a farm and whose rural legal practice had involved him in many a land fight, Regula felt he understood the passions of the Navajo-Hopi dispute. "People are people, and land is land," he said. "I don't care if it's Arizona or New York."

As he talked with a reporter in late 1978, Regula showed an amazingly complete memory of the Navajo-Hopi fight more than four years previous. He had obviously agonized over his decision. "It was an impossible situation, and we did the best we could," he said. "I don't think there was any question that the Hopis were legally entitled to possession of the land. We were down to basic property rights on this. If you and I own ten acres, and I'm on eight, you're still entitled to five. I tell you, though, I'm glad I don't have to be the marshal that has to carry the Navajos out. I could visualize that."

In February of 1974, both sides knew the Interior Committee vote would be close. Each side kept scorecards that showed which congressmen had committed themselves and which were still un-decided. The lobbying became frantic. When the Meeds Bill failed (in a 20–20 tie vote) the Navajos were stunned. The tally showed that the land dispute had become a partisan issue. Lloyd Meeds and COPE had persuaded sixteen of the twenty-three Democrats on the committee to vote for the Meeds Bill; Sam Steiger and Ralph Regula brought in thirteen of the seventeen Republicans against it. The Owens Bill then passed on a voice vote. Steiger indignantly told the *Arizona Republic* that the Indian subcommittee had voted eleven to two against the Meeds Bill before COPE got involved. It was another case of Steiger blurring the issue. The subcommittee vote against Meeds had been eight to six.

Manuel Lujan's Letter

During James Haley's chairmanship of the Interior Committee, bills that survived the committee almost never lost on the House floor. The Hopis were so confident the Owens Bill would pass there that they turned their attention to the Senate. Then Manuel Lujan reversed the Hopi momentum.

Lujan sent a sizzling "dear colleague" letter to every member of the House just before the Owens Bill came up for a vote under a procedure known as suspension of the rules that limits debate to one hour and requires a two-thirds majority for passage. Written in the tone of a man shouting from the rooftops, the Lujan letter warned of bedlam should the Owens Bill become law. "Enactment of this bill could result in a blood bath in northern Arizona that would make the My Lai massacre look like a Sunday School picnic," Lujan wrote. He said the bill would force the relocation of seven to eight thousand Navajos and continued, "the Navajo families have served notice on Congress that they will not abandon their homes and land peaceably. They will resist, which means the government will have to haul them away at gun point."

The Owens Bill provided money for relocation benefits, but no place for the displaced Navajos to go, Lujan observed. He said forced relocation would be "the most shameful act this government has perpetrated on our Indian citizens since Colonial days. . . . The American public would not permit us to treat coyotes the way the bill orders the Navajos treated. . . . And the most shameful aspect of the Navajo-Hopi land dispute is that it has been created entirely by the U.S. Government itself. Having created the problem over the past 100 years, we now order the Navajos to take the blame and pay for our mistakes by giving up their homes, their land, and very possibly their lives."

The New Mexico Republican visualized the form Navajo resistance would take and anticipated it would result in an international scandal. "My dear colleagues, think for just one moment of the image our nation will gain for itself in the eyes of the international community when the TV cameras report the spectacle of armed American soldiers routing thousands of poverty-stricken and helpless Indians out of their sod huts at gun point, clubbing down or shooting those who resist, and hauling them off like so many stunned and bleeding animals. . . .In the name of justice, humanity, and national honor, I urge you to join me in voting down H.R. 10337 [the Owens Bill] and demanding the right to let the Congress vote on the alternative and non-violent solutions that have been proposed."[44]

The letter was an extended hyperbole, an exaggeration for effect from a man whose proposal for a Navajo buy-out of Hopi interests had received no attention. It was stunningly successful. On the House floor two congressmen expressed disbelief that a bill that would require relocation of several thousand Indians at a cost exceeding $28 million had been brought up under suspension. Far from winning a two-thirds majority, the Owens Bill was voted down, 133 against and 100 for.

Sam Steiger grumbled that the Lujan letter was "a lot of emotional garbage."[45] And Abbott Sekaquaptewa issued his own very quotable warning at a Salt Lake City press conference. "I don't propose a war, and I don't want that tactic," the Hopi chairman said. "But I don't sit here to guarantee that my people will keep the peace. If it takes blood and guts, that's what we'll do." Two days after his Salt Lake City appearance, Sekaquaptewa was in Phoenix to tell newsmen, "There comes a time when people have to defend themselves. And we are prepared to do that. We have been pushed beyond the limit of endurance."[46]

The House Passes the Owens Bill

The Hopi chairman's press conference remarks were the first salvoes in a public relations war with the Navajos that raged across the Southwest in March, April, and May of 1974. There was activity on other fronts as well. With help from Barry Goldwater, the Hopis managed to persuade the House leadership to schedule the Owens Bill for vote under a regular rule, which would require a simple majority for passage and allow unlimited debate and floor amendments. Meanwhile, the COPE voter registration drive was in full swing on the Navajo Reservation. Peter MacDonald told a Phoenix news conference that a major thrust of the Navajo voter effort would be to oust Sam Steiger. "Steiger is the biggest liar I have ever come across," MacDonald said. "He is the only man I know who can look you in the face and lie to you. I am very disappointed we have a man like him in the Congress. To me, people who are reckless with the truth are as bad as the persons involved in the Watergate scandal."[47]

On another occasion MacDonald said the Owens Bill demonstrated a double standard for Indian land claims. If the Hopis were to be allowed to force Navajos off the JUA, the Navajos should be allowed to force non-Indians out of Farmington and Gallup, New Mexico, he said. "The Navajos believe that everyone should play by the same rules and that if Indians are not allowed to take over their claims because Anglos live on it, then the Hopis should be prevented from doing it."[48] This was one of the Navajos' most compelling arguments, and they advanced it repeatedly.

Abbott Sekaquaptewa got a dig in at Manuel Lujan and U.S. Senator Joseph Montoya of New Mexico for supporting a Navajo buy-out of the JUA. "The land is not for sale, and we will not give it up," he said. "Let them appropriate public funds to buy out the Spanish land grants and give them to the Navajo."[49]

Wayne Sekaquaptewa's *Qua Toqti* provided some welcome relief from the verbal heat with a cartoon depicting MacDonald in a chef's hat presiding over a "bullburger" stand at a Navajo hogan. The chef's hat was labeled "Big Mac," and the hogan carried two arches over the slogan "Over Two Served." Two mudheads, comic figures in Hopi religious dances, were slumped over a table, feeling the effects of the bullburgers, and the caption quoted MacDonald as boasting, "My bullburgers are gobbled up so fast, especially in Washington."[50] Even the Navajos appreciated the cartoon.

Navajo relations with Barry Goldwater, which had begun to deteriorate in 1972, worsened steadily in 1974 because of the tribe's alliance with the AFL-CIO. A front page story in the *Phoenix Gazette* quoted Goldwater blasting MacDonald for "spreading lies about the land dispute." Asked for his reaction to MacDonald's effort to get out the vote for Democrats, Goldwater snapped, "If he wants to go after my seat, fine. I just may go after his."[51]

MacDonald lost no time responding. He compared the Owens Bill with the Long Walk to the Bosque Redondo. "I had thought the day of Bosque Redondo had passed, along with the day of Kit Carson," he sniped in a news release issued by the Phoenix office of George Vlassis, general counsel for the Navajos. "But apparently

Kit Goldwater has revived the old tradition of driving the Indian to the point of starvation to gain his voluntary acceptance of federal programs."[52]

The "dear colleague" letters were flying on Capitol Hill in the weeks before the Owens and Meeds bills were brought up again. A letter from Meeds insisted that negotiation or forced arbitration of the land dispute would be the only way to avert bloodshed.[53] Steiger feared the Meeds Bill would result in a Navajo buy-out, which he said "would constitute a blanket endorsement of economic and cultural genocide of our country's oldest surviving Indian tribe."[54] Goldwater and Fannin claimed to "know in great detail the relative merits of the century-old dispute" and said their knowledge "demanded support for the Owens Bill."[55] Owens wrote that the Navajos who would be forced out by his bill "would have to leave the land anyway because of the overgrazing."[56]

While the Navajos and Hopis were competing for space in the newspapers, and while the letters were circulating on Capitol Hill, Peter MacDonald was quietly deciding not to commit his tribe's lobbying resources to the Meeds Bill. Tribal elections would be held in the fall, and MacDonald was expecting a stiff challenge from the man he had defeated in 1970, Raymond Nakai. Politically, the safest thing for MacDonald was to hold the hard line of the Lujan buy-out approach, even if it obviously had no chance in Congress. And so, while Owens and Steiger pressed singlemindedly for the Owens Bill, Meeds and Lujan were at cross purposes. Richard Schifter repeatedly called on the Navajo chairman to get behind the Meeds Bill, insisting it could win with an all-out effort. MacDonald ignored Schifter until the week before the House vote, when he okayed a Navajo push for the Meeds Bill. By this time, however, the Navajos had been outmaneuvered by the Hopi lobbyists—teams of lawyers and people from the villages who visited every congressional office. The effect of MacDonald's indecision was to sacrifice the Navajos' best hope to personal political expediency. Had the Meeds Bill become law, the required negotiations between the two tribes would probably have failed, but there would have been a chance for the federal arbitrators to order unequal partition of the JUA that would have allowed the Navajos to retain more than half the land. The Hopis could have been compensated for whatever portion less than half they received.

Another quiet but pivotal decision was made by Congressman

Morris Udall. As Barry Goldwater was Arizona's most influential senator, Udall was the state's most respected member of the House of Representatives. Both sides tugged hard at the Tucson Democrat, aware that he could swing dozens of votes. Udall recalled his quandary in 1977.

"I was being torn by two considerations," he said. "I really felt the damn thing had to be settled. It was festering, and it would continue to fester unless we took some action to settle it. It seemed to me that the Owens approach had some merit. On the other hand, I was very close to the Navajos. My closeness to the unions was another factor in my decision. The unions talked about a permanent alliance between labor and the Navajos that could have a great impact on elections in Arizona. And I was in the early stages of cranking up a presidential campaign in which labor was important to me. One of the wrenching things from a personal standpoint was that my mother had a close relationship with the Sekaquaptewa family. [Mrs. Udall had helped Mrs. Sekaquaptewa write her autobiography.] The week she died we talked about the land dispute, and she asked me to take the side of the Hopis. By the time the Owens Bill got to the floor the last time, I had made up my mind that I was not going to be out front twisting arms against it. One of the union guys called me and wanted me to fight it. But I told him I just couldn't."

Udall's decision not to commit his considerable prestige on behalf of the Navajos was a relief to the Hopis, who were doing quite well without him. Sam Steiger said Udall told him, "I can't help you, but I won't hurt you."

Although Udall did not take an active role in the debate on the House floor, he did make a brief statement in support of the Meeds Bill. And he did counter the misconception persistently nurtured by Steiger that the Owens Bill was the only way Congress could conform to the *Healing* decision. For example, when Congressman Roy Taylor of North Carolina asked if the Supreme Court would not overrule any decision by federal arbitrators for a less than equal split of the JUA (assuming passage of the Meeds Bill), Steiger hastened to agree. "I think the gentleman is correct," Steiger responded. "That would be exactly my definition of what would happen. It would be the only possible circumvention of the Supreme Court decision, and it would be done in the name of expedience, I will tell the gentleman. It seems to me that that is not worthy of this body."[57]

Udall intervened with the facts. He explained that the Supreme Court decision upholding the *Healing* court had not conferred upon the Hopis an absolute right to possession of the land, but rather a 50 percent ownership of the land which could be recognized through monetary compensation. "So, if the arbitrators decide that the fair decision is to give more land to the Navajos, then we can have the Navajos pay more money to the Hopis to make up, or we can have an appropriation to make up the difference," Udall said.[58]

The whole Navajo effort in the House of Representatives was a case of too little, too sloppily, too late. Few of the 435 congressmen who would vote on the Meeds and Owens bills had time to consider the complexities of the land dispute. They and their staffs carried an enormous burden of legislation affecting their constituents. They voted upon the advice of colleagues or according to how the two tribes had presented their cases in a few hurried minutes of explanation. The Hopi lobbying effort, teaming Owens, Steiger, tribal lawyers and officials, and several people from the villages was far more efficient and coordinated than the Navajo effort with Meeds, Lujan, lawyers, and tribal representatives.

The votes were not even close. The Meeds Bill went down 199 to 128. Then the Owens Bill, in what was little more than a post-mortem formality, was adopted, 290 to 38. At about the same time, Judge Walsh was in his Tucson courtroom, issuing an order that found the Navajos in contempt of court for failing to reduce their livestock in the JUA.

6
Congress, Round Two

The Washington atmosphere was charged with reports and rumors about Watergate in the midsummer of 1974, when eighty Navajos and six anticouncil Hopis came to the nation's capital in three Greyhound buses to fight the Owens Bill. Most of them had no idea what the scandal was about. They were elderly, traditional Indians whose world did not encompass the meaning of break-ins and cover-ups and articles of impeachment; anyway, they had their own crisis to worry about. Many were making their first trip beyond the towns that border the reservation. Nearly a dozen were medicine men. On the way east they sprinkled corn pollen into the Rio Grande, the Mississippi, the Missouri, and the Potomac to pray for a successful journey.

The group held press conferences at several cities. Samuel Pete, director of the Navajo Tribe's Land Dispute Commission, outlined the purpose of the trip to reporters while photographers clicked pictures of the Arizona Indians holding hand-lettered cardboard signs that read "Navajos Will Not Be Moved Like Cattle," and "Indian Justice." Inevitably, the news stories ran under headlines that told of "Indians on the warpath" to Washington.

Each time the buses stopped at a Greyhound terminal for food or a change of drivers, some of the elderly men clustered around game-room machines pulsing with light and sound in simulation of submarine warfare or a ping-pong match. They stared in astonishment at white bleeps that glided across glass screens to blow up enemy shipping or tie the score. Then they walked back to the bus, shaking their heads and muttering softly to themselves in Navajo.

Three days and twenty-one hundred miles from Window Rock, the buses arrived in Washington. Several of the medicine men asked to be taken to the ocean so they could pray and gather water for ceremonial use back home. Before dawn one morning, two cars set out on the three-hour drive to the Maryland resort town of Ocean City, where they conducted a short ritual at the water's edge and left offerings of turquoise, jet, abalone, and shell—the four sacred stones used in Navajo ritual. Carlos Castaneda's books on the Yaqui medicine man Don Juan were quite popular at the time, and the Indian jewelry fad was peaking in the East, so the Indian medicine men from Arizona in turquoise beads, concho belts, and wide-brimmed hats caused quite a stir. For their part, the Navajos were startled to see women in bikinis. A television crew interviewed Samuel Pete, and a local woman invited the group to her restaurant for lunch. But it was a seafood restaurant, and the medicine men were not about to eat anything from the ocean to which they had just prayed. They were chagrined to learn that the menus, which they could not read, featured such dishes as baked flounder, crab cake, and clam chowder. Fortunately, the restaurant also served a few items not from the sea. All the Navajos ate steak.

Several dozen Indians walking the halls of the two Senate office buildings couldn't help but draw a lot of attention. The large contingent from the reservation irked Senator Goldwater, who released to the *Washington Post* a statement chiding the Navajos for "attempting to overwhelm Congress by sheer numbers and political strength."[1] In a meeting with the Navajos on the day the story ran, Goldwater angrily denied that he had made the statement and condemned the *Post* for running it. But a reporter attending the meeting obtained a copy of the release from Goldwater's office and learned that the *Post* had quoted him correctly.

The people from the reservation were in Washington less than a week. But the Navajos had a battalion of other lobbyists in the nation's capital throughout the summer. There were Richard Schifter and Rick West of the prestigious Washington law firm of Fried, Frank, Harris, Shriver, and Kampelman. There were Al Barkan, head of the AFL-CIO's Committee for Political Education, and other union officials instrumental in the alliance with the tribe. There was the public relations firm of Maurer, Fleisher, Zon, and

Anderson. The Navajos also retained free-lance lobbyist Joe Miller, a former chairman of the Democratic National Campaign Committee. And they opened a congressional liaison office, whose primary assignment was to work against the Owens Bill.

While the Navajo representatives bustled about, the Hopis deliberately kept a low profile. Several of the lawyers in John Boyden's law firm flew in from Salt Lake City and teamed up with two or three Hopis to make the rounds of Senate offices. The lawyers made a brief presentation of the land dispute's history, and the Hopis followed with a short speech asking for understanding and help. It was all very deft and economical, and it contrasted stunningly with what the Navajos were doing. Some Senate aides found themselves resenting the Navajos. Their instincts told them there could be little moral force behind the Navajo position if it had to be presented by so many non-Indian professionals. Because it was so excessive and desperate, the Navajo effort backfired. "The Navajos were very heavy-handed," said Tom Imeson, aide to Senator Mark Hatfield of Oregon. "If it had been a test of lobbying skills, the Hopis would have won hands down." Dorothy Tennenbaum of the staff of Montana's Senator Lee Metcalf was downright offended. "It was a case of overkill," she said. "The Navajos came on like gang busters."

Another plus for the Hopis was that Abbott Sekaquaptewa came across far better than Peter MacDonald. Senate aides later recalled Sekaquaptewa as intense but gracious, MacDonald as stuffy and arrogant. Sekaquaptewa was grateful to anyone who would listen to him and understood that he would often have to tell his story to legislative aides. MacDonald spoke condescendingly to aides, expecting to be ushered into the company of the senators. Sekaquaptewa was deferential, MacDonald often cold. The Hopis made a point of reminding the aides that MacDonald had been held in contempt of court for not reducing Navajo stock in the JUA.

The effect of Navajo lobbying ineptitude was to lose friends and disillusion people. It cheapened the story of the people of the JUA. But it was a story too real to be shunted aside, regardless of what one thought of the way it was presented. The traditionalists who came to Washington were effective. Kennedy aide Wendy Moskop recalled the perplexity she felt after meeting with Navajos and Hopis. "I had a strong sense of the distress of each group, but I also had the feeling that I didn't really know what was going on out there in Arizona," she said. "It seemed to me that the Hopis didn't really need the land. But it was also apparent that the Navajos were seriously overgrazing the land. I was upset that I couldn't decide which was right. Both sides talked as if it was a life-or-death matter."

Moskop's reaction was understandable. It was impossible to get a feel for what was going on out there in Arizona by meeting for a few minutes with the two sides and then reading their position papers. She and other aides simply didn't have time for more. So in their minds the land dispute took on an appearance like that of much of the JUA itself, flat and featureless, without reliable points of orientation. For every Navajo sign pointing east, there was a Hopi sign pointing west. The land dispute baffled understanding and defied informed judgment.

According to the distribution of responsibility in the Senate, it was the job of the Interior Committee to sift the arguments of the two sides in the land dispute. Had the committee made a careful study in the field, it would have discovered that fallacies underlay some of the basic Hopi arguments. The Hopis claimed that the Navajos would be forced off the JUA by overgrazing, if not by partition. In fact, the Navajos would never sever their attachments to the land without partition. They would remain in the only life they knew, traveling away from home for seasonal work or even taking work in a nearby town, but always returning to home and family. The Hopis said they would be overrun in District 6 if the Navajos were not pushed back by partition. In fact, it was the Hopis who had refused the Navajo offer to fence the District 6 boundary, and without a fence there was no way to prevent Navajo stock from straying across the line. The Hopis said the Navajos were a rich Goliath and that they were a minority within a minority threatened with cultural extinction. In fact, as Hopi-Tewa Albert Yava pointed out in his book *Big Falling Snow*, only a handful of already affluent Hopi cattle ranchers stood to gain from partition. The Hopi Tribal Council, then, was a minority within a minority within a minority. The Navajos had wealth as a tribe, but the people of the JUA had a per capita income of less than $1,000. They, not the Hopis who pushed so effectively for partition, were the true underdogs of the Navajo-Hopi land dispute.

By failing to recognize the dimensions of the land dispute and the implications of massive relocation, the Interior Committee failed the entire Senate. The only person associated with the committee who made more than a token visit to the disputed lands was staff member Bill Chandler, who spent several days there and came to the foreboding conclusion that relocation "would be fraught with enormous if not insurmountable difficulties." None of the documents published by the committee during its investigation of the land dispute made mention of the Chandler report.

The Navajos and Hopis trotted out their best arguments at the Interior Committee hearings at the end of July. By this time there was nothing new either side could contribute to the record. The most interesting occurrence was the sniping between Senators Abourezk and Fannin, who criticized each other for bias in the land dispute. Hopi general counsel John Boyden was the star of the hearings, hammering away at the Navajos with eloquent indignation. He concluded his plea for justice with a Biblical quotation: "How long, O Lord, how long?"[2] Abourezk announced that the Supreme Court had just voted eight to zero to require President Nixon to surrender the tapes of his Oval Office conversations. It was a turning point of the Watergate scandal. The order brought forth information that would force Nixon to resign two weeks later. Boyden chimed in immediately, "I move to amend it so that the Navajos turn over to the Hopis their land, too."[3] A former bishop in the Mormon Church, a member of the International Academy of Trial Lawyers, an unsuccessful candidate for the Utah governorship in 1948 and 1956, John Boyden was an impressive man who seemed larger than he was. He charmed the Congress with his small-town-lawyer style, he exuded competence and righteousness, and he could fill up a room with his powerful presence.

Only Senators Abourezk, Fannin, and Dewey Bartlett of Oklahoma heard most of the testimony. Five of the other committee members sat in only briefly. They and the other seven members had commitments elsewhere. In addition to the Owens Bill, the committee had before it two other proposals to settle the land dispute. The first, sponsored by Abourezk, would have partitioned the JUA equally, but would have avoided large-scale relocation by allowing a life estate for those born on the land and by allowing those who moved there to remain for a period equal to the time they had already lived there. New Mexico's Joseph Montoya sponsored the second, the one the Navajos really wanted, which provided for a buy-out of the Hopi interest. The committee gave serious consideration only to the Owens Bill. Passed by the House, endorsed by both Arizona senators, it had considerable momentum going into "markup," the name given to the meetings where committees iron out the language of bills for report to the Senate floor.

Then the momentum was abruptly checked. Committee chairman Henry Jackson was determined to get the land dispute settled by the end of the year, but the Owens Bill troubled him for two reasons. First, Al Barkan, whose help Jackson needed to run for president in 1976, was still lobbying for the Navajos. And, second, Jackson didn't want to endorse a bill that would later blow up in his face. He thought the Owens bill was too heavy-handed, too direct an imposition of Congress in the Navajo-Hopi fight. At the first markup session, Jackson said he wanted the tribes to try negotiations one last time, and then, should negotiations fail, he wanted flexible guidelines for a court decision. The specter of massive relocation haunted Jackson, and he hoped to avoid it. But then the committee staff drafted a bill for the second markup that had none of the flexibility Jackson had called for. It merely provided for a plug-in of the Owens formula for 50-50 partition if negotiations failed. Jackson let the staff bill stand. Perhaps he did not want to risk a fight with Paul Fannin and the other Republicans on his committee or perhaps he did not want to appear to be unduly influenced by COPE. He adopted a posture of fence-sitting between the two sides in the land dispute.

The Dispute over Moencopi

One of the causes of the land dispute was the ambiguous language of Chester A. Arthur's 1882 order setting aside land for the Hopis " and such other Indians as the Secretary of the Interior may see fit to settle thereon." Similarly troublesome language appeared in a 1934 act of Congress that defined the exterior boundaries of the Navajo Reservation in Arizona, reserving the land for the Navajos "and such other Indians as are already settled there." The Hopis, of course, had long been settled in the center of what became the Navajo Reservation. When they took the JUA dispute to Congress, the Hopis saw a chance to turn the tables on the Navajos. They reasoned that if the 1882 order had allowed the Navajos to establish equal rights to the JUA, then the 1934 act gave the Hopis as much right as the Navajos to most of the Arizona portion of the Navajo Reservation. The Owens Bill provided for direct partition to the Hopis of a quarter of a million acres west of the JUA around the Hopi village of Moencopi, in return for which the Hopis would give up their claim to the rest of the area covered in the 1934 act. It was another clever bit of maneuvering by John Boyden, and it would have forced at least another thousand Navajos to relocate.

As it marked up the Owens Bill, the Interior Committee took a long, hard look at the "Moencopi Dispute." First the committee disagreed with the Owens approach, adopting by an eight to seven vote an amendment to refer the dispute to the federal court in Arizona. Then Senators Metcalf and Alan Bible of Nevada, who had voted with the majority, switched their votes. The amendment was killed, and the original language for direct partition was restored, only to be deleted after a shootout on the Senate floor.

Senator Metcalf's Dilemma

One of the keys to committee approval of the Owens Bill was Paul Fannin's ability to keep the six Republican votes solidly in line against James Abourezk's attempts to make the bill less harsh on the Navajos. A second key was the decision of Democrat Lee Metcalf to support Fannin and the Hopis. Respected as one of the finest legal minds in the Senate and as a humanitarian vitally interested in preserving Indian culture, the Montanan carried a lot of weight with other Democrats.

A year before his death in 1978, Metcalf spoke with a reporter about the land dispute. He was exhausted, his physical vitality sapped by an overloaded work schedule. "This is a young man's job," he said wearily. "The experiences you gain and the memories you acquire don't balance the physical effort required of a senator." Despite his fatigue, he grew energized as he talked about the land dispute, recalling in detail the events of three years past. He recalled that the AFL-CIO's Al Barkan and Andy Biemiller, both long-time friends, had urged him to support the Navajos. "They told me this issue was vitally important to labor's relations with Indians," Metcalf said. Metcalf rebuffed the powerful union lobbyists. He had defined the land dispute as a question of Hopi survival, and he had been determined to give the Hopis all the help he could. "Here we

had one of the richest tribes against one of the poorest," Metcalf
said. "It was a David and Goliath situation. I was concerned about
the vitality of the Hopi culture and way of life." But Metcalf said
he also had firsthand knowledge of relocation and found the prospect of uprooting Navajos disturbing. "During World War II, I was
an officer in charge of transferring people back and forth between
the zones. The Russians demanded that the Estonians and Latvians
be sent back. They were sent back, and it was terrible. The Ger-
mans had sent French, Belgians, and English to camps in the east
and Russians to camps in the west. I saw the heartache of being
dislocated. I well remember the anguish of those people." Metcalf's
eyes were sad. He was easily able to relate the land dispute to his
own experience. "What were we going to do in the Navajo-Hopi
situation? Were the Hopis to be squeezed out of existence? Were
the Navajos to be allowed to take away traditional Hopi land and
threaten their culture? It was a situation in which someone's heart
was going to be broken." Senator Metcalf was a man of extraordinary sensitivity and compassion. He had struggled with his conscience before deciding that the Navajos would have to be moved.
He acted with absolute integrity.

The Navajos Vote Their Frustrations

In the congressional elections of 1974 the Navajos gave dramatic expression to their own strong feelings in the land dispute.
Across the reservation, and particularly in the JUA, they turned out
with a vengeance to cast ballots against Barry Goldwater and Sam
Steiger, who had so stridently opposed them. In 1970 one person
had voted at the Hardrock precinct; 336 came to the polls in 1974.
The Navajos regarded all Republicans as enemies.[4] Arizona's Democratic candidate for governor, Raul Castro, received 9,006 of the
10,274 votes cast on the reservation and it is likely that many of the
reservation votes for the Republican gubernatorial candidate were
cast by non-Indians living there. When Castro won the governorship by a margin of 4,113 votes, political observers noted—some in
shock—that the Navajos had clinched his victory. "With a potential
block of 25,000 votes, the tribe will no longer remain mute or
passive in federal and state elections," Steve Auslander of the *Arizona Star* wrote. "The candidates for these offices will have to
reckon with the tribe, which now constitutes a well-organized, well-
financed political machine."[5]

Both Goldwater and Steiger won reelection. Goldwater was an easy victor over Scottsdale newspaper publisher Jonathan Marshall. ("It's tough to run against a national monument," Marshall was fond of saying.) But Goldwater was furious that 90 percent of the Navajo vote had gone against him. He blamed it all on Peter MacDonald and COPE, claiming they had engaged in "a conspiracy" to get out the vote. Goldwater said the Navajos had been lured to the polls by promises of free beer. "They're not interested in the white man's elections, but they voted by the thousands last month."[6] Peter MacDonald called Goldwater's remarks "an insult to every Navajo who exercised the right of a citizen to vote." Goldwater presented no evidence to support his claim.[7]

The Debate on the Senate Floor

The Hopis were counting on the principle of "senatorial courtesy" to carry their bill over its final obstacle. One of the unwritten rules of the Senate, senatorial courtesy calls for deference to senators from the state affected by legislation when the legislation is not of national significance. Senators Goldwater and Fannin had made it clear that they wanted their colleagues to vote for the land dispute legislation reported out of the Interior Committee. Senators Abourezk and Montoya tried, nevertheless, to weaken the committee bill on the Senate floor by proposing two amendments that became the focal points of the afternoon's debate. Both amendments concerned controversial points in the markup deliberations. The first would refer the Moencopi dispute to the federal court. The second would allow the court flexibility from the 50–50 partition guideline.

The Moencopi debate was relatively restrained, offering little hint of the drama that would follow when the Senate voted on the amendment. The debate on partition, however, was hot and heavy, an intriguing battle of wits on the meaning of Section 5-D of the bill, which read: "In any partition of the surface rights to the joint use area, the lands shall, insofar as is practicable, be equal in acreage and in quality: Provided that if such partition results in a lesser amount of acreage, or value, or both to one tribe such differential shall be fully and finally compensable to such tribe by the other tribe." It was the kind of language that drives people who aren't lawyers wild and makes legislative drafting an arcane science.

Primary antagonists in the debate were Lee Metcalf and James Abourezk. The report prepared by the committee staff interpreting the bill's convoluted language clearly supported Metcalf's position that partition of the JUA should be 50–50. He read an excerpt: "The committee does believe that if judicial settlement is to be equitable and fair, any division of the lands of the Joint Use Area must be equal."[8] Paul Fannin joined in with an equally concise passage which said the committee wanted to allow the court flexibility for "a minor divergence from an equal partition" that would "preserve to one or the other tribe a particularly densely populated area, thus significantly reducing the necessity for relocating households and minimizing social, economic, and cultural disruptions."[9]

Abourezk repudiated the staff report, insisting that it contradicted the intent of the committee. "Apparently the committee has no control over what the staff writes as far as the report is concerned," he said. "It is totally contradictory to what was decided by the majority of the committee." Abourezk found the prospect of relocation repugnant. He cautioned that the Hopis did not intend to live on the land and said that by moving Navajos, Congress would be "replacing human beings with livestock, and I do not think that is fair."[10] His amendment to 5-D would have made it clear that the primary consideration the court should observe in drawing the partition line was not equality of acreage, but minimizing relocation.

Senator Jackson's position was unclear, as it had been in committee. He spoke gravely of the impacts of relocation. "We need not speculate on what these impacts might be," he said. "We need only review the truly disgraceful history of past Indian removal efforts."[11] But Jackson shed no light on the troublesome "insofar as is practicable" language. First he moved toward the Hopi interpretation, saying equal partition would be consistent with the *Healing v. Jones* decision; then he came over to the Navajo side, pointing out that the standard for an even split of the JUA was "strongly conditioned" by the committee's desire for flexibility. Chairman Jackson summarized the arguments of both sides without saying where he stood; the net effect was ambiguity. Metcalf and Fannin held the high ground with the committee report, however, and Abourezk and Montoya reluctantly withdrew the amendment to 5-D.

Few senators heard the debate. They were working in their

offices or in hearing rooms and were summoned to the Senate floor by a series of bells that signaled it was time for a vote. As they stepped off the elevators behind the Senate chamber, they were met by aides who told them what the debate was about and where key senators stood. Joe Miller, a lobbyist for the Navajos, button-holed his friends and asked that they vote for the amendment to send the Moencopi dispute to the federal court. There was no question that the partition bill would pass. Backed by the House of Representatives, the two home-state senators, and the Interior Committee, it was a cinch. The only question was, Who would win what the Navajos later called "The Battle of Moencopi"?

Steve Bell, press secretary for Senator Pete Domenici of New Mexico, later outlined the process by which a hypothetical senator walking onto the Senate floor decided which way to go. "Suppose you are a senator on the Public Works and Foreign Relations Committees and another small committee. It's near the end of the session, and you've just come back from a hard campaign. There's a lot happening in the short time before recess. You've got to be familiar with what's coming out of your committees, and here comes this damn bill about some place you don't know about and aren't concerned with. You get off the elevator and one of your aides comes up to you and says this is the Montoya-Abourezk amendment. Then one of the senators you know and respect comes up to you and tells you he'd like you to vote his way. Chances are you will."

How many votes were cast as favors is impossible to measure, but certainly some were. On the first roll call, John Tower of Texas voted for the amendment and Lawton Chiles of Florida voted against. Then Barry Goldwater talked with Tower and Pete Domenici talked with Chiles, and the votes were switched on the second and final call. Domenici talked on the floor with Sam Nunn of Georgia and got Nunn's vote. Each side kept a tally as the ayes and nays were recorded. The vote was close throughout, very nearly even. Abourezk stood next to Phil Hart of Michigan, holding onto his arm. Hart had voted against the amendment on the first roll call at the request of Barry Goldwater, following the principle of senatorial courtesy. But when Abourezk insisted that the amendment must be passed, Hart told him he would switch if his vote were needed.

It wasn't. The amendment passed, 37–35. Thirty Democrats and seven Republicans voted for; twenty-four Republicans and eleven Democrats voted against. Barry Goldwater was furious. He took passage of the amendment as a personal affront, an insult to his knowledge of Arizona Indian affairs, and a victory for Peter Mac-Donald and COPE. Goldwater was particularly upset with the Republicans who had gone against him. One of them was Mark Hatfield of Oregon, whom Goldwater upbraided on the Senate floor and again in the Senate cafeteria. "It pained me to find Republicans voting for an amendment that had absolutely nothing to do with any state in the nation but Arizona," Goldwater wrote in a letter to Republican leader Hugh Scott.[12] *Newsweek* took note of Goldwater's anger, reporting that the senator was so upset he had drawn up an "enemies list" of the Republicans who had voted against him. Besides Hatfield and Domenici, the list according to *Newsweek*, included Oregon's Bob Packwood, New York York's Jacob Javits, Vermont's Robert Stafford, Pennsylvania's Richard Schweiker, and Connecticut's Lowell Weicker.[13]

Having won the Battle of Moencopi, pro-Navajo forces pulled back and joined in the 72–0 vote that passed the land dispute bill. When the House and Senate pass differing versions of the same legislation, an ad hoc conference committee comprising members of the two congressional wings normally meets to work out the difference. But House leaders agreed informally to accept the Senate version and brought it to a floor vote for unanimous consent. The bill was then sent to President Ford, who signed it during a skiing vacation in Colorado.

The Navajo-Hopi Land Settlement Act directed that representatives of the two tribes begin a six-month period of negotiations, assisted by a federal mediator, in an attempt to resolve their dispute. Any agreement reached during the negotiations would become law. If no agreement were reached, the mediator was to submit to the federal district court in Arizona a suggested boundary for a 50–50 partition of the JUA that would "include the higher density population areas of each tribe within the portion of the lands partitioned to such tribe to minimize and avoid undue social, economic, and cultural disruption insofar as practicable." The mediator would also recommend that "in exceptional cases where necessary to prevent personal hardship" life estates be granted to the members of one tribe living on lands partitioned to the other.

In another key provision, the act established a three-member Navajo and Hopi Indian Relocation Commission, whose members were to be appointed by the Secretary of the Interior. Within two years of the court-ordered partition of the JUA, the commission was to submit to Congress a plan for the relocation of members of one tribe living on lands partitioned to the other. Thirty days after the commission submitted its plan to Congress, a five-year period was to begin during which relocation was to be completed. In order to encourage relocation, the act authorized payment of incentive bonuses. Heads of households who contracted to relocate during the first year of the relocation period would be paid $5,000, and the bonus would decrease by $1,000 each year thereafter so that $2,000 would be paid to those who contracted to relocate during the fourth year. The commission was authorized to purchase the property of relocatees and to provide a replacement home whose value was to depend on the size of the relocatee family. Up to $17,000 could be spent on a new home for a family of three or fewer persons, and a $25,000 limit was placed on the purchase of a home for a family of four or more—figures that would be raised several times after 1974 because of inflation. The act authorized the appropriation of $37,000,000 to carry out relocation.

In two other important provisions, the act directed the secretary of the interior to reduce livestock in the JUA to the carrying capacity of the range and to sell to the Navajo Tribe at fair market value up to 250,000 acres of lands under the jurisdiction of the Bureau of Land Management. The land was intended to be a relocation site for those forced to move from the JUA.

The Goldwater-MacDonald Feud Examined

Of all the influences that shaped the will of Congress to adopt the Navajo-Hopi Land Settlement Act, Public Law 93-531, the most substantive were the federal court decisions. First there was the *Healing* decision. Handed down by a district court in Arizona, upheld by the Supreme Court, it was the legal backbone of the drive for partition. Then there were the 1972 stock reduction order and the 1974 contempt ruling, extensions of the *Healing* decision that added a sense of urgency to the Hopi plea. But these decisions did not make partition inevitable. They suggested but did not require that Congress take the ultimate step; they were not a legal imperative. In the mind of Congress, the land dispute was an equation in which Hopi rights as defined by the courts were balanced against Navajo rights as defined by generations of occupancy. The Hopis finally succeeded in unbalancing the equation with their shrewd public relations and lobbying campaigns. They blurred the vision of the nation's lawmakers, claiming that war was about to engulf the Arizona range, that any action short of partition would violate the court decisions, that they could survive as a tribe only if they received half the Joint Use Area. In portraying the Navajos as marauding bullies unworthy of compassion, the Hopis received an unwitting boost from the Navajo lobbyists.

The Hopis had effective spokesmen in Abbott Sekaquaptewa and John Boyden. More important, they had hard-working advocates in Congress. They had Wayne Owens and Sam Steiger in the House, and over in the Senate, they had Paul Fannin, Lee Metcalf, and—most important of all—Barry Goldwater. When he left neutral ground on the land dispute in 1972 following Peter MacDonald's public courtship of George McGovern, Goldwater took a lot of Republican votes with him. Because the Goldwater-MacDonald feud was a pivotal influence in the land dispute, it must be examined further and explained in its full context.

The antagonism that flowed between the two men like jolts of electricity from 1972 to 1974 did not subside with the passage of the land dispute legislation. Goldwater stayed in contact with MacDonald's critics on the reservation, who expressed to him their concern that MacDonald was misusing tribal money. In February 1976, while a federal grand jury was conducting an exhaustive investigation of tribal finances, Goldwater released to newspapers a copy of a letter he had sent to the General Accounting Office, requesting an audit of Navajo financial affairs. "Serious questions have been raised as to whether or not the Navajo tribal funds have been properly and legally expended and there is uncertainty and confusion among the Navajo people themselves as to the actual fiscal position of the tribe," Goldwater said in his letter to the Comptroller General, Elmer B. Staats.[14] MacDonald said the Goldwater request represented "the latest attempt to bring down the tribal government."[15] He later called the federal investigation "a political witchhunt."[16]

After a two-year investigation costing hundreds of thousands of dollars, MacDonald was indicted on charges that he had defrauded the Tucson Gas and Electric Company by submitting false travel vouchers for trips he made on the reservation speaking in favor of a power line the company wanted to build there. The charges had nothing to do with tribal finances and were almost ludicrously insignificant in the wake of the rumors that had churned across the reservation that federal agents were onto something big. But Mac-Donald took no chances with the federal courts, which he felt were being used as a political weapon. He hired F. Lee Bailey to defend him in the federal court in Phoenix. The U.S. attorney's case was so weak that the judge did not even send it to the jury, but instead issued a directed verdict of acquittal.

The Goldwater-MacDonald story became bizarre in February 1977 with sworn testimony of John Harvey Adamson, the man who confessed to planting the bomb that blew up the car of *Arizona Republic* reporter Don Bolles in a Phoenix parking lot in June 1976, wounding Bolles so gravely that he died several days thereafter. Adamson testified that he had discussed the idea of planting a bomb in MacDonald's offices with Neal Roberts, a Phoenix attorney and Joe Patrick, a former Phoenix television newsman who worked on the Navajo Reservation in late 1976 and early 1977 as a consultant with the Navajo Area School Board Association. Then came the real shocker.

Adamson recalled asking Roberts what Patrick did on the reservation. "Mr. Roberts said Mr. Patrick was a spy on the reservation—that he was a spy for Senator Goldwater and reported directly to Senator Goldwater what happened on the Indian reservation, especially in regard to Peter MacDonald," Adamson said. Adamson's testimony became even more unsettling as he recalled that he, Roberts, and Patrick also discussed planting a bomb "in a car one Indian drives back and forth to Phoenix, where he stays at the Granada Royale Hotel." He said the plan was to rig the bomb in such a way that it could not explode. Later it was learned that the "other Indian" who drove back and forth to Phoenix was Tony Lincoln, who was director of the Bureau of Indian Affairs on the Navajo Reservation. Explaining the rationale for planting a bomb that could not explode, Adamson said, "They wanted some havoc to be raised on the reservation." He said the ultimate goal was to discredit MacDonald and bring about "martial law on the reservation."[17]

It was a terrifyingly rational scenario. Lincoln, a Goldwater protégé, did not get along with MacDonald. If a bomb were found on Lincoln's car, MacDonald could be blamed. Then, if federal officials stepped in to impose martial law (as they had considered doing during the Wounded Knee takeover in 1973) MacDonald would be pushed aside and Lincoln, the highest federal officer on the reservation, could assume control of the Navajo government.

Goldwater called Phoenix reporters to his home immediately after Adamson's testimony. He acknowledged that he and Patrick had flown together in the National Guard, but insisted that Patrick was not a spy for him. "He's no more informant than if I might say, 'Joe, what happened on your last flight to Germany or your last flight to Saigon,' or 'How's the National Guard going.' " Relaying information he had received from federal investigators, it was Goldwater who revealed that Lincoln was the "other Indian" of Adamson's testimony.[18]

Whether or not Patrick was a spy, there was a clear connection among Patrick, Lincoln, and Goldwater. Lincoln arranged for Patrick to work for the Navajo Area School Board Association, which is funded by the BIA. He had first attempted to find work for Patrick with the BIA but gave up when personnel director Lee Shearin pointed out that Patrick could not be hired because he was not on a Civil Service Register. Shearin was asked by a reporter if Lincoln had mentioned why he wanted to find work for Patrick. "He mentioned something about Barry Goldwater referring him," Shearin replied.[19]

It is difficult to believe that Senator Goldwater wanted bombs planted and havoc raised on the Navajo Reservation. But despite the senator's denials, it is obvious that Patrick came to the reservation with Goldwater's help. The real damage of the Goldwater-MacDonald feud was that it alienated the senator from the Navajos and gave the Hopis a powerful ally in the land dispute. Goldwater wrote a letter to *New York Times* reporter Molly Ivins in early 1979, denying that he had sought the federal investigation into MacDonald's handling of tribal finances. "I can assure you that at no time did I have anything to do with it," Goldwater wrote, "because I believe, as the Indians believe, that the white man has done enough to mess up their lives and I would leave any decisions as to his dishonesty or lack of it up to the Indians."[20]

A Troubling Navajo Claim

Another sensitive aspect of the land dispute is the Navajo claim that energy interests worked for partition of the JUA. The claim was first advanced in 1972, three weeks before the House passed the Steiger Bill. Navajo officials noted that the partition line included in the bill would turn over to the Hopis the portion of Black Mesa in the northwest JUA, which they said was potentially rich in oil and gas reserves. "Even an untrained mind such as mine can see why the Hopi want control of the specified area," Navajo tribal official Marshall Tome told the *Navajo Times*. "It will give them basis for control of future development of some of the richest potential oil and gas formations anywhere." Tome went on to charge, "There appear to have been some payoffs somehwere. Why else would deception of this nature occur?"[21]

The land dispute legislation passed in 1974 left to the courts the responsibility for partitioning the JUA. Nonetheless, when the land was partitioned in 1977, according to legislative criteria designed to minimize relocation, the line closely resembled that proposed by Steiger. While the Navajos do not dispute the fact that the Hopi partition area is the area of least Navajo population density, they remain convinced that energy interests are at least partially responsible for partition. By 1979 the Navajos had stopped talking about the oil potential of the northwest JUA and were drawing attention to the proven coal wealth of the area. Attending a meeting of the National Conference of American Indians in Albuquerque in October 1979, a group of Navajos from Big Mountain renewed the old energy conspiracy charge. "It is our feeling and the feeling of our Moqui (Hopi) allies that the American government created the land dispute so that it would be easier for American energy corporations to exploit the vast mineral resources in the land," Big Mountain spokesperson Roberta Blackgoat said.[22]

Samuel Pete, assistant to Peter MacDonald, shares this view. "Everybody was aware of the coal reserves on Black Mesa," he said. "Once the Navajos are relocated, it will be easier to make minerals deals, because you won't have to worry about relocation." Pete points out that Harrison Loesch—who was instrumental in shaping the Interior Department's propartition policy in 1972 and who worked on the land dispute legislation in 1974 as minority counsel for the Senate Interior Committee—became an executive for the Peabody Coal Company in 1976.

At his Washington office, where he was Peabody's vice-president for government relations, Loesch said any implication that he was looking out for Peabody's interests while he was a federal employee "is a lot of nonsense." As to his role in shaping Interior's policy on the land dispute, Loesch said, "After reviewing the legal aspects of the matter way back, I came to the definite conclusion that the Hopis had just been wronged, that's all, and that they ought to get it back. And the only way to do that was partition it and kick the Navajos off." Loesch pointed out that Peabody's two leases in Arizona—one in the JUA and one on the exclusive Navajo Reservation—"ought to keep us happy for a long, long time." Peabody does indeed have considerable coal-bearing lands under lease from the Navajos and the Hopis. However, at least three other coal-mining companies have expressed interest in mining the Hopi portion of the former JUA.

Questions have also been raised about the involvement of Jerry Verkler, staff director of the Senate Interior Committee in 1974, in the land dispute legislation. Navajo general counsel George Vlassis expressed surprise at the intensity of Verkler's work on behalf of the legislation. "I never saw such a vigorous sustained effort from a man in such a position," Vlassis said. Mark Panitch, whose story for the *Washington Post* in 1974 reported on Hopi contracts with the WEST energy consortium, spoke with Verkler while he was preparing the story. "I had an interview with him for about a half-hour, and within three hours of the time I talked with him, the PR man for the Hopis in Salt Lake City called me up and practically read a verbatim transcript of the interview and told me that it was their obligation to try to get the story killed," Panitch said.

As staff director of the Senate Interior Committee in 1974, Verkler worked at the direction of chairman Henry Jackson, who avoided taking a clear position on the land dispute. Verkler, therefore, might have been expected to follow the lead of his boss. But as Sherwin Broadhead, a member of the committee staff in 1974, recalled, Verkler "gave an emotional appeal for the Hopis" at the first markup session on the bill in August 1974. Richard Schifter, Washington counsel for the Navajos, said he thought Verkler "was very emotionally involved" on behalf of the Hopis. A second Washington source who worked for the Navajos in 1974 asked not to be identified in print. "There was no question about Verkler's open lobbying activities," he said.

Both Schifter and the second source said Verkler had spoken against Peter MacDonald to at least one Democratic Senator on the Interior Committee, reminding the senator as he pleaded the Hopi cause that MacDonald was a Republican. They also said Verkler worked to have the bill brought up to a vote on the Senate floor before November, when the Navajo tribal elections were held. "He was pushing like hell for a vote before the election," the second source said.

During most of 1974, a corporation known as WESCO, a consortium of the Texas Eastern Transmission Company and Southern California Gas, was negotiating with the Navajo Tribe to construct coal gasification plants on the New Mexico portion of the reservation. WESCO representatives found Peter MacDonald unresponsive to their project, which they ultimately abandoned in 1979 after investing some $30 million. MacDonald's opponent in the 1974 election was the man he had unseated in the previous election, Raymond Nakai. WESCO general manager Bob Rudzik recalled in 1979 that Nakai "said he could get it [the WESCO project] approved in about two weeks."

In January 1975, Verkler became the manager of the government affairs office of Texas Eastern Transmission Company in Washington. In 1980 he was the vice-president for government affairs and had moved back to the company's headquarters in Houston. Verkler said he had not taken an active role in the land dispute legislation and scoffed at the Navajos' suggestion that there might have been improprieties in his work on the legislation. "I never heard of coal gasification until 1975," he said, adding, "I believe I stood for an objective settlement of that issue, as fair to both sides as it could be." Verkler also claimed to have been instrumental in the decision at the end of 1972 not to allow the Steiger Bill to come up for a vote on the Senate floor.

Peter MacDonald was asked in early 1980 if he believed energy interests were involved in the passage of the Navajo-Hopi Land Settlement Act. "Definitely," he responded. "I think not just the fact that there is coal and possibly uranium and oil in that area, but also my position, a strong position against the energy companies, were factors. In other words, one thing was to get the resources and the land, as much of it as possible, through partitioning it and taking it away from the Navajos. That's one objective, I feel, with the energy companies. The other was to punish me and the Navajo Tribe for refusing to let the energy companies steal our resources again. So it was a double-barreled attack."

The Navajo claim that energy interests were involved in the land dispute cannot be substantiated with conclusive evidence. It is, however, a matter of historical record that the Hopis were courting energy interests in the early 1970s, while Peter MacDonald was speaking against them. Samuel Pete pointed out that if the land dispute legislation had been passed before the tribal election, Peter MacDonald would have suffered a political embarrassment on the reservation and Raymond Nakai would have gained an advantage. As events turned out, the Navajos managed with their allies in Washington to have the Senate vote put off until December 2, well after MacDonald had been elected to a second term.

7
The Battle for
House Rock Valley

The uproar over Navajo attempts to buy land for relocation did not begin until long after Wayne Owens had eased into his land dispute legislation an amendment authorizing the secretary of the interior to sell the Navajos 250,000 acres of federal land. The issue stirred no controversy in either house of Congress in 1974. However, the news articles, public hearings, position papers, and government studies that have poured forth since then amply demonstrate the shortsightedness that pervades the 1974 act.

Owens introduced the amendment as the House prepared in May 1974 to vote on his bill a second time. "Mr. Chairman, I think the amendment speaks for itself," he said as the floor debate wound down. "There are allegations, founded or unfounded, that those 800 to 900 familes required to move under this bill would have no place to go because of the way the 15 million or 16 million acres in the Navajo Reservation are already divided. If so, this 250,000 acres, I think, would solve the problem."[1]

There was no indication on the House floor of the implications of the amendment—no anticipation that citizens' groups would form to oppose it, that it would embarrass the Arizona and New Mexico congressional delegations, lead to nearly a dozen public hearings, require an exhaustive and costly environmental impact study, and contribute to the defeat of Sam Steiger in his 1976 bid for the Senate. Democrat Lloyd Meeds spoke briefly in favor of the amendment. The only remark from the Republican side of the floor came from Ralph Regula, who said simply, "The minority has no objection." The House wanted to have done with the troublesome legislation. Impatient cries of "Vote! Vote!" demanded an end to debate, and a few minutes later the Owens Bill had passed.

The trouble began the following July, just as soon as Peter MacDonald informed the Bureau of Land Management that the tribe would apply for a quarter of a million acres in the House Rock Valley and on the Paria Plateau, in an area known as the Arizona Strip because it is cut off from the rest of the state by the Colorado River and the Grand Canyon. The valley and plateau are joined by the spectacular Vermillion Cliffs—massive, jagged sandstone ramparts that glow molten in the slanting rays of the afternoon sun. The land around the cliffs is austere. Its sparse vegetative cover consists largely of rabbitbrush, snakeweed, blue gramma grass, and big sagebrush. Despite the land's apparent undesirability as a relocation site, Navajo officials insisted it was the best available. It was just across the Colorado River from the reservation, they pointed out, and therefore met the act's requirement of being contiguous or adjacent to Navajo land.

Much of the history of the American West is the story of Indians fighting to keep white settlers from taking over their hunting grounds. And so it was ironic that Bill Morrall, whose Flagstaff home is filled with the stuffed heads of the Cape buffalo, spotted hyena, and other game he has taken on hunting expeditions around the world, was determined to keep the Navajos from gaining title to land grazed by the Kaibab deer herd and prized by outdoorsmen for its rugged beauty.

During his career as an electrical engineer, Morrall had helped build Saudi Arabia's first television station. In retirement, he wrote an outdoors column for the *Arizona Daily Sun* in Flagstaff and sat on the board of the Arizona Wildlife Federation. In the second half of 1975 he organized the Save the Arizona Strip Committee, a coaltion of hunters, ranchers, and environmentalists who claimed to have a half-million-dollar war chest for legal challenges to Navajo attempts to buy House Rock–Paria.

In 1976 Morrall made life miserable for Sam Steiger, blasting him for not blocking the land purchase amendment. Steiger was in the thick of a fight with Democrat Dennis DeConcini for the Senate seat that Paul Fannin's retirement would put up for grabs, and the last thing the conservative Republican from Prescott needed was to be ridiculed for allowing Navajos to remove land from the public domain. *Arizona Republic* outdoors writer Ben Avery said Owens had caught all the state's representatives asleep,[3] but Steiger caught most of the heat because he had pushed so hard for the land dispute legislaton. Steiger wrote to Morrall promising to do "everything I can to prevent the Navajos from gaining control of this land."[4] He admitted, however, that there was little chance to change the legislation so that the Navajos would not be allowed to buy public land.

Ducking for cover from a barrage of criticism, Steiger tried to find some way to explain his failure to challenge the land purchase amendment. First, he said he had not even discussed the amendment with Owens. A year later he changed his story, saying he had asked Owens about the amendment before the House vote and had received assurance that it was intended to allow the Navajos to acquire federal lands in the New Mexico Checkerboard area— lands that are interspersed with private, tribal, and state lands in a checkerboard pattern.[5] The story did not check out.

"The Checkerboard had nothing to do with it," Owens said in a phone interview from Montreal, where he had gone to direct a Mormon mission following his unsuccessful campaign for the Senate in 1974. Owens pointed out that the Navajos had long been settled on the Checkerboard. "My intention was to get new lands that would allow the Navajos who would be forced out some place to live," he said.[6] In an interview with Robert Thomas of the *Arizona Republic* Owens elaborated on his thinking in 1974. "I felt they were the victims of government inaction for the past 100 years," he said of the JUA Navajos. "In the interest of justice, I felt this was the rational solution."[7] Morrall thought Owens's rationality was perhaps a bit too calculated. He pointed out that the land purchase amendment said the Navajos must choose land in either Arizona or New Mexico, and he noted that Owens had left Utah out of the land purchase picture. This only compounded his conviction that Steiger had been taken on a ride.

Robert Thomas was not placated either. He made the amendment sound almost treasonous. "So, for the first time, public land, the birthright of all Americans, is being used as a payoff to induce one side to go along in settlement of a strictly intertribal dispute,"

he wrote, displaying in the phrase "strictly intertribal" an unfortunate lack of awareness of the federal government's role in the land
dispute.[8] A state wildlife official saw the proposed sale as part of a
pattern of government limitations on individual freedom. He claimed
sale of the land to the Navajos would be "just another restriction on
the public's ability to move around."[9]

If the Owens amendment smacked of treason to Morrall's group,
Steiger's failure to challenge it amounted to giving aid and comfort
to the enemy. The pressure on Steiger increased as the election
drew near, and he finally snapped. When Steiger attended a meeting of the Arizona Wildlife Federation, he was handed a list of ten
questions, one of which asked if he supported repeal of the land
dispute legislation. Weary of saying Congress would not consider
repeal, the harried Steiger shot back an angry handwritten response,
"No—and you idiots had better understand what you are doing
before you do it." An Associated Press story on the meeting quoted
Federation president Doug Baker suggesting that Steiger was something of an idiot himself for allowing the land purchase amendment
to go through.[10] Steiger said his "idiots" remark was a joke, "just
my way of being funny." But the joke was on Steiger, who admitted after he had lost to DeConcini that the land fuss had cost him
plenty of votes.

Mina Lansa, kikmongwi of Old Oraibi and opponent of the
Hopi Tribal Council, offered Morrall support he hadn't expected.
"We should all work together against Washington to revoke this
bill," she said. "The Hopi council favors the bill. But as a Hopi
chief, I say no. The Hopis and Navajos can live right where they
are."[11] Morrall said he and the traditionalists of both tribes shared
"a common cause, which is fighting bad legislation."[12] But in his
column for Flagstaff's *Arizona Daily Sun*, he showed different feelings for Indians. Morrall attacked the concept of Indian reservations, declaring that the Navajos' "future lies in forgetting their
'Separate Nation' status and become [*sic*] dues paying Americans
like the rest of us." This is the gospel of those who believe that
Indians should climb into the American melting pot, who regard
reservations as willfully and dangerously un-American, and who
demand that tribally owned land be allotted to individuals and put
on the tax rolls. Morrall ended his column with a stirring warning
of the Red Peril on the Arizona Strip. "It's time to circle the
wagons," he wrote.[13] So much for solidarity with Indians.

Morrall stirred only cynicism in George Vlassis, general counsel for the Navajos, who called Morrall "the worst kind of self-
seeking person who is really only putting up a front of looking out
for other people."[14] A lot of non-Indians in Arizona appreciated
Morrall's crusade, however. He won the 1975 Governor's Award as
Conservationist of the Year.

The Mormon Ranchers

A dozen Mormon families operated ranches on the lands the
Navajos wanted to buy from the BLM. None of the families depended on the ranches for their livelihood; most worked at jobs in
northern Arizona or southern Utah or had their own businesses
there. But the family ranch is a special tradition in this part of the
West; it has an importance far beyond economics. The ranches
serve "as a gathering place for personal identification, for solitude,
for refuge," one of the ranchers said. "You could document how
everyone pulls together to make it go, their religious feelings and
responsibility to improve and beautify the land."[15] Like the Navajos,
the Mormons draw a sense of individual worth and family unity
from the land they hold together.

One of the ranchers using House Rock–Paria with BLM grazing permits was former Utah state senator and former mayor of
Kanab, Utah, A. D. (Dunc) Findlay, who had become wealthy with
real estate holdings in Utah just north of the Arizona Strip. Like his
fellow ranchers, Findlay was infuriated that he might have to give
up his ranch to make room for relocated Navajos. The Owens amendment had added insult to injury by neglecting to authorize compensation for those who used the land purchased by the Navajos,
and Findlay promised to fight the proposed land sale all the way
"to the highest court in the land."[16]

Individualism as rugged as the Paria Plateau is part of the
chemistry of western ranchers. So is pride in their heritage. Those,
like Findlay, who have prospered in the American economic system tend to look upon Indians on reservations as economic conscientious objectors who would be better off if they gave up values
impractical in a world of harsh realities.

At a public hearing on the proposed land sale, Findlay expressed his feelings with compassion, without the demagoguery of
Morrall's column. "We must educate our Indian population of this

country that they will be able to make a living like all other Americans, without any more acquisition of public lands, because there aren't any," he said. "They must be urged and encouraged to use the lands they already have in a more beneficial manner. They must be urged and encouraged to all speak English. This is a competitive world. One must speak the language of the country to be able to compete."[17] It was a crisp but restrained statement of the belief that Indians must be assimilated into the American mainstream. At times, assimilationism is a facade for racism. But when it is preached by men like Findlay, it is an economic theory. Developed with firsthand knowledge of the poverty on Indian reservations, it is a statement of conviction and concern.

Assimilation is taking place. Indians of the Southwest are slowly taking on Anglo ways while seeking some formula that will permit them to retain that which is most precious in their own values. The difficult accommodation is being made, with varying degrees of success, especially by the young, and particularly on the fringes of the reservation, where contact with the off-reservation world is most common. But there is no possibility of accommodation for those who have grown up in the geographical and cultural center of the Navajo Reservation—the JUA. Assimilation is a process of erosion that occurs with the passage of generations. It cannot be achieved by a dynamite blast of social engineering, regardless of Paul Fannin's confident assertions. Federal mediator William Simkin, who probably came to know the people of the JUA more intimately than any other federal official in the history of the land dispute, recognized this fact of Navajo life in his report to Judge Walsh. He knew that land must be made available to Navajo relocatees.

Simkin estimated that 700 Navajo families would be forced to relocate if Judge Walsh adopted the partition line he recommended. He estimated further that House Rock–Paria would accommodate only 60 families with livestock and 60 families who would find work in the wage economy. An additional 30 families would qualify for life estates on the JUA, he said.

That left 550 families of relocatees. The mediator estimated that 200 of these would move, either off the reservation, to the Navajo partition area, or to the main body of the Navajo Reservation. The quarter of a million acres authorized for Navajo purchase would not be enough to accommodate the remaining 300 families, Simkin said. He recommended that the tribe be allowed to purchase an additional 270,000 acres.

Simkin's visits to the JUA, his meetings with the Navajos there, and his own common sense dispelled any notion he might have had that Navajo relocatees could be assimilated. He departed from the generally dispassionate language of his report to urge sale to the Navajos of House Rock–Paria, which, he said, appeared to be the only lands available to the tribe under the "contiguous or adjacent to the Navajo Reservation" language of the act. "If this is the case, and if no adequate presently known alternative land can be found, there is no alternative but for the Secretary of the Interior to 'bite the bullet' and make House Rock–Paria available for purchase," he said. Simkin pointedly observed that the land dispute act did not just authorize the secretary to sell the Navajos land, it *directed* him to do so. A long delay in finding a place for Navajos on the Hopi side of the partition line would have "ominous effects," he said, because it would heighten the anxiety and distrust of the prospective relocatees. "Moreover, time is of the essence and such action should be taken at the earliest possible moment."[18]

Simkin's call for quick, decisive action was drowned out in Washington by the protests of the Save the Arizona Strip Committee. Responding to the pressure, Secretary of the Interior Thomas Kleppe ordered that an environmental impact statement (EIS) be prepared to measure the likely effects of Navajo settlement of House Rock–Paria. It was a sweet victory for the committee and a bitter setback for the Navajos. Tribal official Samuel Pete called Kleppe's order "yet another example of the government's failure to fulfill its commitments." He said the tribe would press for the land sale "not as a matter of charity but as partial payment for what is to be taken from us."[19] Four years would pass before the EIS was completed in 1979. The Navajo application for House Rock–Paria lay frozen in a bureaucratic glacier. Simkin's suggestion for additional land was ignored by Interior. The Navajos wondered where their relocatees, the casualties of the Navajo-Hopi land dispute, were to go.

Farmington in an Uproar

When Secretary Kleppe ordered the EIS task force to examine lands other than House Rock–Paria for possible sale to the Navajos, the tumult over the Owens amendment moved beyond the borders of Arizona. Two of the alternative tracts examined by the task force were in San Juan County, New Mexico, near the northeastern corner of the Navajo Reservation. One was just out-

side the town of Bloomfield; the other lay on the northern edge of
Farmington, a town bordering the reservation, where relations
between Navajos and non-Indians were still strained after the ra-
cial tensions of 1974.

In April of 1974, the severely beaten, burned, and mutilated
bodies of three Navajo men were found in the wooded hill country
outside Farmington. They had been dumped there by the murder-
ers, three teen-age students at Farmington High. In June, three
thousand Navajos and a few non-Indians came to town for the first
of five marches to express outrage at the murders and at what an
instructor at Navajo Community College said was racism "running
rampant in this town."[20] Rumors that Indians and non-Indians
were plotting mayhem ran up and down the streets like so many
pickups. The season of outrage climaxed at the annual Sheriff's
Posse Parade, which a young Navajo called "a demonstration of
cruel and stupid insensitivity to the feelings of Indian people."[21]
The New Mexico Advisory Committee to the U.S. Commission on
Civil Rights described the parade in its "Farmington Report: A
Conflict of Cultures": "Conspicuous among the participants in the
parade was a mounted ceremonial unit from Fort Bliss, Texas,
dressed in cavalry uniforms similar to those worn by the Indians'
original oppressors."[22]

Images of Kit Carson and the Long Walk, stories told by
grandfathers on winter evenings of the exile to the Bosque Redondo
flashed in the minds of young Navajos who watched the parade.
When four of them stepped into the street to block the way, tear
gas cannisters flew and a scuffle broke out. Thirty-one Navajos
were arrested.[23] The April murders and June parade shredded
Navajo sensibilities. Fred Johnson called Farmington "the Selma,
Alabama of New Mexico." Wilbert Tsosie told *Time* magazine that
"Farmington has more rednecks than anywhere else in the world.
They kill you with their eyes first, then pick a secluded spot to beat
you up." Farmington city councilman Jimmy Drake told *Time* he
thought the Navajo protests might have been organized by com-
munists.[24]

While suspicion and hostility toward Indians are part of the
emotional makeup of all the towns bordering the Navajo Reservation, nowhere are the feelings more virulent and close to the surface than in Farmington. Mayor Arlo Webb said in an interview
with the *Navajo Times* that the problem was due in large part to
the influx of new residents that accompanied the energy boom of

the 1950s and 1960s. "Many of our residents have come from other areas of the country where they had no knowledge of Indian culture and history, and where they had never met an Indian," Webb said. "They come here and have little contact with our Indian residents. And when they see Navajos lying drunk in the streets, they make the generalization that all Navajos are drunks. Longtime residents know that this is a false stereotype and must do what we can to educate our fellow citizens to the dignity of the vast majority of Navajo people." Webb lamented the Sheriff's Posse Parade as "a case where no one thought beforehand what such a parade might cause."[25]

In early 1977, Navajo official Samuel Pete didn't know what to think before he met with 350 San Juan County residents who felt that sale of county lands to the Navajos would limit the growth of Farmington, strain community services, restrict recreation and hunting, displace ranchers already there, and involve them unfairly in an Arizona land dispute. One angry woman recommended that a fence be built around the reservation to keep the Navajos from acquiring more land. Most of those at the meeting listened politely to Pete's brief history of the land dispute, however, and to his explanation that the Navajos in the JUA would prefer to stay right where they were. "I think our feelings and concerns here are mutual," Pete said. "We did not want relocation, but it was forced down our throats. Instead of fighting the land transfer, you should fight relocation. If cowboys and Indians can join together, who's to oppose?"[26]

It was a graceful performance under pressure by an articulate, attractive young Navajo. Before the evening was out, Citizens Opposed to Public Law 93-531 had been created. A management and motivation consultant named Norm Lamb was hired to head the group's lobbying effort in Washington. Lamb said he thought Citizens Opposed would probably fight relocation even if the San Juan lands were ruled out of consideration for sale to the Navajos. But he admitted candidly, "It probably would be hard to keep everyone excited about that one for very long."[27]

The Showdown at Kanab

In the second half of 1978, after a draft of the Navajo Land Selection EIS had been written, a round of public hearings was held in Arizona, New Mexico, and Utah to receive public comment for inclusion in the final version. The most interesting hearing by far was in Kanab, Utah, a town established in 1865 as a fort for protection from Indian raids. The two hundred Mormons who assembled in the Kanab High School gymnasium on a Friday evening in November came to discuss a raid they believed would be no less dangerous than those of a century before. This time it was an attack by the bureaucrats of the federal government on the land they or their friends used for grazing in the House Rock Valley and on the Paria Plateau.

The Mormons who settled Utah in the mid nineteenth century had been driven steadily west by religious intolerance and hostility in New York, Ohio, Missouri, and Illinois. Brigham Young, their leader, feared the United States government would try to hound them even from their refuge in the Rocky Mountains. The Mormons needed friends in their harsh new world, so when Young dispatched Jacob Hamblin to colonize southern Utah, he instructed Hamblin to seek alliances with the Indians there. "Continue the conciliatory policy toward the Indians which I have ever commanded, and seek by works of righteousness to obtain their love and confidence." Young wrote, "for they must learn that they have either got to help us, or the United States will kill us both."[28]

Hamblin had only limited success in his attempts to teach farming to the Paiutes, and the missionaries he sent to the Hopis had to return home in 1859 after a dispute arose among the Hopis as to whether the Mormons were the white brothers who had left the Hopis long ago and whose return would signal an era of peace.[29] In the Black Hawk War of the 1860s, the Mormon settlements in southern Utah were put under siege by Paiutes and by Navajos who had escaped Kit Carson's roundup.

No curtain rose on the Kanab High School stage at the start of the hearing to discuss the draft EIS, but perhaps one should have. For what took place was more a drama than a public hearing, a play in two acts about the feelings of local citizenry for the federal government. If a title were needed for the hearing transcript, "The Bureaucrats Get Theirs" would probably be as good as any, although a lot was said about the Navajos, too.

The two villains, the bureaucrats, had taken their positions behind desks on the stage. They were the Interior Department solicitor from Phoenix, William Lavell, and the EIS editor, Carle Hodge. The heroes, the Arizona Strip ranchers and their friends, sat on metal chairs below, where the Kanab Cowboys play their basketball games. They came ready to shoot holes through an EIS they regarded as outrageous and through the bureaucrats responsible for it. The bureaucrats had assembled a considerable document—over 800 pages in two volumes covering the land and its geology, topography, archaeology, mineral resources, climate, air quality, history, vegetation, soils, water resources, and so forth. The document also talked about the Mormons who used the land with BLM permits and the Navajos who had asked to buy it.

The land would support forty-three families in the sheepherding economy, the EIS reported, and the people relocated there would need gravel roads, a school, clinic, utility systems, and quarters for BIA personnel. Not that the Navajos wanted to move there. "Very few of the Navajos in the former Joint Use Area want to leave," the EIS said. "Most who must leave will do so with reluctance and bitterness. Those who move to House Rock Valley and the Paria Plateau must bear the added burden of the resentment of the residents of the nearest towns and the hostility of their traditional enemies, the nearby Paiutes. The adjustment this will require defies precise prediction but it will be difficult."[30]

The EIS reported that the ranchers holding BLM grazing permits for the Arizona Strip "are bonded together culturally to an extent that would be remarkable in most of the United States." It said that because the strip is settled by Mormons and is detached from the main body of Arizona by the Grand Canyon and the Colorado, the area "is culturally and fiscally bonded more to southern Utah than to Arizona."[31] Seven of the fourteen ranchers would lose at least half their grazing area if the land were sold to the Navajos, according to the EIS, and the others would lose considerably less.

When they spoke the word "bureaucrat," the people at Kanab spat it out, as they would such words as "communist" and "liberal." Bureaucrats are a plague, they feel, and when they come up with harebrained schemes for the land, as bureaucrats in those parts do with regularity, they must be confronted. These convictions derive inevitably from federal ownership of most of the land in Utah, where one district manager for the Bureau of Land Management has been labeled a "colonial lord" and a "federal carpetbagger."[32] The BLM is forever coming up with new plans to restrict grazing or turn grazing lands into a federal preserve. It is all maddening to the independent, tough-minded, and proud ranchers.

To Dunc Findlay, the EIS was particularly outrageous—"the biggest joke I've ever heard of." He issued a warning about the bureaucratic threat. "If they can take land away from us out there, they can take your home right here in Kanab."[33]

Utah State Senator Ivan Matheson was next to take up the cudgel. "What we've got, gentlemen and ladies, is a bureaucratic dictatorship that lives between the government and the people," he said, insisting that the only people who wanted the land transfer were the bureaucrats. "It's a tragedy if you move forty-three families into House Rock Valley and expect them to eke a living out of there. They can't do it. If they don't want to go, they hadn't ought to be put there." Matheson took a few more swipes at the bureaucrats. He suggested that if the bureaucracy did not respond to the needs of the people, then the people should have "a thirteen-state Western tea party and tell the federal government this is our land, and when you come, you come on our terms."[34]

This was the emotional climax of the evening. The people of Kanab were angry and restless in their chairs. Matheson was talking about revolution, expressing the rage of a movement against federal controls that has become known as the Sagebrush Revolt. At this point Lavell could have leaped to his feet, seized Hodge by the shoulders, and screamed, "Will you take Barabbas?" And the crowd would have shouted as one, "Never! Give us Bureaucrat!"

The hearing was saved from chaos by rancher John Rich, his son Steve, and his adopted Navajo daughter Bonnie. The Riches are rightly proud of their family's history on the Arizona Strip. John's wife is a descendant of Edwin Wooley, an early settler who built the Bright Angel Trail into the Grand Canyon in 1901 and who entertained Buffalo Bill, Zane Grey, and Theodore Roosevelt.[35] John's father-in-law built a lodge near the North Rim of the Grand Canyon, naming it the Jacob's Lake Inn, after Jacob Hamblin. The Riches had studied the EIS carefully. When they spoke, they generated as much light as heat.

John Rich pointed out that the bureaucrats were not to blame for the proposal to sell House Rock. Congress had passed the authorizing legislation, whose sponsor was Utah's own Wayne Owens, and the bureaucrats were simply observing the law, he noted. Rich went on to take polite exception to what he called "slurs and innuendos" about Mormons in the EIS.[36] He was particularly offended by the statement that Mormons believe they must master the land because "the earth was under a curse which could be exorcised only by subjugating nature's bounty."[37] To prove that Mormons have long had a strong aesthetic sense he read from the writings of explorer F. S. Dellenbaugh, describing an 1873 visit with Jacob Hamblin:

> We had an excellent dinner of rich cream for the coffee which was an unusual treat. In all Mormon settlements the domestic animals were incorporated at once and they received special care; butter milk, and cheese were consequently abundant, but in a "Gentile" frontier town all milk, if procurable at all, was drawn from a sealed tin. The same was true of vegetables. The empty tin was the chief decoration of such advance settlements, and with the entire absence of any attempt . . . to start fruit or shade trees, or do any other sensible thing, the "Gentile" frontier town was a ghostly hodge-podge of shacks in the midst of a sea of refuse. As pioneers the Mormons were superior to any class I have ever come in contact with, their idea being home-making and not skimming the cream off the country with a six-shooter and a whiskey bottle . . . .[38]

Bonnie Rich had become part of the Rich family at the age of five when her family on the Navajo Reservation broke up. She was a grown woman in 1978, the mother of five children and manager of the gift shop at Jacob's Lake. Bonnie had been brought up within Mormon culture. She had made a clean break with traditional Navajo ways, but her emotional ties to the reservation remained strong. She gave John Rich a letter to be read at the hearing in Kanab.

In the letter Bonnie pointed out that purchase and development of the House Rock–Paria land as envisaged in the EIS would cost $22 million, or $500,000 for each of the forty-three relocated families. "Spending $500,000 for each family to give each one a little band of sheep and put them in a dead-end, hopeless settlement would be a terrible thing to do to them," she wrote. She insisted that the Navajos must be encouraged to seek training for jobs in the cash economy. "I don't know of one young Navajo under the age of 35 who wants to spend the rest of his life on a little pasture with a small herd of sheep and let the world pass by him or her. . . . We are great people and as able to do things as any other people. We have been held back too long. We don't want more picturesque hogans where the women run a few sheep and weave rugs and the

men try to find work, and when they can't find it, they become
alcoholics because of the endless monotony and despair. There was
a time when a few sheep and weaving rugs was a life-saver for our
people. But that time has passed for the younger Navajos."[39]

While Bonnie's statement carried a great deal of truth, it was a
reflection of the worst in Navajo society, a description of what
happens when the traditional system breaks down completely. The
statement would not be endorsed by even a significant minority of
young Navajos. Most young Navajos want to make an accommodation to new economic realities by entering the job economy, but
they do not want to sever their ties to their own immediate past.
They remain tied to the land and to livestock. They see the challenge for survival as a challenge to improve old patterns of land and
stock use, to develop a modern economy, and still to retain the
language, religion, and family ties that have bound the Navajos for
centuries.

Steve Rich, a twenty-seven-year-old University of Utah graduate, an accomplished sculptor, and a good enough kicker in his
school days to try out with the Dallas Cowboys, startled everyone
at Kanab by drawing a parallel between the relocation of Navajos
from the JUA and the Jewish holocaust. "In this case the government proposes to kill its victims more slowly," Steve said. "It is
legal, but it isn't right. . . . Imagine what history would be like if
every time some idiot gave a morally unjustified command the
answer was simply, 'No, it's wrong, I won't do it.' " Steve criticized
the EIS for burying the human complexities of the proposed land
sale and relocation under a mound of technical descriptions. He
called on the EIS writers to present the story "in human terms
which the Secretary [of the Interior] could understand."[40]

The statement of Bill Leach at Kanab had little to do with the
Environmental Impact Statement. But it is an important part of the
story of the land dispute. For it is representative of attitudes toward Indians held by many people living near the Navajo Reservation, attitudes shaped both by practical experience and by ignorance
and that in turn help shape the fear and distrust many Navajos feel
toward the off-reservation world. Here are some excerpts:

> The Navajo Indians has [*sic*] immigrated into our culture
> long enough to go along without having any more reservations.
> Let's make them 100 percent Americans and pay taxes like
> the rest of us. It's foolish for the white people to have to keep

everybody else. The Navajo Indians and other Indians are getting smart enough that they don't have to be babied like that. Let's make them humans. They are humans. . . .

A few weeks ago, I went to the store out at Page to buy a few groceries. And there's a Navajo boy ahead of me, and he had a great deal of groceries, several bags full. And he's paying for them with what? Food stamps. And he had to have 14 cents more, so he pulled out a roll of bills and he had a hell of a job finding a one dollar bill to make the change for paying the 14 cents. Now, he went outside and got in his vehicle, a $9,000 or $10,000 four-wheel drive, and drove off. Yet he paid with food stamps and money enough to choke a dying horse. His bagging pockets stuck out with the money he had in there. . . .

Like one Navajo boy says, he said, "The dumb white man, we'll take anything he'll give us." And that's about right. When are we going to start waking up?

Now, I have nothing against the Indians. In fact, I have some good friends amongst the Indians. And they come and talk to me quite a bit because I have worked with quite a few Indian boys. And there's some pretty doggone smart and sharp.[41]

When the EIS was completed in mid 1979, Interior Department officials assured Navajo leaders that a decision on their application would be made soon. Then Morris Udall stepped in with a legislative proposal aimed specifically at blocking Navajo purchase of land in the House Rock Valley and on the Paria Plateau.

8

The Aftermath
of the Land
Settlement Act

In 1979, Assistant Secretary of the Interior for Indian Affairs (a position known as Commissioner of Indian Affairs before the Carter administration) Forrest Gerard recalled the turbulence that accompanied congressional consideration of the land dispute. Gerard, who was on the staff of the Senate Interior Committee in 1974, said the land dispute legislation was "the most emotionally charged and argued bill in the six years I was there." That emotion has hardly dissipated since passage of the Land Settlement Act. Rather, it has spread out from Congress to swirl in a number of less conspicuous whirlpools. There were the six months of tense negotiations between the two tribes in 1975, the initial ineptitude and confrontational spirit of the federal relocation commission (which will be explained in detail in the next chapter), Judge Walsh's partition order of 1977, the hysteria that followed partition when Abbott Sekaquaptewa defied the court and ordered the impoundment of Navajo stock on the Hopi side of the partition line, and the confrontation between Navajos and Senator Goldwater on Big Mountain in 1978. And then there was the return of the land dispute to Congress in 1978, 1979, and 1980 with attempts to amend the 1974 legislation and provide for more reasoned and humane relocation. This discussion of the aftermath of the Navajo-Hopi Land

Settlement Act begins with the intertribal negotiations convened in March 1975 by federal mediator William Simkin.

The Navajo and Hopi negotiating teams hardly met on equal terms. The land dispute legislation had said that if negotiations failed and the dispute were sent to the courts for final settlement, the Joint Use Area was to be divided equally. This, of course, was what the Hopis had sought all along; all they had to do was hold firm for six months. Negotiations very nearly collapsed early on over a story in the *Gallup Independent*, a daily paper widely circulated in the eastern half of the Navajo Reservation, indicating that the Hopis might be willing to settle for less than half.

Independent reporter Bill Donovan got his information for the story from Samuel Pete, head of the Navajo negotiating team, who gave a decidedly Navajo slant to the framework established for the talks. But the story read as if the reporter had also spoken with Simkin, especially the part that attributed to Simkin the statement that while the Navajos "will turn over a portion of the land to the Hopis, how big that portion will be has yet to be determined."[1]

The Hopis were furious, accusing the Navajos of duplicity and threatening to end negotiations right then. They were soothed only when Simkin repudiated the story with the insistence that "any implication that the Hopis would receive less than one-half the land surface area is completely false."[2]

Simkin was impressed with both teams. In an interview with a mediators' journal after the negotiations had ended, he said "The Indian negotiators did not in any way take second place to Anglo labor negotiators as respects native intelligence, perception, astute weighing of the realities, and other aspects of good negotiators."[3] The two sides exchanged maps proposing various partition schemes. The Navajos first suggested that the JUA be divided piecemeal, assigning scattered, thinly populated tracts to the Hopis to keep relocation to a minimum. The Hopis drew a much neater line that encompassed a single block of land and would have required far more Navajos to relocate. At several points feelings ran high and Simkin called a recess and caucused with the two sides separately. The low point of the negotiations came with a statement, which Simkin noted was probably written by a lawyer for the Navajos, that the Hopis should be willing to accept the Navajo proposal because "had it not been for the grace and forebearance of the Navajos, the Hopi Tribe would not even exist today."[4] It was a gratuitous bit of arrogance that infuriated the Hopis once again. Abbott Sekaquaptewa returned the insult by not showing up for the last scheduled session at Salt Lake City.

Right from the start, Samuel Pete had little confidence that the tribes could come to an agreement. He reluctantly accepted the negotiating framework in order to keep Simkin coming to the JUA. Throughout the negotiations, Pete took Simkin to chapter meetings so that the mediator could meet traditional Navajos face to face and learn firsthand the implications of relocation. "We wanted to keep the negotiations going to educate him about the people," Pete said later. Many of the residents of the JUA did not understand Pete's strategy and accused him of cooperating with the partition process. "I got the impression that Sam and the other members of the Navajo team were doing a tough job with their own people," Simkin said. He also recalled that several times during the negotiations the Navajos asked the Hopis exasperatedly what they intended to do with the land. "They didn't respond in precise terms," Simkin said. "They just said they needed it for agriculture and grazing."

The suggested line of partition Simkin submitted to the court at the end of 1975 reflected his agonized attempt to balance the twin congressional mandates for equal partition and minimal relocation. The line moved with calculated irregularity across the JUA map. Its most striking features were a Navajo island around the community of Jeddito and a Navajo peninsula at Hardrock, both areas of high density population. Simkin estimated that 3,495 Navajos lived on the land he proposed for partition to the Hopis. "This is a surveyor's nightmare, but so be it," he told a reporter for the *Navajo Times*.[5] Simkin, a former head of the Federal Mediation Service, said he thought the line "was about as good as could be done" under terms of the legislation. "You can't help but feel concerned about those people who have to move," he said. "But if it has to be, it has to be."

Predictably, neither tribe was pleased with the Simkin line. Abbott Sekaquaptewa called it "a big giveaway program, primarily for the Navajos" and claimed the Jeddito island went against the legislative provision that each tribe receive areas densely populated by its people.[6] Sekaquaptewa had a point: the only Hopis in the JUA lived within the island. Simkin estimated their number at thirty-four; he thought the island was justified by the settlement of several hundred Navajos there. Peter MacDonald called the partition proposal "a victory for property rights and a defeat for human rights."[7] Samuel Pete looked upon the line philosophically, noting that it could have been much worse for the Navajos. He was anguished at the prospect for large-scale relocation, but without his dedication the partition line could indeed have been a lot worse.

Trouble After Partition— "This Thing Could Bust Wide Open"

Judge Walsh adopted the Simkin line on February 10, 1977, and three weeks later Hopi rangers moved into the Hopi partition area and impounded forty head of Navajo cattle. Chairman Sekaquaptewa said it was just the beginning of a Hopi push to clear the range. According to the land dispute legislation, the Navajos would not have to leave the Hopi area for several years, but Sekaquaptewa intended to encourage their early departure by making sure they had no stock. As feelings rose among owners of the impounded cattle, the Navajos sent twenty policemen into the Hopi area. When George Vlassis ominously told a reporter the police had been ordered to "protect the lives and property" of the Navajos there, it sounded as if the Navajos were preparing for battle.[8] However, Police Chief Philip Meek said he had instructed his men merely to preserve the peace by keeping irate Navajos from confronting Hopi rangers. In the meantime, lawyers for the Navajos went to court in an attempt to block further impoundment.

The cause of the uproar was an ambiguity in the part of Judge Walsh's partition order that concerned livestock control. "Law and order administration of the lands hereby partitioned shall hereafter be the responsibility of the tribe to which such lands are partitioned, provided, however . . . that during the period when the Secretary is engaged in livestock reduction and range restoration, he shall give such supervision and attention to the areas partitioned to each of the tribes as will assure the maintenance of law and order and make certain that the civil rights of persons within the area are not obstructed." The Hopi leaders interpreted the order as allowing them to enforce the tribal regulation against Navajo stock on Hopi land. They said they would sell the impounded stock if impoundment fees were not paid within ten days. Tension mounted; it was rumored that the Navajo stock owners were preparing to free their animals, by force if necessary. John Artichoker, head of the BIA's Phoenix Area Office, which oversees the Hopi reservation, called BIA superintendents across the West, and soon forty policemen were flown to Keams Canyon to supplement his own force around the impoundment corral there. Artichoker had the police supplied with enough arms to repulse a tank assault. Weapons flown in from a special BIA arsenal in Utah included grenade launchers and automatic rifles. The land dispute was spawning another nightmare.

At his office in Flagstaff, the BIA's JUA director, Bill Benjamin, received a call from an employee at the Utah arsenal, warning him that "something terrible might happen" unless the powder keg were defused quickly. Abbott Sekaquaptewa seemed almost eager for a shootout. In a meeting with lawyers for the two tribes, Judge Walsh said his partition order did not allow for the impoundment, and the Hopi lawyers agreed to return the Navajo stock. But Sekaquaptewa had other ideas, announcing that the Hopis "can't just have an ordinance around without enforcing it."[9] Even after Judge Walsh issued a formal injunction forbidding impoundment and ordering the return of the stock, Sekaquaptewa persisted and Artichoker kept his men stationed at Keams Canyon.

Phone wires had been buzzing between Arizona and BIA headquarters in Washington since the beginning of the crisis. "I called Washington and said this thing could bust wide open and the BIA would be in a position of defending an illegal seizure of livestock," Benjamin recalled later. In a four-way conference call linking Benjamin in Flagstaff, Artichoker in Phoenix, the BIA's Navajo Area Office in Window Rock, and Acting Indian Commissioner Ray Butler in Washington, Benjamin flatly rejected Artichoker's suggestion that the Joint Use Office pay the impoundment fees to the Hopis. Benjamin came up with an alternative, saying he would be willing to purchase the impounded stock from their Navajo owners. "Then I said I'd tell Abbott that if he went ahead with the sale, he'd be selling government property," Benjamin recalled. Artichoker balked at the idea and finally offered to have his office pay the $2,200 in impoundment fees. Not wanting to challenge the furious Hopi chairman, Butler agreed, and the crisis was eased.

Butler bowed to Sekaquaptewa once again when he agreed to Sekaquaptewa's demand that the BIA remove all Navajo stock from the Hopi partition area within a year of the partition order. When Benjamin received the news, he reacted angrily and on the record

to the Gallup *Independent*, saying the impoundment of Navajo
stock had disrupted his program to bring Navajo livestock in the
JUA down to half the carrying capacity of the range, in accordance
with the Land Settlement Act and orders of the federal court. "I
don't know what I can tell him," he said after receiving word of
Butler's order. "I may tell him we'll need 200 policemen. We could
run into armed resistance and even see some group like AIM come
in.[10] Benjamin recalled his first contact with Abbott Sekaquaptewa,
at a 1973 meeting with the Hopi Tribal Council. He said Sekaquaptewa had some advice on how to conduct the stock reduction program. "He said, 'My advice to you is to get the Army and some
machine guns out there, because that's all the Navajos understand.' "

A tough-minded, independent career BIA employee and a
Chippewa Indian, Benjamin was not afraid to oppose an order that
he regarded as an unconscionable provocation of Navajos already
faced with stock reduction and expulsion from their homes. In the
first year of a planned five-year program to reduce Navajo stock in
the JUA, Benjamin's office had purchased 67,000 of the estimated
120,000 Navajo sheep units there, he said, and the Navajos were
cooperating with him.

Benjamin had another reason to be frustrated with Washington.
In a trip to BIA headquarters there, he had insisted that the United
States had a moral obligation to ease the hardship of stock reduction and had received oral approval of his proposal for a two-million-
dollar aid package for the JUA Navajos. Confident that the money
was on the way, Benjamin visited the JUA to tell the people he
would be able to help them. Then, without warning or explanation,
the funds were denied in Washington. Benjamin was crestfallen.
"Those people are under tremendous strain," he said. "They are
facing the unknown of relocation, and as their stock is taken away
they are losing a bank account and a way of life. Traditionally, their
day was planned around the needs of the flock, and if they needed
money they could sell a sheep or two. But as things are now, we
can expect a lot of personal and family problems." He also lost face
among people who wanted very much to trust him. "All I know is
that now I can't deliver on a promise I made to people in a very
difficult situation," he said.

Abbott Sekaquaptewa was so upset with Benjamin's public
statements that he chartered a plane to have newsmen flown into
Oraibi, first from Phoenix and then from Albuquerque, to hear him

read a tribal council resolution demanding that Benjamin be "immediately reassigned and replaced by a person who is effective and impartial and who will publicly commit himself to carrying out the orders of the United States District Court."[11] Benjamin was not reassigned, however, and the stock reduction program went ahead under his direction. In order to encourage sales, the BIA paid 150 percent of the market value as well as the costs of transportation to the stock reduction camps. BIA personnel made home visits and sent out notices by registered mail to inform Navajos that their stock would be impounded if it were not sold. In May 1977, Benjamin said, "I think we've done a remarkable job, with the full cooperation of the Navajos." Sekaquaptewa was openly skeptical and pressed constantly for more dramatic federal action to clear the range. He was upset when the BIA decided in 1979 that the Navajos would be allowed to retain a few sheep right up until the time they relocated.

"At Some Point I Think We Are Going to Resist"

On May 3, 1977, aides to Senator Dennis DeConcini attended a meeting at the White Cone chapter house and heard Navajos describe the effects of stock reduction and tell how they felt about the impending relocation program. Mary Lou White cried when she asked what had happened to the financial assistance Benjamin had promised. Then Miller Nez spoke somberly of the possibility of violence. "This is very emotional, and at some point I think we are going to resist any further attempt by Washington to take away our only source of support," Nez said. "I think sooner or later there will be killing of individuals."

The chapter house was crowded, mostly with elderly Navajos who had come to meet the men from "Washindoan," that place that had so much control over their lives. "Livestock reduction means starvation to us," said eighty-four-year-old Emma Nelson, whose son had died in World War II. "Washington has taken our livestock without replacing it with any other way of making a living." Chester Morris wore the blue cap of the White Cone American Legion Post. His statement was powerful, even chilling. "The enforcement of Public Law 93-531 means starvation, homelessness, mentally disturbed [*sic*], alcoholism, destruction, family dislocation, crime, and even death for many," he said. "That is what I call a cruel law. And these people don't understand what they are getting us into. . . . These things really hurt, hurt the old people. They don't have anything to look forward to. They used to see their sheep coming around the hill in the evening. Some of them had 100 or 200 head of stock for their livelihood, their children. Now what do they have for their children? I wish the people of America and Arizona would understand these things, give it thought, and place themselves in there, where we are right now."[12]

Seven weeks after the White Cone meeting, DeConcini introduced amendments to the 1974 act to slow down the relocation process. DeConcini proposed that heads of households on the wrong side of the partition line be allowed to chose a "life estate," during which they and their dependents could stay at their homes. As the older Navajos died, their children, presumably better able to adjust to a new life, would have to relocate, and the homesite would be turned over to the tribe to whom it had been partitioned. DeConcini's legislation would have supplanted the life estate provisions handed down by Judge James Walsh. Judge Walsh imposed restrictions so severe—allowing for life estates of five acres on which no stock could be grazed, and forbidding visits of more than twenty-four hours—that they made the program unworkable. DeConcini found Judge Walsh's order unreasonable. "I'm trying to make it a little easier for the people to live with the legislation," DeConcini said during a break in hearings on his amendments in Winslow in March 1978. "I'd like to soften the blow, and the main ones that need help are the old ones."[13]

Abbott Sekaquaptewa said "political considerations" were behind the amendments, implying that DeConcini was doing the bidding of the Navajos, who had voted overwhelmingly for him in his 1976 senatorial campaign against Sam Steiger.[14] DeConcini was obviously aware of the Navajo voting strength, but had he merely wanted to do a favor for Peter MacDonald, he would have introduced legislation for outright repeal of the 1974 act. At the Winslow hearings, MacDonald, who faced tribal elections at the end of 1978, was indifferent toward the DeConcini Bill. Had he endorsed it, MacDonald would have been implicitly accepting relocation and would have opened himself to a barrage of criticism from the people of the JUA as well as from his political opponents. James Abourezk joined DeConcini at Winslow, and MacDonald thanked them both for their efforts to help his people. But he asked that they attempt to "fashion a more complete solution to a problem that was not created through the fault of the Navajos or through the fault of the

Hopis." MacDonald was unnerved by the politically risky life estate concept. He was much more comfortable with the hard line against partition and relocation. But as DeConcini noted repeatedly in 1978, Congress was in no mood to repeal the act it had passed four years previously after so much emotional deliberation.[15]

The most striking thing about the Winslow hearings was that they were attended by about thirty Hopis and five hundred Navajos. The Hopi witnesses were primarily members of the extended family of Harrington Navasie, whose father built a home near Jeddito in 1912. They told how they had been bullied and harassed by Navajos who stole their stock and crops. "Harassment has become to us a day-to-day thing, and we don't want to put up with it any more," Claudina Cedarface said, opposing the life estate concept. "We want to have peace and rest from these problems. We can get this only if we live on Hopi land with the Hopi people and without the Navajos living there also." Like the other Hopi residents of the Jeddito island, Mrs. Cedarface was planning to relocate to the Hopi partition area and was upset with the prospect that Navajos might remain there for years.[16]

The Navajos who testified came from all across the Hopi partition area. Most were elderly, like Emma Nelson, who spoke briefly in Navajo and submitted a statement in English. "We, the old folks, had no choice but to learn the livestock business in our youth," she said in the prepared statement. "We could not go to school because we were needed at home, and education in the white man's way was hardly heard of at that time. . . . Further, as you might be aware, our livestock have been reduced and nothing has been offered to us to support ourselves. . . . Since the land dispute has evolved, all the actions taken to resolve the dispute have been to our disadvantage. The laws that have been made only harmed us. As I said before, I am uneducated. Only my children and my grandchildren are educated. They have the opportunity of learning the white man's life. They can adapt to other alternative ways of making a living. I cannot."[17]

The Equation of Suffering

The relative attendance of the two tribes at the hearings and the testimony they presented raised once again the question of the land dispute's equation of hardships. The courts had written that Navajo hardships in settling the dispute would have to be balanced by past hardships suffered by the Hopis. Abbott Sekaquaptewa invoked this argument at Winslow, urging the senators "not to forget about those people who are not testifying but who cannot do so because they have been forced off the land."[18]

It is easy to see the Navajo side of this equation of suffering. Several thousand Navajos, many of them of the generations that grew up without acquiring job or language skills that would allow them to cope with the non-Indian world, are to be expelled from their homes and deprived of a way of life. They are poor, but they are emotionally whole in a way of life they understand. That way of life, which is dying to be sure, has been stamped for early extinction by an act of Congress.

As the history of the Navasie family (see pp. 69–70) poignantly illustrates, the Hopi side of the equation is also weighted with suffering. Two questions, however, must be asked about the land dispute. First, how many Hopis were harassed by Navajos from the land beyond their mesas? Second, what use will the Hopis make of the lands from which Navajos are to be removed? The first of these cannot be answered with any statistical accuracy, but it is clear that only a few Hopis wanted to live away from the mesa communities. The answer to the second question is known. As Senator Abourezk noted during the debate on the 1974 act, the Hopis have never intended to occupy the partitioned land in any numbers. They plan to use these lands primarily for cattle grazing. The northern part of the Hopi area seems destined for strip mining. Abbott Sekaquaptewa has said that the tribe will need several years to develop a land use plan for its partition area, but he acknowledged in 1977 that financial considerations would force the tribe "to seriously consider additional coal leases."[19]

The Demoralizing Effects of Stock Reduction

In 1977 social scientists at Northern Arizona University made a study of the stock reduction program, documenting in straightforward, unemotional language its demoralizing effects. They reported, "There can be no argument that the residents of the Joint Use Area are experiencing a general depression, a sense of lack of achievement, and a relative pessimism for the future." Some of the Navajos, they said, had cooperated with stock reduction in the desperate hope that if they gave up their sheep the government would allow them to stay on their land. Another interesting observation of the NAU study is that livestock help to ease the transition into the job economy represented by urban centers on and off the reservation. The researchers quoted another study that said, "The flocks provide them with some cushion against the vicissitudes of a market economy where many Navajos can participate only at the lowest levels. On the other hand, when wage opportunities are good, it becomes reasonable to subsidize livestock activities with wage income."[20]

The last point raises an important question about Navajo livestock ownership during the transition to the job economy. A number of Navajos who earn good salaries in the urban centers still own livestock at the family camp. The burden on the land would be eased considerably if the tribe established rules whereby grazing rights would diminish as income increases. Such an action would meet stiff resistance among a people long tied to sheep, and to some extent it might discourage entry into the job economy. But it would certainly help those Navajos who have no choice but to follow the old ways and who are involved in a holding action against a future they are not equipped to enter.

Senator Goldwater Baffles Big Mountain

The DeConcini Bill went nowhere after the Winslow hearings. A general reluctance in Congress to reopen the wounds of 1974, coupled with the conviction in some quarters that the DeConcini Bill was too sweeping in its approach to the problems of relocation, caused the bill to languish in the Senate Select Committee on Indian Affairs. It wasn't until Senator Goldwater made a visit to Big Mountain that there was any movement on the bill. Goldwater's official lines to the Navajos were badly frayed because of his feud with Peter MacDonald, but Roberta Blackgoat and Violet Ashke reestablished contact when they traveled to Washington at tribal expense in July 1978 as part of the "Longest March" demonstration of Indian concern over an anti-Indian backlash that had seen the introduction of legislation to curb Indian water and fishing rights and even to break up reservations into taxable, individually owned plots. They stopped at Goldwater's office and asked the senator to come to Big Mountain and talk with the people there about the land dispute. Goldwater accepted and later said the invitation was "the first time the Navajos have ever asked me to discuss the dispute with them."[21]

At the end of July, Goldwater cleared room in his busy Washington schedule and flew by helicopter from Phoenix to Big Mountain for a four-hour meeting with some 220 Navajos under the shade of a brush shelter. The senator, without whose support the land dispute legislation probably would not have passed in 1974, showed an almost total lack of awareness of what the bill was doing. "There has been no decision that says you have to move or what you have to do," he said, unmindful of the partition order. "And until that happens, and I don't think it's very close to happening or the way it looks now will happen, I won't say don't worry, but nobody can push you around."

As the Navajos who understood English shook their heads and muttered disbelief, the senator compounded his mistakes. The relocation commission had been receiving funding for more than three years, but he insisted, "No money has been appropriated for relocation." The BIA had removed over half the Navajo stock from the JUA, but the senator said he knew of no federal stock reduction program since the one organized by John Collier in the 1930s. Goldwater said the major thrust of the land dispute legislation was to establish a commission to develop a plan for partitioning the JUA. He said he would talk with the Rev. Paul Urbano, one of the commission members, about the hardships of the people of Big Mountain. "The commission, I might add, can make no binding agreement. They can merely say 'Here's an agreement that we've reached.' " Then he added reassuringly, "Most of us will probably be dead before they reach any decision. And I expect to be coming back out here and seeing you for quite some time."

The elderly Navajos received Goldwater with elaborate courtesy. They served him lunch of mutton stew, peaches, and fry bread, and when they came up to the front of the brush shelter to speak, they shook his hand gravely. Translation into Navajo was spotty, so most of the people there did not understand what Goldwater was saying. But the English-speaking young expressed exasperation. "So what you are saying is that Public Law 93-531 is no good, or it's vague, or *what is it?*" Annie Holmes said. Percy Deal, new director of the Navajos' Land Dispute Commission, got down to specifics. "Sitting here among my people and listening to you this morning, it became apparent to me that either your staff down here in Phoenix or up there in Washington is not doing their homework," Deal said. "I can tell you right now that relocation is in progress, livestock reduction is in progress, fencing is in progress, and you are here telling us that this has not come about yet. I would suggest that you go back to the Phoenix office or your D.C. office and tell your staff to get on the ball and keep you current on information going on out here."

The senator responded defensively. "Well, for your information, I helped write that act. I sat through the debate in the Senate, I listened to the debate in the House." Obviously knocked off stride now, he tried to recover his balance, acknowledging that, yes, partition had occurred, but still, relocation was a remote prospect. Then he added, "If you people are willing to force your tribal government to accept the court decision that they don't like, then you can live with it. But it is not my decision to tell your tribal government what to do."[22]

It was a baffling, disturbing performance. Senator Goldwater was absolutely out of touch with the consequences of the Land Settlement Act. Apparently he was suggesting that the Navajos didn't have to go along with the court decision if they didn't want to. Daniel Peaches, a Navajo member of the Arizona legislature, and a Republican, suggested sarcastically that Goldwater's statements were up to the usual level of Washington's understanding of the land dispute. "The people here have suffered because the politicians in Washington, especially our Republican leaders from the state of Arizona, failed to understand, failed to recognize, failed to see that if the land was to be divided 50–50, it was inevitable that tragedy was going to fall on the shoulders of the Navajo people."

Goldwater may have sensed that Peaches had been sent to ambush him by Peter MacDonald. "That was a good political speech," he said, becoming increasingly tense. He made an abrupt departure from Big Mountain then, stalking to the helicopter past Navajos who called on him to stay and listen to them. Before he flew away, Goldwater angrily told a reporter for the *Navajo Times*, "I've lived here fifty years, and I probably know this land better than most of these Navajos here today do." He had given his fellow congressmen the same assurance back in 1974.[23]

Reports of Senator Goldwater's appearance at Big Mountain prompted an *Arizona Star* editorial entitled "Goldwater's Confusion":

The episode recalls speeches Goldwater delivered two years ago on a legislative proposal for settlement of disputed Indian water rights in Central Arizona. Water rights between Indians and non-Indians had been agreed upon decades before, Goldwater said, and there was no reason for new law. At that time, two major lawsuits had been filed by Arizona tribes against non-Indian users. More suits have been filed since then.

Goldwater, who either has uninformed or inaccurate sources on Arizona Indian affairs, has not spent enough time gathering firsthand information or he has simply lost interest in the subject. If the latter is true, the senator should refrain from public comment. . . .[24]

Back in Washington, Senator Goldwater kept his Big Mountain pledge to do what he could to ease the pain of relocation. He told Senator DeConcini he would not get in the way of an attempt to broaden the provisions for life estates. Goldwater wanted to keep a low profile on his decision to support a major change in the 1974 legislation, however, so he made no public comments as DeConcini revived his life estates initiative. Goldwater did make it known to the people who mattered that it was OK to go along with DeConcini, however. Those people were his administrative assistant, Jack Murphy, and the staff of Dewey Bartlett, ranking Republican on the Indian committee.

The DeConcini bill moved quickly through committee and was passed by unanimous consent on the Senate floor before the Hopis had time to organize their opposition. Fewer than ten senators were in the Senate chamber when the DeConcini Bill was introduced and passed in a process that took less than ten minutes. Then the bill was referred to the House of Representatives, where its fate lay in the hands of Morris Udall, chairman of the House Interior Committee.

Life Estates "For the Truly Elderly Navajos"

Wayne Owens, sponsor of the 1974 legislation, had lost his 1976 bid for the Senate, and was now a member of John Boyden's law firm. The morning after the DeConcini Bill was passed by the Senate, Owens was in Udall's office complaining that DeConcini had pulled a fast one. After the meeting with his friend and former colleague, Owens expressed confidence that he had been heard by "understanding and sympathetic ears."[25] Meanwhile, back in Arizona, leaders of both tribes were booking passage on flights to the nation's capitol. The land dispute was coming to Washington once again, and once again Morris Udall was a man in the middle.

To make a long story short, Hopi leaders attacked the DeConcini Bill for undermining their hard-earned rights, Peter MacDonald told Udall he didn't want life estates because he thought the entire 1974 act should be repealed, and Morris Udall said he would accept no significant change in the formula to settle the land dispute without first visiting the JUA and holding hearings. Udall said that while he recognized a need for life estates "for the truly elderly Navajos," he would not support legislation granting life estates to forty-year-olds, as provided in the DeConcini Bill. "I'm talking about an age that is really just elderly Navajos," he said. "That's the justification for it, and a forty-year-old Navajo is not an elderly Navajo in my book." Udall also said he expected the Navajos to accept partition and relocation if Congress passed any life estate legislation. The Navajos responded that they would never stop working to block their removal from the former JUA.[26]

Although the DeConcini life estate initiative was halted in 1978, the two houses of Congress did agree on a bill that made a number of less substantive changes in the 1974 act. President Carter subsequently vetoed the bill because he did not like two of its provisions. He objected first to the provision that either house of Congress could veto the plan of the federal relocation commission to move Navajos and Hopis. Second, Carter objected to the provision that would have made elected officials ineligible to serve on the relocation commission. The aim of that provision was to remove from the commission Hawley Atkinson, a man whose unfortunate conduct had further embittered the Navajos of the former JUA.

DeConcini Tries Again

Nineteen seventy-nine was year ninety-seven of the Navajo-Hopi land dispute, and it was the fifth year in which congressional hearings attempted to sort out how it should be resolved once and for all. In April, Senator DeConcini reintroduced his life estate bill, quoting from a letter he had received from the McCabe family of Tolani Lake—part of the Hopi partition area. The McCabes said they had been relocated in the 1930s and 1940s, when District 6 was established and then expanded. "Our grandmother and her family have been moved three times for the same problems," they wrote. "It is high time that we, the children and grandchildren, put our foot down and demand our rights. So this is where we all stop and stay for the rest of our lives. . . . We know every foot of our land. Our relatives and friends live close by, and this is our happiness."[27]

When the Senate Select Committee on Indian Affairs held hearings on the DeConcini Bill in May, Peter MacDonald said Congress would be guilty of a double standard if it did not allow the Navajos to buy the Hopi half of the former JUA. He referred to the land claims of several East Coast tribes that were in the process of being settled without forcing non-Indians to relocate. "Why in the name of God do you insist on moving Navajos?" MacDonald asked in exasperation. "Why is there a double standard in which, when Anglos displace Indians, Indians get money and Anglos keep the land, but when Indians displace Indians, Indians must be moved?" Hopi spokesman George Nasoftie said his tribe's leaders had become frustrated by Navajo attempts to repeal the 1974 legislation and DeConcini's attempt to amend it. "The Hopi people lost faith in us and in Washington when nothing happens like Washington promises," Nasoftie said. "The Navajos still have our land. We obey the law and have no land. The Navajo disobeys the law and is rewarded with millions of dollars. What are we to do? What do we tell our children?"[28]

Just before his visit to the former JUA in July, Morris Udall made it clear that his position had not changed since the previous fall. "While I will not support any proposal to repeal the basic settlement terms, I do not feel that Congress has given adequate attention to the heavy burden of relocation, and I am looking for reasonable proposals to ease those burdens," he said.[29]

California Democratic Representative George Miller accompanied Udall to Arizona for a one-day tour of the former JUA and for a second day of hearings in Winslow. The hearings were a clear victory for the Hopis. Tribal officials, who had been embarrassed by the scant Hopi turnout for the Senate hearings fifteen months earlier, urged their supporters to make the trip to Winslow, and transportation was provided for those who needed it. As a result, about half of the 700 persons in attendance were Hopis, and they vigorously applauded the testimony of their representatives. Meticulously prepared in advance, Hopi testimony was presented by men and women, young and old, and indicated a sharp shift in the tribe's strategy before Congress. In all the hearings leading up to passage of the 1974 legislation, the Hopis said quite frankly that they wanted the JUA land for its grazing potential. In 1979, however, newspaper stories were reporting the misery of the Navajos, and the Hopis were becoming increasingly sensitive to the charge that they were going to replace people with livestock. At Winslow they listed additional plans for the partitioned land: agriculture and community development. In a briefing paper prepared for Udall and Miller, the Hopis argued, "The issue before Congress is not the hardship of relocation; the issue is the survival of the Hopi culture. The question of hardships and equity were argued in the courts in 1962 and in Congress in 1974. In both instances just decisions were made. There is no reason to expect that if argued again there will be a different outcome. The only amendments to the act of 1974 which should be considered are those which will accelerate its implementation, not hinder it."

The Hopi presentation was forceful and articulate; however, it does not stand up to careful examination. In the first place, even if the Hopis were experiencing a population explosion—and they are not—new communities could not take up more than a fraction of the 911,000 acre Hopi partition area. Second, Hopi interest in farming is declining with each successive generation. And third, there is now plenty of evidence to support the argument that the basic premises of congressional action in 1974 were false, and that the Land Settlement Act has created problems far more severe than anything anticipated by Congress.

Instead of challenging the Hopi contentions, the Navajos spoke of their heartache. Their testimony was uncoordinated and impromptu, but nonetheless poignant. Bessie Allen described the effects of the 1974 act on her father. "He has been depressed since the passage of the public law," she said. "He is senile, he no longer talks, and he has lost all feelings of self-worth. Many of the community members are in the same state." As the hearings came to an end, Udall reaffirmed his support for partition of the JUA. "Congress is not going to repeal the 1974 act," he said. "It was passed after long deliberation and careful consideration."[30]

A Veto Threat from the Carter Administration

After the Winslow hearings there was no further movement on the land dispute in Congress until September. By that time Udall had decided to sponsor his own life estate legislation. His bill proposed to limit life estates to 28 acres and to allow them only to fifty families, whose heads had to be at least seventy years old. Another key provision would have allowed the federal relocation commission to purchase up to 50,000 acres to help carry out the resettlement of the Navajos. Responding to pressure from the Save the Arizona Strip Committee and to his own conviction that House Rock–Paria was inappropriate as a relocation site, Udall also included in his bill a provision that would have expressly prohibited the Navajos from buying land there or anywhere else in the Arizona Strip.

Udall's bill passed the House of Representatives in September, shortly after the Senate passed a modified version of the De-Concini Bill. The Senate version proposed to grant up to 160 life estates of 150 acres each to families whose heads were at least forty-five years old. DeConcini's bill set a 200,000 acre limit on the land the relocation commission could buy. It did not include a prohibition on Navajo purchase of House Rock–Paria.

The Navajo and Hopi Indian Relocation Commission lobbied hard for authorization to buy as much land as possible. They wanted to avoid the situation in which relocatees would be forced to move into towns or communities against their will. In a position statement, the commission argued: "The most critical consideration is the absolute requirement of maintaining the traditional lifestyles of certain Indian people impacted by the partitionment—namely those families who in fact do not possess the ability to accommodate a major change in their present situation or the capacity to adjust to a new situation."[31]

With his usual candor, Udall said his position on life estates and land acquisition was not necessarily as hard line as his bill indicated. He said he had anticipated the need to compromise with the Senate and wanted "a little bargaining room" going into a special House-Senate conference committee. "The key element in this is finality," Udall said. "I'd be willing to give a lot of ground if we knew this was the end."

Udall continued: "I really feel that both [the tribes] would welcome it if someone moved in and said, 'This is the settlement.

It's not perfect, but it's fair, and there won't be a run at Congress next year to have it upset.' Indian and non-Indian politicians, especially at election time, tend to say to the Navajos, 'Stick with us and we'll find a way out of this.' But once the people who have to move accept the fact that they have to move, then all these relocation problems become very easy. We've got generous assistance for them. It's kind of a psychological thing. After the first four families move, the next group will be able to move a lot more easily. I'm trying to fine-tune the 1974 bill. But I want a sense of finality to come out of this, so that the people will say that for better or worse, it's settled and let's get on with our lives."[32]

An ad hoc House-Senate conference committee was expected to convene in December 1979 to work out a compromise between the two bills. Then the Navajos made a surprise announcement through their public relations firm, Hill and Knowlton, whom the Navajos had retained earlier in the year after the tribal council authorized spending up to a half million dollars in a last-ditch fight to repeal the 1974 legislation. Picked up by both the Associated Press and the United Press International, the Hill and Knowlton press release said the two tribes had privately come to an agreement to end their dispute. As explained in the press release, the Navajos had agreed not to seek life estates if a total of about 600,000 acres were made available for relocation. The "settlement" also called for the Hopis to receive additional land sufficient to graze 3,500 sheep units.

There were two problems. First, Hopi counsel John Kennedy repudiated the press release. "We just don't have an agreement," Kennedy told Ben Cole of the *Arizona Republic*.[33] Representatives of the two tribes had been meeting for several months, Kennedy said later, but talks had been broken off a month previously after apparently irreconcilable differences had developed. The second problem was that congressional staff reacted with horror to the "settlement." Estimating that it could cost taxpayers $100 million, they said it had no chance of being ratified by the Congress.

As 1980 began and this manuscript went to press, the conference committee was expected to meet soon and work out compromise language for life estates and land acquistion. However, the Navajos were still trying to persuade Udall that if relocation had to be done, the most reasonable approach was to drop life estates and increase the amount of land the relocation commission could buy.

Regardless of Udall's position, the Navajo initiative faced almost certain opposition from the Carter administration. In a letter to Montana's John Melcher, chairman of the Senate Select Committee on Indian Affairs, an official in the Interior Department said relocation should be carried out "in the most cost-effective and efficient manner." Assistant Interior Secretary Larry Meierotto informed Melcher that Interior favored limiting the land the relocation commission could buy to 25,000 acres. Addressing the life estate provisions in the House and Senate bills, Meierotto found the House bill too restrictive and the Senate bill too generous. He recommended that life estates be granted only to heads of households who were at least sixty-five and that the estates be large enough to graze fifteen sheep units. Without these changes, Meierotto said, new legislation "would not be in accord with the program of the President."[34]

The Carter administration's budget-conscious position was cause for consternation and bitterness among the staff of the Senate Indian Committee. "Without a doubt, they are mindless, and they probably are heartless as well," one staff member said. The staff of the relocation commission talked cynically about the men in Washington who had shaped the administration's position, doubting they had any idea of the dimensions of the relocation program. They recalled the testimony of commissioner Sandra Massetto at the Winslow hearings in July: "If the United States government can spend billions of dollars to settle the dispute between the Egyptians and the Israelis, they can spend whatever dollars are necessary to settle this land dispute which it created."

Pauline Whitesinger. *Photo by John Running*

Rick Lavis of the Department of the Interior meeting with Navajos at Big Mountain, November 1977. *Photo by Jerry Kammer*

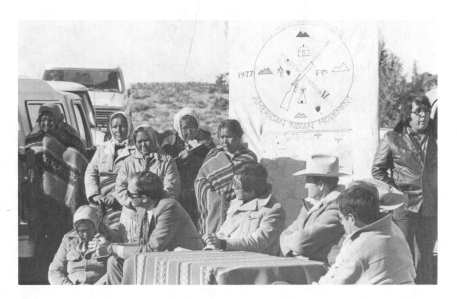

Effie Begay's son herding sheep near Big Mountain. *Photo © 1980 by Dan Budnik, Woodfin Camp & Associates*

Peabody Coal Company mine, Black Mesa. *Photo © 1980 by Dan Budnik, Woodfin Camp & Associates*

A Navajo trading post, 1970s. *Photo by Abigail Adler*

Big Mountain Navajos outside abandoned Wide Ruins trading post, 1977. *Photo © 1980 by Dan Budnik, Woodfin Camp & Associates*

Arizona Senator Dennis DeConcini (left) with Navajo Tribal
Chairman Peter MacDonald. *Photo by Jerry Kammer*

Hopi Tribal Chairman Abbott Sekaquaptewa. *Photo by Mark
Lennihan*

Wayne Sekaquaptewa,
1956.

John Boyden, General Counsel for the
Hopi Tribe.

George Vlassis, General Counsel for the
Navajo Tribe. *Photo by Paul Natonabah*

Hopi snake dance, Walpi Pueblo, August 17, 1889. *Photo by Ben Wittick courtesy of the Museum of New Mexico.*

Navajos and Hopis meeting at Shongopavi, May 1972, to discuss the Steiger Bill. Left to right: Chief Claude (Hopi), Thomas Banyacya (Hopi), Daniel Peaches (Navajo), Mina Lansa (Hopi), unidentified man with tape recorder. *Photo © 1980 by Dan Budnik, Woodfin Camp & Associates*

Hopi Tribal Council meeting, May 1972. Tribal Chairman Clarence Hamilton (upper left), Assistant Secretary for Land Management Harrison Loesch of the Department of the Interior (laughing), and Indian Commissioner Louis Bruce (lower right). *Photo © 1980 by Dan Budnik, Woodfin Camp & Associates*

Cartoon from *Qua Toqti* ("The Eagle's Cry"), Hopi newspaper, April 1974.

Cartoon from *Navajo Times*, August 1, 1974.

Congressman Wayne Owens.   Senator James Abourezk.

A reporter interviews Samuel Pete, director of the Navajo Tribe's
Land Dispute Commission, during the journey to Washington by
traditional Navajos and Hopis lobbying against the Owens Bill in
1974. *Photo by Jerry Kammer*

Senator Barry Goldwater at Big Mountain, July 1978. *Photo by Mark Lennihan*

Sign near Jeddito Springs, 1979. *Photo © 1980 by Dan Budnik, Woodfin Camp & Associates*

Congressman Morris Udall visiting Navajos at White Cone, 1979.
Photo by Paul Natonabah

Hawley Atkinson of the Navajo
and Hopi Indian Relocation
Commission.*Photo by Jerry
Kammer*

Big Mountain Navajos in 1979 discussing the line partitioning the Joint Use Area with BIA official Lynn Montgomery (seated left, chin in hand). *Photo © 1980 by Dan Budnik, Woodfin Camp & Associates*

Harrington Navasie. *Photo by Mark Lennihan.*

Roger Attakai at his home near Star Mountain. On the wall hang (left to right) Navajo wedding basket and Native American Church rattle and prayer fan. *Photo by Abigail Adler*

Ashike Bitsi of Big Mountain. *Photo by Abigail Adler*

Katherine Smith's basket holds ritual objects. White buckskin bundle
is her Mountain Earth Bundle. Big Mountain is in the background.
Photo © 1980 by Dan Budnik, Woodfin Camp & Associates

Leonard Deal standing on Big Mountain, overlooking the land dispute country. *Photo by John Running*

9
The Relocation Commission

The battle for House Rock Valley was one of the inevitable unhappy results of the legislation to settle the Navajo-Hopi land dispute. It was the product of conflicting passions for land and a way of life. A second unhappy result was far from inevitable. It came about through an exercise of political cronyism to find a job on the Navajo and Hopi Indian Relocation Commission for a man not well suited to do the commission's sensitive job.

Hawley Atkinson attended the University of Washington for three years before returning home to Idaho in the 1930s to work in his family's building supply business. He sold the business in 1964 and moved to Arizona to get away from the cold of the north country. For two years Atkinson worked for the Navajo Tribe, helping to reorganize the tribal warehouse. Then he did economic planning for a consortium of seventeen Arizona tribes before joining the staff of Republican Arizona Governor Jack Williams. As president of the Republican Club in Sun City, a huge planned retirement community near Phoenix, Atkinson presented the profile of a fiscal conservative and critic of the federal bureaucracy. His tone was fervent. When Atkinson ran for the Maricopa County Board of Supervisors in 1976, he told Phoenix newspapers he was seeking office because he wanted "to restore fundamentals to our local government, in hopes that the fire which will start by our example will shed its light all the way to Washington with one clear, resounding message—here the people are once again sovereign."[1]

Back in mid 1975, Democrat Raul Castro was Arizona's Governor and Atkinson was out of work. He asked Senator Paul Fannin for a job. Fannin had nothing for Atkinson on his staff but came up with something else. Appointments to federal commissions are usually made upon the recommendation of Congressmen who belong to the party of the president and who represent the state where the commission will work. Gerald Ford was president in 1975, so Fannin arranged to have Atkinson appointed to the Navajo and Hopi Indian Relocation Commission, which had the task of developing a plan for resettling those expelled from the JUA. The three commissioners were to be paid at the GS-18 level, $140 per day in 1975, for each day or part of a day they worked.

The commission's work would have challenged a saint. It required tact, patience, and sensitivity. The other two appointees—the former governor of New Mexico's Zuni Pueblo, Robert Lewis, and a Phoenix Episcopal priest, the Reverend Paul Urbano—had at least some of those qualities. Atkinson seemed to lack them in abundance. He proved to be an abrasive, combative man whose style was that of confrontation. It was inevitable that the Navajos would be suspicious of the commissioners, the men who would plan their removal. When Atkinson encountered suspicion, he went on the offensive, thrusting his jaw forward and lecturing in terse, clipped phrases. He relished the authority of his position but was unable to use it gracefully.

The first meeting between the commissioners and the people who were to be relocated was a representative Atkinson performance. It took place at the Coal Mine Mesa chapter house, in the treeless, flat immensity of the western JUA where the horizon is broken only by an occasional hogan and the massive electric transmission towers that send power to southern Arizona. For five hours on a warm afternoon in the summer of 1976, about sixty Navajos, mostly middle-aged or older, sat attentively as each question, answer, and statement was conveyed in both English and Navajo.

The mood in the chapter house was tense. Samuel Pete of the tribe's land dispute commission said he was disappointed that the commission had not supported the Navajo application for House Rock–Paria. "Time and time again," Pete said, "Navajos have asked this question: if we are going to be relocated, where are we going to go, what lands are available? It is critically important that lands be made available and that support be obtained from the relocation commission."[2] Atkinson gave a brusque response. He spoke at the people rather than to them, in the manner of a rigid school principal.

"In my opinion, the relocation commission has no proper place in either the selection of land by the Navajo Tribe or the granting of land by the Bureau of Land Management," he said, his left hand clutching a microphone, his right hand punching the air before him on every third or fourth word. Several Navajos expressed anger and frustration with the commissioners. "I'm beginning to think the white man won't help us much," Tribal Councilman Joe Dayzie said.[3] Atkinson left the meeting shaken and did not pause to engage anyone in informal conversation. He climbed into Father Urbano's Mercedes sports car for the 250-mile drive to Phoenix.

Atkinson's refusal to involve the commission in land acquisition apparently contradicted the land dispute legislation, which directed the commission to identify relocation sites. But it was perfectly consistent with his own political interests. Maricopa County elections were just a few months off, and Bill Morrall's Save the Arizona Strip Committee had been active in southern Arizona. Atkinson didn't want to antagonize anybody. For him the safe position was no position. He even refused to allow a commission staff member to attend a hearing in Flagstaff over the proposed sale of House Rock–Paria to the Navajos.

Atkinson changed his mind about land acquistion the day after he had been elected to the County Board of Supervisors, announcing that he felt the commission should help find a relocation site after all. "It is not a question of whether there is a legal responsiblity for the commission to identify sites," he said, like a man who had seen the light. "There is a higher responsibility to achieve a successful relocation for those unfortunate Navajos and Hopis who have to relocate." When an incredulous reporter asked when Atkinson had changed his mind, he replied that he wasn't sure. "It just dawned on me that someone had to do this." He added, however, that he wasn't enthusiastic about House Rock–Paria as a relocation site.[4]

Atkinson also irritated a lot of people who were not being forced to relocate. In early 1978, *Arizona Republic* reporter Glen Law wrote that the board of supervisors had ended the previous year "in confusion and disharmony" largely because of Atkinson and that Republican members of the board had met "to tell Atkinson to get his act together." Law offered insight into the Atkinson style: "Atkinson, 61, is a tall, rangy, graying man who sometimes dresses conservatively and sometimes flamboyantly in cowboy boots and a neckerchief. He seldom hesitates to give a subordinate a dressing down. At times he displays a knack of attacking people without making it appear to be a personal attack."[5]

After the Coal Mine Mesa meeting, both Atkinson and Reverend Urbano skipped the next two meetings with Navajo relocatees. Robert Lewis was the only commissioner at the meeting in Forest Lake, where Joe Biakeddy, a middle-aged seasonal railroad worker spoke through tears about the commissioners, the House Rock furor, and relocation. "We don't believe you have the qualifications to understand the underdeveloped Navajo people," Biakeddy said in halting English. "We are suspicious that you will treat us unfairly. We are suspicious of your thoughts and your ways. I say this with all apology." About House Rock he said, "We feel and we understand that nobody wants us anywhere out of the Executive Order Reservation. There is no place for us. Even though we suffer here, we like it. We don't want to suffer anywhere else. Years ago they set this area aside as a concentration camp. Now they're fighting over it. We don't want to leave here. Wherever you take us, it's wrong. That's the way I feel. We don't want to push anybody, and we don't want anybody pushing us."[6] It was one of the most incisively truthful moments of the land dispute—and two of the commissioners weren't there.

The Navajos were offended by Atkinson's and Urbano's failure to attend chapter meetings. "The only way to learn the feelings of the people is to meet with them and discuss with them," the tribal councilman from Forest Lake said.[7] The chairman of the tribe's Land Dispute Commission called upon the secretary of the interior to replace the two men with Navajos or others experienced in relocation and community development. "We want the commission to meet our people because it is evident that at least two of them know nothing about the Navajo people and Navajo problems," Marlin Scott said in a press release. "Instead, the only commissioner who has any knowledge of the Navajo people shows up, and the ignorant twosome becomes the ignorant and absent twosome." Scott charged Atkinson and Urbano with continuing a legacy of neglect in high places. "If one lesson is clear from the Navajo-Hopi land dispute, it is that this tragic chapter in Navajo and Hopi history was caused by Anglo indifference and Anglo ignorance."[8]

Atkinson responded to the charges with disbelief. He was "shocked and dismayed," he said and explained that he had missed chapter meetings because he had not received the three weeks advance notice he required. He was, in fact, still busy campaigning for the board of supervisors.

All three commissioners made it to the meeting at Red Lake where chapter president Joe Klain said he intended to stay right where he was. "I am not planning to be relocated, and I am not planning to get the money," he said, "I want to stay on my land. That is my plan." Army veteran Yodell Billaha said proudly that his ancestors had eluded Kit Carson's troops and had not been taken to Fort Sumner. "What do you think about relocating people who didn't go on the Long Walk?" he asked defiantly. Marie Attakai talked about differing conceptions of land. "The Anglos sell land in a small patch and pay taxes on it," she said. "But this is our land. No money will buy it. We don't have much use for money. We exist on our land and our livestock."[9]

Robert Lewis did most of the talking for the commission, making repeated expressions of concern for the relocatees and asking for their advice. The Reverend Urbano, a dignified, sophisticated man with a gray goatee, said he regarded relocation as "a serious human tragedy." "I am not pretending that any amount of money can make up for the emotional loss of the land one loves," he said. Hawley Atkinson invited the future relocatees to come to his office in Flagstaff.[10] The invitation was sincere; Atkinson is much more comfortable meeting people individually than he is in a group. But to elderly Navajos who have infrequent access to transportation, the suggestion that they travel 140 miles to talk with Atkinson was yet further proof that Atkinson had no idea of who they were and how they lived.

Goldwater Intervenes to Save Atkinson

Trouble had been simmering between Lewis and the two non-Indian commissioners for some time before it finally came to a boil in the late summer of 1976 over the decision of Atkinson and Urbano to fire the commission's staff director, John Gray. Gray and Lewis had been close friends ever since Lewis was governor of Zuni and Gray was the top BIA official there. Lewis was so upset at the firing that he told Atkinson he intended to resign. Instead of resigning, however, Lewis stopped meeting with the other two commissioners and attempted to convince the Interior Department that they should be replaced. He made no public comment for the next two months.

In the meantime, relations between the Navajo tribal government and the commission were growing steadily more antagonistic. With good reason, tribal lawyer Larry Ruzow criticized the regulations drafted by the commission as "unclear" and "awkward." He then went on to say the "best thing that could be done with the proposed regulations would be to flush them, a luxury that the indigent Navajos of the Joint Use Area can only contemplate."[11] Father Urbano called the remarks "gratuitously insulting" and "a vulgarity unworthy of comment." In a letter to Ruzow he said, "I hope I will not have the displeasure of encountering you again. But if I do, I trust I will find your manners improved. You should not find that difficult to accomplish."[12] And so the long-distance spitting match between Flagstaff and Window Rock continued.

The Hardrock and Low Mountain chapters in the JUA joined the fray with petitions to the secretary of the interior asking for the removal of Atkinson and Urbano. Navajo Vice-chairman Wilson Skeet recalled seeing Atkinson "point his finger and yell" at Navajos during a chapter meeting. The Navajos responded by booing and telling Atkinson to go home, Skeet said. "When I saw that, I wrote to the secretary and told him he ought to consider replacing Atkinson," Skeet continued. "This is a touchy problem and can only be done by having the right people to do it."[13]

Robert Lewis broke his public silence by releasing to the press copies of a letter he had sent to Atkinson, with copies to Interior Secretary Kleppe, the Navajo and Hopi tribes, and the Arizona and New Mexico congressional delegations. Lewis said his refusal to work with the other two commissioners "represents the sum total of the frustration, despair, and actual disgust" he felt over their actions. "As you well know," he continued, addressing Atkinson, "I feel the last year and a half of activities by the commission have been a total waste. Far worse is the fact that the commission's policies, which have been dominated by you and Commissioner Urbano, have been totally ineffective in bringing about an orderly approach to our mission." Lewis said the other two commissioners had ignored his suggestions. He claimed the commission "is totally unacceptable to the people you are expected to serve." He said his absence from their meetings "should not stop you from continuing the relatively insignificant chores of the commission you seem to have a preoccupation with."[14]

Atkinson's reply was typically brusque. He called Lewis "kind of an egomaniac as regards publicity"—a strange statement to make about a man who had refused to speak to reporters for two months—and said Lewis was frustrated that the commission "can move progressively and successfully without him."[15] A year later, ironically, Atkinson was criticized back home in Phoenix for using the county Public Information Office to prepare personal news releases not related to county business. Atkinson had other problems in Maricopa County. *Arizona Republic* political editor Bernie Wynn reported that Atkinson wasn't getting along with the other Republicans on the Board of Supervisors. "Atkinson is kicking up his heels like a prima donna and creating dissension on the board, which gives the whole operation a public black eye," Wynn wrote.[16]

One thing reporters liked about Atkinson was that he was quotable. He snapped at opponents and critics in Maricopa County, calling one of the other supervisors "a master politician in smoke-filled rooms."[17] When he talked about the relocation program, he tried to present himself as a self-sacrificing public servant with a strong sense of history and his place in it. Some examples:

On the commission's work: "Would I want to do this again? Listen, would Joan of Arc want to fuel another bonfire?"[18]

On the land dispute legislation: "[It is] the greatest political setback for the Navajo Tribal Council since the Kit Carson war of 1863."[19]

On the importance of his work: "When I was first appointed and people told me they didn't envy my position, I didn't know what they meant. Still, the Lord gives us few opportunities to serve our fellow man. When we do receive such an opportunity, we have to grasp it just as firmly and as solidly as we can."[20]

Navajos were puzzled at the Atkinson-Urbano alliance that had frustrated Lewis. If Atkinson had antagonized them with his bluster, Father Urbano had impressed them with statements that relocation must be carried out with utmost care and that relocation was "a serious human tragedy." The Navajos hoped that the Reverend Urbano would join Lewis in pressing for Atkinson's removal. But the two non-Indian commissioners were united by their political conservatism and mutual friendships with Arizona's Republican leaders.

A member of the commission staff shed light on the Atkinson-Urbano relationship at the end of 1976. "Father Urbano sits there and tells you about how he wants to help these people. Then he gets in front of Atkinson and folds, just literally folds," the staffer said, not hiding his frustration. "They've spent $180,000 in a year and a half. You show me what they've done other than pay salaries and furnish the office. There's been absolutely no progress." The staffer was worried as well as frustrated and predicted that unless Atkinson and Urbano were replaced, "relocation is not only going to be a disaster, it'll be a national embarrassment." The staffer criticized the commissioners for staying holed up in Flagstaff with insignificant paperwork. "They should be willing to throw a sleeping bag into the back of a truck and go out there and live with the people."

The Interior Department finally responded to the Navajos' complaints by sending an investigator to look into the commission's work. Then Barry Goldwater wrote two letters to Secretary Kleppe, stating in both that he had lived with the land dispute his entire life and expressing confidence that all was right with the commission. "I urge you to the point of being insistent that these two men not be terminated because, frankly, you are not going to be able to get the kind of thinking provided by these two gentlemen anywhere else," Goldwater wrote in the first letter.[21] In the second letter he wrote, "I believe you will find most of the difficulties raised by an Interior Department member; Robert Lewis, a Commission member who is not even an Arizona Indian but a Zuni from New Mexico; and, I am afraid, by the machinations of Mr. Peter MacDonald of the Navajo Tribe."[22] Goldwater did not identify the Interior Department member, nor did he explain what he meant by the "machinations" of MacDonald. MacDonald had, in fact, stayed out of the fight with the relocation commission.

Kleppe kept Atkinson and Urbano on the commission. He announced that the findings of Interior's investigation "do suggest a history of delays, personality clashes, petty bickering, and poor judgment in personnel matters and in delegation of responsibility, which in its cumulative effect raised questions as to the potential effectiveness of the commission in carrying out its mission."[23] But these multiple indictments were apparently not enough to overrule the will of Barry Goldwater. Kleppe said he had decided that "the best interests of the relocation program for the Navajo and Hopi Indian people are served by continuing the present members in their current positions."[24]

Without directly mentioning Goldwater's intercession on his behalf, Atkinson expressed his thanks to the senator in a letter to the *Arizona Republic:*

Senator Goldwater has walked the extra mile for the Republican Party—he has knocked on the doors of all independents—he made the word *conservative* the rallying point of those who believe in sane, economical, efficient government. He has been a bulwark of resistance against the encroachment of Washington in local government. *He has fought the battle for any Arizonan who needed personal help to survive the Washington bureaucracy* [emphasis added].[25]

The *Republic* was not as willing as Senator Goldwater to defend Atkinson. In 1978, after Democrat Dennis DeConcini had managed a bill through Congress which would have disqualified political officeholders from the relocation commission, the paper ran an editorial debunking Atkinson's claim that DeConcini was out to get him because he was a Republican. Noting Atkinson's earnings for the year in his two jobs, the *Republic* editorialized "we do doubt that he could do $19,600 worth of work for the taxpayers of Maricopa County and still find time to do $31,190 worth of labor for the federal government. Atkinson's party registration, despite the sham he's trying to foist on the public, is not of any great concern to anyone. Dollars to donuts most of his constituents would tell him no person should be on two public payrolls, especially a second job hundreds of miles away. Of course, if Atkinson wants the Indian commission job so badly, he can always resign as a county supervisor. Your move, Atkinson."[26]

Just as he had survived the Interior Department investigation, Atkinson survived the DeConcini Bill. President Carter vetoed it, explaining that he disapproved of the provision to disqualify elected officials from membership on a federal commission and of a second provision that would have allowed either house of Congress to veto the relocation commission's plan.[27]

"A Cultural Disaster"

At Kleppe's urging the commissioners buried the hatchet and, after a traumatic and expensive two-year shakedown cruise, they finally began to take a hard look at their enormous task. Their staff director, Leon Berger, won the respect of the Navajos for his hard-working, low-key style; he also knew how to handle the sensitive ego of Hawley Atkinson.

Anthropologist and relocation expert Thayer Scudder of the California Institute of Technology was instrumental in getting the commission on track. Scudder agreed to advise the commission because he felt anthropologists have an obligation to be of practical value to the Indian people they spend so much time studying. But Scudder refused to be paid for his services and made it clear from the outset what he thought of relocating Navajos from the JUA. "I have been dealing with compulsory relocation for twenty years, and it's about the rottenest thing you can do to people, especially low-income people who are relatively illiterate and relatively immobile and tied to the land," he said in a telephone interview with the *Gallup Independent*. "It is a cultural disaster. The response of those Navajos when they are moved will be equivalent to the reaction you or I might have to the loss of a wife or son. I'm just 100 percent against this kind of thing."[28]

Scudder predicted that most relocatees would want to stay on the reservation and noted that the overgrazed reservation was in no shape to absorb them, especially the Navajo portion of the JUA, where the land dispute had frozen development. He told the commission they must help not only the relocatees but also the "host population," the reservation communities that would be called upon to accept relocatees under the commission's plan to construct resettlement communities on the reservation.

"The host population doesn't realize the stress of those who have to move," Scudder said. "What they see is that these people get new houses, better houses than they have, which of course will be built next door to their not-so-good houses. They will also see that these people put more pressure on what are already limited grazing areas, schools, and medical and social services. In my opinion, the only solution to the problem is to incorporate the host chapters into the development program for the relocatees so that they can see the tangible benefits that will come to them when they are willing to absorb relocatees."[29]

The commission made this idea of combining relocation with economic development the keystone of its plan. The staff went to work setting up planning committees in the chapters of the JUA that partition had divided between the Navajo and Hopi reservations. They made the offer Scudder recommended: if the chapters would accept relocatees, the commission would ask Congress to appropriate funds for roads, schools, clinics, and economic development projects.

The Navajos responded ambivalently. They still distrusted the commissioners, and they hoped Congress would repeal the land dispute legislation. One of the commission staff members angered the Navajos by ignoring their ideas and forcing his own upon them. Only three of the eleven chapter planning committees approved a set-aside of land for relocation and economic development, and these approvals were withdrawn in 1978, when Dennis DeConcini proposed to grant life estates to certain Navajos provided on-reservation sites could not be found for them. The DeConcini Bill put the senator and the commission at cross purposes. Why, the Navajos wondered, should they set land aside if that would block life estates? The Navajos stopped working with the commission.

Even before it ran up against the DeConcini life estate proposal, the commission's plan had problems. In the first place, the plan envisioned housing developments for relocatees in planned "resettlement communities." That meant the relocatees would have no room for grazing. Tribal people accustomed to life on the land would be living in small, suburban-style residential plots with no means to support themselves. The commission itself recognized the danger that the relocatees would become demoralized in their new environment and completely dependent on the government—that the communities would become welfare ghettos. "There's not much sense in giving a person a good dwelling with modern conveniences if he doesn't have a job which will permit him to keep the machinery going," Urbano noted.[30] And so the commission pledged to do all it could to persuade Congress to appropriate funds for community development. Hawley Atkinson said he would "hard sell lobby" for the program in Washington.

The commission's plan was possibly the best one available, but Navajo skepticism was well founded. The plan challenged, one might even say dared, the commission to accomplish in some of the remotest areas of the reservation what the tribe and various federal agencies had been unable to do even in the reservation's small towns—attract light industry and develop the small business sector of the economy. Second, the commission said between $200 and $250 million would be needed to do the job. Congress could hardly be counted on to come up with six times the $37 million it had okayed in the 1974 legislation. Unless Congress broke out of the fiscally conservative mood brought on by California's Proposition 13, the commission would be left with a very pretty plan and a disastrous program. Even if Congress gave the commission all the money it wanted, chances for a successful relocation program were shaky at best. Fortunately for the commission, its time for developing the relocation plan was extended when the Ninth Circuit Court of Appeals directed Judge Walsh to consider a Navajo appeal of the line partitioning the JUA. The appeal failed, and in April 1979 Judge Walsh reinstated the line he had originally adopted. But since the Land Settlement Act had given the commission two years from the date partitioning finally took effect, the commission received an additional two years—until April 1981—to study the problems of relocation.

A Bonanza for the Bahes

In mid 1977 the commission finally found something to celebrate. As reporters munched cake and sipped punch and listened to Hawley Atkinson say confidently that relocation would be done and done well, the commission marked the relocation of the Joe Bahe family into a brand new $34,000 home in Gallup, courtesy of Uncle Sam. The resettlement of the first Navajo relocatees was not without irony.

The Bahes were not included in the 700 families federal mediator William Simkin had said would have to be moved from the Hopi partition area. They had been living for the past fourteen years in government housing at the Fort Wingate boarding school, just east of Gallup. Mrs. Bahe worked as a recreation specialist at the school, and Mr. Bahe worked for the Navajo Tribal Utility Authority in Fort Defiance. They had just poured the foundation for a new home near the JUA residence of Mrs. Bahe's mother in 1972 when Judge Walsh ordered a halt to Navajo construction. In early 1977 they began talking with a construction company in Gallup about building a new home there. They had no idea they would be eligible for the relocation benefits of the Navajo-Hopi Land Settlement Act.

Then they attended a chapter meeting in the JUA and met Hawley Atkinson, who told them they were entitled to a new home at government expense because the land dispute had stopped them from building and, technically, they were relocatees. The Bahes were excited. That All-American custom of celebrating the final mortgage payment would not have to wait thirty years. The relocation commission had the cash. With their $5,000 bonus for moving

quickly, the Bahes bought a houseful of furniture. For them relocation was a bonanza.

Two of the three Bahe children missed the housewarming.
They were in Salt Lake City living with Mormon families on the
Mormon Church's placement program for Indian children. Only
eight-year-old Josephine joined her parents for the celebration with
the commissioners, reporters, and Gallup Mayor Edward Junker.[31]

Gallup has grown long and slender on both sides of Route 66,
the fabled transcontinental highway that is giving way to Interstate
40. It has grown wealthy from a variety of sources; from the cars
and semi rigs that flow through town by the thousands every day
on the way to Los Angeles or Chicago and all points in between;
from the Santa Fe Railroad; from the coal and uranium mines
nearby. But most of all Gallup is a trade center for the Navajo
Reservation. Saturday is the day the reservation comes to town,
the day Gallup proves its claim to be the "Indian Capital of the
World." Downtown Gallup on Saturday afternoon is a Navajo happening. The sidewalks bulge with old ladies wrapped in Pendleton
shawls, old men with hair tied back in a bun under flat-brimmed
hats, girls in T-shirts celebrating rock groups or bull riders, boys in
cowboy hats, jeans, and rodeo belt buckles. The Navajos come to
town to socialize and shop. They make the rounds of the stores, see
a movie at the Chief Theater or at the Aztec, get their pickups
repaired, have a meal at one of the national fast-food franchises that
have proliferated in town since the early 1970s. Radio stations
KGAK and KYVA do Navajo-language remotes from the Big O Tire
Store or Little Bear's shopping center. The window at Trice's Western Wear is blotted out by posters announcing the rodeos sanctioned
by the All Indian Rodeo Cowboys Association. Santo Domingo
Indians stand in doorways selling turquoise necklaces to secretaries
who work in tribal offices at Window Rock, twenty-six miles to the
west. In an interview before his death in 1979, Mayor Junker
estimated that half the retail sales in town are made to Navajos,
some of whom make payments on pickups with sheep, rugs, or
jewelry.

Some Navajos despise Gallup. They condemn the town's big
annual event, the Intertribal Ceremonial, claiming that it exploits
Indian religion for the benefit of businessmen. They say the dozens
of Indian traders buy cheaply from Navajo craftsmen and make
unconscionably high profits selling to tourists. They say some car

salesmen prey on Navajos who don't speak English and don't know that the sticker price on a pickup is not as final as the price tag on a sack of potatoes. The focus of their anger is liquor. For if thousands of Navajos come to town to take advantage of services and entertainment not available on the reservation, hundreds of others come for the booze that is illegal back home. Gallup is ready for them with more than three dozen bars. Some of those who hitchhike in for the weekend pass out in the streets and alleys downtown, which truckers on their CB's call "Indian Dizzyland." Townspeople criticize the tribe for exporting its alcohol problems rather than legalizing liquor and facing up to those problems on the reservation. All Navajos are embarrassed at the public degradation of their people. They are ashamed of the "Drunken Indian" stereotype and embittered by it.

When the group known as "Indians Against Exploitation" was active in 1975, it accused Gallup of "a long history of racism and exploitation of the American Indian—our people."[32] The group made the accusation when the militancy aroused by the takeover of Wounded Knee and the death of Larry Casuse was still strong. For the most part, those acutely hostile feelings have dissipated. Gallup now has a reputation on the reservation for treating Indians better than any other border town does. Given the tribe's economic importance to Gallup, that can be viewed as an example of enlightened self-interest. But it is also the result of hard work by men of goodwill, including Mayor Junker, a survivor of the Bataan Death March and a kind man who became upset when he heard people in Gallup say "the Indians" in the same scornful way some people in Texas say "the Mexicans." He preferred to speak of "our Indian neighbors."[33]

At the Bahes', Mayor Junker unintentionally recognized the tension between town and reservation. "We welcome people from the reservations here," he said. "We want them to trade with us and consider Gallup their town. Our police department has orders to see that they are not beaten up, ripped off, or have things taken."[34] There is an undercurrent of suspicion between Indians and the people of Gallup; there is fear between two worlds that know little about each other. Families like the Bahes—educated, skilled, upwardly mobile families—are comfortable away from home and can indeed call Gallup their town. The great majority of Navajos, however, don't want to spend more than a few hours at a time in town. They are ill at ease in the white world, that bewildering if interesting world of bustle and noise and tension that begins in Gallup and Farmington and Holbrook and Winslow and Flagstaff and stretches over a cultural infinity to places named Phoenix and Los Angeles and New York and Washington. They have no illusions that they could ever become city people.

"Nothing to Do with Her Time"

By the end of 1978 the commission had relocated sixty-eight Navajo families, over half of them to Flagstaff. Like the Bahes, most of the relocatees were young and comfortable with the off-reservation world. Most were relatively affluent. Only 35 percent had incomes under $9,000, and 19 percent had incomes over $16,000.[35] In a few cases, parents of the younger Navajos moved also. Most remained on the reservation, however, like the mother of Mrs. Bahe, who wanted nothing to do with relocation.

For the most part, the relocations were moderately successful. But as the Interim Report published by the commission in early 1979 pointed out, some did not adjust well to the new life. "Some have lost or quit jobs, some have applied for and received debt consolidation loans with their [new homes] as collateral, some have not paid their property taxes on the due date, and there have been instances of family discord."[36]

There were indications of even more deep-seated problems with the off-reservation relocation program, although they were not documented in the commission report. On March 3, 1979, at a meeting of the Coal Mine Mesa chapter, Mabel Begay talked about the problems she and her husband Ralph had encountered since they relocated to St. Johns, Arizona. "My husband and I are worried about the land from where we moved," she said. "We are not eating well, nor are we sleeping. We are very depressed. We realize what we have done to ourselves. There is no employment for my husband and some of my children. We are not educated and we are not used to living with other races because we don't speak English." Mrs. Begay said she and her husband were hoping to move back onto the reservation.

Near the end of 1979, a Navajo paralegal trainee interviewed Laura Ann Nez, who had relocated to a home at a suburban Flagstaff development known as Fernwood Estates, located just off

State Highway 89. "Mrs. Nez has absolutely nothing to do with her time," paralegal trainee Geneva Lewis reported. "These are the times she cries for the home she left, remembering the times she kept busy with her sheep day in and day out. She said she is barely getting used to being alone. But she also worries about the future. When she gets older, she would like to live the rest of her life on the reservation. She realizes that life can't ever be the way it was. But at least she would be around people of her own kind and not in some other world alien to her. The financial burdens and the communication barrier have aged her. She feels much older and weaker now. She feels that she cannot take the emotional stress any longer."[37]

One of the most interesting facts in the commission's Interim Report was that 1,858 Navajos had applied as heads of households for relocation benefits, representing more than twice the number of families federal mediator William Simkin had estimated would have to move. Some of the applicants had already moved to towns because the land dispute made it impossible for them to live at home. Some had moved as far away as Ohio, Montana, and California. Others were still in the JUA and had a wait-and-see attitude, hoping to stay at their homes but aware that relocation was the law. A small hard core refused even to speak with the relocation commission staff and promised to fight for their homes.

The high number of applicants suggested one of the commission's most difficult problems. Who, the commission had to determine, was eligible for relocation benefits? The commission took a big step toward resolving the problem when it adopted a regulation recognizing that the freeze on development in the JUA imposed by the BIA and the courts had already forced some Navajos to leave home. The regulation extended eligibility not only to persons actually living within the Hopi partition area but also to those who had left and maintained "substantial, continuous contacts with an identifiable homesite when employment or other factors dictate temporary occupancy outside the area." The commission estimated that 4,800 Navajos would be eligible for relocation benefits. By the end of 1979 it had upped its estimate to 5,600. Whatever the ultimate number of relocatees, the commission's estimate that 60 percent would want to move onto the Navajo Reservation underscored the fact that if the resettlement communities failed, the federal relocation program would be a disaster.

No Pleasure in Its Task

Father Urbano died in early 1979 after a lengthy illness. He had been an Episcopal priest for nearly thirty-one years and had been well known as an educator, author, and advocate of political conservatism. Shortly before Father Urbano's death, Robert Lewis resigned from the commission, following his election once again to the Zuni governorship. Because there was a Democratic administration in Washington, Dennis DeConcini and Morris Udall, both of whom are Democrats, were allowed to recommend replacements for the commission. DeConcini recommended Phoenix attorney Sandra Massetto, a specialist in Indian law and an active member of the state's Democratic Party. Udall recommended Roger Lewis, his administrative assistant in Washington for seventeen years, who had moved to Flagstaff in 1978 to become an administrator at Northern Arizona University. Massetto and Lewis were named to the relocation commission by Interior Secretary Cecil Andrus.

Massetto let it be known that she didn't like the law she was to help implement. "I disfavor relocation for Indians, whether they be Navajo, Hopi, or Yavapai-Apache," she said in a newspaper interview. "The policy of the U.S. government historically has been when problems arise, relocate. I don't think it's a good idea."[38] In another interview she said, "It's our responsibility to relocate, and we intend to do that. But we have to be sensitive to the people. . . ."[39] While Lewis did not question the law, he shared Massetto's feelings about the commission's responsibility to the relocatees. "A tough thing has to be accomplished in a way that the least possible hardship is incurred," he said. "There must be a great deal of sensitivity in handling the matter."[40]

With the new commissioners, the commission took on a new personality marked by a spirit of cooperation and goodwill. In private conversations, nonetheless, the ambivalence of the commission staff was apparent. One staff member said a sort of gallows humor had developed. He said he and his coworkers talked of donning cavalry uniforms for a photograph that would be captioned "Your Friendly Relocators."

Another staff member spoke more seriously about the land dispute legislation. "I think it's a crazy solution," the staffer said. "I don't see it working. In the short run you can see it's the Navajos who suffer. But in the long run it will be detrimental to both tribes. This thing is really going to strain the relationships between two people who need to help one another." She talked of the effects of relocation on traditional Navajos, observing, "When the basic underpinnings of a culture are torn apart, that has tremendous implications." Then she spoke of the strain of working on the relocation program. "I don't think there's a person here who doesn't have a conflict about working for an agency that has the responsibility for carrying out a law they think is wrong. I can either choose to be a part of it and try to minimize the trauma, or I can opt out. It's a daily rebalancing."

The best illustration of the commission's anguished sense of responsibility is a meeting between the commission and officials of Navajo chapters in the JUA held in November 1979. Staff director Leon Berger told the Navajos that the commission takes no pleasure in its task. "We feel we've got an extremely difficult job, and our role is to do the best we can with a very difficult situation," he said. "Relocation is not a good thing." The purpose of the meeting was to initiate a new cooperative effort between the commission and the chapters. The commission was especially hopeful that the chapters would revive the program of setting aside land for relocatees. Billy Reese, president of the Red Lake chapter, said he wasn't sure he should go along with any part of the relocation program. "So what we're going to do [if we work with the commission] is set ourselves against our people," he said.

Then came the inevitable question: What did the commission plan to do about the Navajos who refuse to relocate, no matter how attractive the federal benefits were? Responding first, Massetto said the commissioners "don't like to think about that." Then Berger demonstrated his diplomatic skills. "If a man says he's not going to move, all he's telling us is that we can't help him," Berger said. Massetto spoke further on this most delicate of topics, one the commission has obviously had to consider. She explained that once the relocation plan is approved by Congress—presumably in mid 1981—the people on the wrong side of the partition line will have five years to relocate. "What will probably happen is that at the end of the five years, the names of those who have not relocated will have to be given to some law enforcement arm." Then, she said, the Hopis might ask that a federal court direct U.S. marshals to evict the Navajos.[41]

That was the bad news for the Navajos at the end of 1979. The good news came from the Department of Housing and Urban Development, which has the responsibility for setting the maximum amounts that may be spent on replacement housing for relocatees. HUD officials raised the limit that could be spent on a family of three or fewer persons to $38,700, and they said up to $57,000 could be spent for a family of four or more. HUD will revise the figures annually, adjusting them according to the rate of inflation.

The action highlighted the irony of the relocation program. For some of the Navajo young, relocation was a free ticket to the off-reservation world they wanted to enter anyway. For those whose attachment to their land was beyond the measure of dollars, it was a cruelty. "The men who made that law had an incredibly narrow vision," a commission staffer said. "Their sense was that you buy them a house and they live happily ever after. They are not living happily ever after."

As 1979 ended, the commission reported that it had relocated 166 families from the former JUA. It also complained that Navajo tribal officials were not working with them to make the relocation program work. In its fourth annual report the commission cited "a singular lack of publicly visible and tangible action" on the part of tribal officials to implement the Navajo-Hopi Land Settlement Act.[42]

10
The Relocatees

Oh, Brother
When you were born
A holy rainbow encircled you
For protection.

Now you have grown into older years
And aged into trouble . . .
Your eyes cast darkness . . .
Plainly your rainbow is broken
You blindly walk a crooked path
Plainly your rainbow is broken.

Barbara Silversmith
St. Michael High School

Just outside Oraibi, across Highway 264, a dirt road heads
north past a wood sign that reads "Navajo Gospel Mission, 13
Miles." It is October 1978. The road skirts Hopi cornfields where
the crop has been taken in and the stalks are bleached yellow. It
crosses an earthen dam built in the 1930s as part of the federal
conservation program that brought stock reduction to the Navajos
and Hopis. Then it parallels a crumbling sandstone ridge perhaps
thirty feet high and littered at the base with the boulders pried
loose on winter nights when the rain freezes and expands the rock.
An eagle sits atop the ridge, watching the passing car and then
launching itself toward the clouds.

Clouds over the desert. Usually they float on the dry air as
mild and innocent and insubstantial as campfire smoke. Sometimes

in summer they are black and serious as lead, convoys rigged for the mayhem of desert lightning, which Navajos find so malevolent that they purify anything near a place that has been struck. But this is autumn—no sense calling it fall in this emptied landscape—and the clouds are moody gray, lying flat and motionless across the sky like a layer of earth left behind after a flood. The sky will hold this shape another two days before dissolving in the gentle, enduring rain Navajos call "female rain."

At the end of the road three boys are riding bicycles along a tree-lined avenue in the mission grounds. A reporter's car moves past the mission and into the compound of the Hardrock chapter. Inside a small frame building five women are spinning wool that will become Navajo rugs. They are CETA workers, employees of the federal program that is all that stands between hundreds of Navajo families and the welfare rolls. One of the women is Mae Wilson Tso, whose daughter Juanita has just finished her day at preschool and is sitting on the floor next to her mother eating a box of Cracker Jacks.

The reporter had met Mrs. Tso six weeks previously, at the end of an interview with her father, Sam. He was sixty-six years old and lived on the Social Security he had earned through years of work as a clerk for trader Lorenzo Hubbell, then as a laborer for the railroad, finally as a school bus driver. He spoke English in the chopped cadences of Navajos unaccustomed to the language. When he talked about the land dispute, he was anxious, depressed, emotionally flat. He said the stock reduction program had forced his family to sell all but eight of its sheep. He was worried about relocation. "This dispute, what has it done?" he asked, drawing his shoulders into a shrug. "It has hurt our feelings and our hearts and our livelihoods. What are we going to live on in the future? Sometimes I sit up late at night and smoke my pipe and think about it, because it hurts all over."

Sam's daughter, Mae Wilson Tso, speaks no English. She ran away from the mission school in 1945, when she was seven years old, and her parents did not make her go back. She helped them with the sheep, her mother taught her to weave, and she became one of the most talented weavers around Dinnebito. At sixteen she married a man who died shortly after the birth of their son, Larry. Later she married Hoskie Tso, and together they raised Larry and eight other children. Hoskie is gone over half of each year, away in

New Mexico or Texas with a railroad track repair crew. He sends money home every month, but not enough to meet the needs of his large family. Mae began working with CETA after her family lost most of its sheep to stock reduction in 1977. She was one of the lucky few to get a job.

None of the women spinning wool speaks English, so the reporter goes back outside and asks a young man to interpret. Mrs. Tso is eager to talk about the land dispute. She agrees to meet the visitor at the trading post shortly after her son picks her up at day's end. Three hours later the reporter follows in the dusty wake of the Tsos' pickup, past the Dinnebito Gospel Mission and under wire cables thick as hawsers slung from the metal arms of huge electric transmission towers that march eerily across the land from the Four Corners Power Plant to southern Arizona. They look strangely like the Navajo Holy People, the Yeis, as depicted in sand paintings. The pickup leaves a wake of dust in the air as it plunges through gullies and depressions that smack like waves against the tires. It bulls its way onto a plateau studded with pinyon and juniper, a sparse pygmy forest of the high desert. Seven and a half miles from the trading post, a dog lies waiting. He dashes joyfully to meet the truck and then runs alongside it to the Tso camp, where two other dogs join him in a noisy welcome.

The Tso family have built their hogan, corral, and storage shed on a swell in the rolling earth twenty miles south of Big Mountain. A hundred miles to the southwest, the San Francisco Peaks, dusted with the season's first snow, are radiant purple in the slanting rays of the late afternoon sun. Few trees here interrupt the vast circle of the horizon; the plant cover is sage and rabbit brush. No electric wires enter the hogan; the transmission towers leave none of their power here. Mae's son Earl gets out of the pickup and solemnly shakes the reporter's hand. Sometimes young Navajo men in the JUA resent the intrusion of outsiders into the lives of their families, warning them away with hostile looks or angry words. But Earl offers a welcome. He says he is worried about his mother. Earl graduated from Tuba City High the previous June and hopes to find work as a carpenter. But for now he wants to help his mother. "She's been getting sick," he said. "All this talk about the moving gets to her mind."

Built by Hoskie fifteen years ago, the hogan is a pleasant combination of old style and new technique. In the old way it faces east and has six sides, its log walls chinked with mud plaster. In the new way it has a concrete floor, glass windows, and a tarpaper roof. It is about twenty feet in diameter. There is no paint on the walls, no refrigerator, no television or electric lights, no sink, no bathroom. A barrel-shaped wood-burning oven perhaps fifteen inches high and eighteen inches across sits on the floor in the center of the hogan. It cooks the Tsos' meals and gives them warmth in the winter, sending its smoke into a long metal pipe and through the roof into the free air. This is a one-room home, simple, intimate quarters for Hoskie and Mae Tso and their children.

Earl motions for the reporter to sit on a pile of four thin mattresses stacked against the west wall beneath a tapestry of Christ, His chest aglow with the brilliance of His Sacred Heart. The Tsos are Christians in the uniquely Indian way of the Native American Church. Mrs. Tso says something Earl translates as "ten people have to sleep here," and the reporter understands that at night the mattresses are spread across the floor between the bed and the small, tattered sofa. Earl says that in the summer, when all the children are home from boarding school, some of them sleep outside on the ground or in the storage shed. Hoskie had just started work on a new house in 1972 when Judge Walsh handed down his order forbidding new Navajo construction in the JUA. A rectangle of cinder blocks three layers high is as far as he got. It is an empty shell next to the hogan, the symbol of their frustrated hopes. Some Navajos in the JUA defied the order and went ahead with new homes for their growing families.

The Tso hogan is lighted by a Coleman lantern that hangs from a nail driven into one of the two-by-four-inch beams that are the ribs of the domed roof. Because they have no plumbing, the Tsos haul their water in barrels from the Rocky Ridge School, eight miles away. They haul their firewood from Big Mountain. Between the two of them, Hoskie and Mae earn perhaps $8,000 a year. They are making it, if just barely, because they do not pay rent or property taxes or utility bills. Their greatest single expenses are for food and for the pickup truck that, next to the hogan, is their most important material possession. The pickup allows the family access to trading post, chapter house, and town; it hauls their water and wood. It is an import from Flagstaff, domesticated to the purposes of life at Dinnebito.

Mae is sitting on the sofa next to the stack of mattresses, and

Juanita leans across her lap, listening intently to the three-way discussion, questions in English which Earl puts into Navajo, answers in Navajo which Earl puts into English. Drawing from a meager inventory of Navajo phrases, the reporter asks, "Díkwíi nináháah, Juanita?" How old are you? When she answers "Four" instead of the Navajo "Dį́į," Mae and Earl laugh delightedly. After two months in preschool, Juanita is already becoming bilingual and is proud to show her new language skills to her family and to the white visitor.

Mae leans forward and looks through wire-rim glasses at the tape recorder in front of her. Her long black hair is pulled straight back and is gathered at the nape of the neck in a beaded pin. Her expression is intense and anxious. She has been thinking all afternoon of what she wants to say. For the next forty minutes she speaks without pause, hoping to communicate her hurt to the Anglo world, the world of Washington, the world of the land dispute legislation and Judge Walsh's court orders. Her hands move purposefully before her, punctuating her words. Her gestures have no context for the visitor, who must wait for Earl's summary translation.

Later, with a transcribed interpretation of her lengthy remarks, the visitor learned that Mae spoke of the land dispute as her father had, as a living, malicious force breathing sickness into her life. "This thing is immensely strong," she said. "We have pleaded in vain, and it seems we have been forgotten. The time has passed and it turns into hardship and hunger. In my home I have seen disruption and come into being poor. I have sold my animals and have come to see that it is no good without them. It is lonely without them. The land was divided without proper thought of how it would hurt us, the five-fingered people. Washington was foolish. I compare it to the way you treat sheep when you separate the ones you are going to sell." When Navajos say they have five fingers, they are saying they are human beings, worthy of respect.

Mae spoke of her anxiety for the future of her children, her uncertainty of the world they would inherit, her understanding that because of partition they would not be able to live together on this land. She knew that the past was being severed from the future, and she wondered what she could tell her children. "Why have merciful thoughts and make good teachings?" she asked. "Why tell the young this is a place for them to live?" Then she said the land dispute had driven some of her relatives and friends to seek the numbness of alcohol. "Some people have hurt themselves with the liquor. They are pitiful, and we mourn for them. This is the way it has become for us. I worry about it, and I can't sleep because of it. I have become sick. Some have lost hope completely. There is such cause for depression. Only when I think firmly that I will remain here am I well in my mind. If I was beaten unconscious or put to sleep, then maybe I would be taken to the place where we are supposed to move to. But it would not be of my own will, and as soon as I was awake I would get up and come back to this place."

Mae's weaving is a metaphor for her life. She herself is part of the pattern, a pattern of family and land, a pattern that began nearby where her grandfather was born ninety-two years earlier. Now her grandparents, parents, sisters, cousins, aunts, uncles, and her own children live within a few miles of one another. The loom on which they have been weaving the pattern of their lives is being dismantled by "this thing," this law from Washington. The land is being taken away, the sheep have been sold, a new house denied. The family has been told it must disperse. The thought is terrifying. The only defense against despair is the conviction that it will not happen, that she will not let it happen, that she will one day wake up from this nightmare and find that the land is theirs again.

Mae is the oldest of six girls and two boys born over a period of twenty-five years to Sam and Blanche Wilson. The three youngest children still attend school. Colleen lives a few hundred yards away with her husband, who drives a bus for Rocky Ridge School. Lawshia is a jailer for the Navajo Police in Tuba City. Mary and her husband also work in Tuba City, she in a school cafeteria, he in a car repair shop. Blanche is a dispatcher for the police at Tuba City, and her husband works there with the Navajo Tribal Utility Authority. All return home on weekends. All say they will not leave home voluntarily.

Navajos believe that their minds can be fully at rest only at the place where their umbilical cords are buried. They believe that if they move away, their minds will return to that place. If the cord is buried near the corral, their thoughts will be of livestock. If it is buried near a loom, they will think of weaving. "I was born right here, and we're not going to move one inch," Blanche said. "They'll have to jail me first. If they want to build me a home, they can build it right here. I was born and raised here, my cord is here. I have my own family now, and my parents are getting old. I don't want to live any place but here."

Many of the young adults on the Hopi side of the partition line feel as Blanche feels. They leave home temporarily for work. But Tuba City or Window Rock or Flagstaff or Los Angeles can never be anything more than a place to make money so they can keep things going back home. They return home as often as distance permits to reenter the pattern. In late 1978 they were returning home more frequently, returning home with a vengeance in the face of an order that says they must leave, with a heightened sense of who they are and what is most precious to them.

Two of the Tsos' relatives deserve special mention. Billy King is completely disabled as the result of injuries he received in World War II. His brother Taja, a medicine man, walks on crutches because of the wounds he received in a battlefield in France. Both landed at Normandy. Shortly after Taja was drafted into the Army, the officers at boot camp in Texas gave him the opportunity to return home because he understood little English. But Taja stayed on. "I feel that we have done valuable things for the country and now they want to move us from this simple piece of land," he said. He was concerned that young Navajos might resist relocation with force. "Who can tell about the young people? They tell us there will be trouble. And I believe the government is forcing us to this possibility." In late 1978 one of Taja's nephews talked of grabbing a gun if anyone came to force them off the land.

"This Is Our Church"

At the end of 1978, while Mae Wilson Tso's grandfather, Hosteen Manybeads, lay near death at the Indian Health Service hospital at Tuba City, fifty members of his family gathered in a hogan for a service of the Native American Church on his behalf. All night long they sat and knelt on the hogan's earth floor before an altar that had been molded from the earth into a long, slender crescent by the peyote priest or "roadman," Doran Bitsui. They chanted to the throbbing of a drum, shared the peyote buttons, and prayed for the recovery of Hosteen Manybeads.

Anthropologist David Aberle suggests that the Native American Church achieved wide acceptance among the Navajos in the 1930s as a result of the stock reduction program then in force. He calls peyotism "an accommodation to the post white man situation after destruction of a system in which all was directed toward the extended group and found meaning in this context." He says peyotism "provides special gifts which compensate for the Indian's lack of status and privilege. If the white man has the Bible and his church, the Indian has direct access to God. If the white man has learning, the Indian has revelation." Aberle says church members believe peyote is a gift from God to Indians, a sacrament, a source of grace and comfort.[1]

The reporter entered the hogan early Sunday morning, at the end of the ceremony for Hosteen Manybeads. Around the hogan's perimeter, against its walls of wood and mud, the children, grand-children, and great-grandchildren of Hosteen Manybeads sat on sheepskins and blankets. They were three generations together, sharing the warmth of each other's presence, praying that they would not lose someone dear to them all. Mae was dismantling the altar with the help of two nieces no more than five years old. Together they pounded the altar with their fists and took the loosened earth outside, from where it had been gathered the day before.

Sitting against the west wall, Doran Bitsui ended a long prayer in Navajo with the English words, "Jesus, God, Amen." A young man distributed cups for the ritual sharing of water. Finally, every-one took part in a meal of mutton stew, fry bread, and coffee. Dwight Bedonie and his brother Dan wanted the reporter to un-derstand their religion, wanted him to understand why they believed in it. Dan recalled the competition among Christian missionaries when he attended boarding school in the early 1960s. All stu-dents were required to attend religious instructions on Wednesday and services on Sunday, he said, and the missionaries worked zealously to win new recruits. Dan was baptized by the Catholics, Mormons, and Presbyterians, all of whom spoke scornfully of the competition and warned him of the evil of other churches. "I went to all those churches," he said with surprising good humor. "I saw the white man's way. He dresses up fancy and carries a Bible into a fancy church." With a sweep of his arm, Dan drew in the circle of the hogan and said proudly, "This is our way, this is our church." The Native American Church allows Dan to be a Christian while remaining Indian; it allows him to see God in terms consistent with his own history and values. It fortifies a belief he knows he must have: that it is good to be an Indian, that Indians have a special status in the eyes of God. It is a belief that is often assaulted in the off-reservation world. The single most dramatic achievement of the Native American Church on the reservation is that it has rescued hundreds of Navajos from the despair of alcoholism and has persuaded many others never to begin drinking.

Dan's brother Dwight is about thirty-five years old. He attended elementary school at the Hardrock mission before being sent to a BIA boarding school in Oregon that emphasized vocational training. After he graduated, the BIA's program for finding Indians work off-reservation helped him find a job as a machinist in Los Angeles. Dwight stayed in Los Angeles four years before returning home. Now he lives in Tuba City and operates heavy equipment on road construction projects. "The BIA, they're always trying to take us off," he says. "But we're used to these ways, we're comfortable here."

Things were not always comfortable for members of the Native American Church on the Navajo Reservation. Their long fight for legitimacy began in 1940, when the Tribal Council, by a 52–1 vote, passed a resolution banning peyote and authorizing a jail sentence and fine for anyone convicted of bringing it onto the reservation.[2] The antipeyote movement was led by Tribal Chairman Jacob Morgan, who was also a Christian missionary and who condemned peyote as contrary to Navajo tradition. NAC members began to organize politically in the 1950s in response to arrests by tribal police. They managed to elect several tribal council delegates sympathetic to their cause but not enough to overturn the antipeyote resolution.

In 1959 the tide began to turn. The New Mexico legislature passed a bill legalizing the use of peyote for religious purposes, and a year later an Arizona judge declared that state's law against peyote use unconstitutional. Raymond Nakai was elected Navajo chairman in 1962 with strong NAC support after he campaigned for religious freedom. Three years after that President Johnson signed a law which upheld the legal right of "any bona fide religious organization to use the herb peyote as a religious sacrament." But still the tribal ordinance was the law of the reservation, and although arrests of NAC members stopped under Nakai, church services were still in violation of tribal law. Finally, in 1967, the Native American Church was recognized on the Navajo Reservation. By a vote of 29–26, the tribal council passed a resolution permitting church members on the reservation to use peyote in connection with religious practices.[3] In 1978 the *Navajo Times* estimated that over half the members of the tribe belonged to the Native American Church.[4]

The Native American Church is a pan-Indian religion. Among the Navajos, it is an institutionalization of the tribe's greatest strengths, the ability to learn from others, give what they have learned a distinctly Navajo character, and make it a part of their equipment for survival. From the Pueblo Indians of New Mexico they learned weaving and became the most accomplished weavers in the Southwest. From the Pueblos they also learned rituals which became the basis for their own rich ceremonialism. From the Spanish they learned to work silver and outstripped their teachers in the brilliance of their silversmithing. Now they have a religion that allows them to embrace the God of Christianity in a way consistent with their own traditions and values. The Native American Church accepts the good news of the Christian Gospel within a ritual environment at once unpretentious and mystical. They pray for health. They have special services at Easter, Thanksgiving, and Christmas to give thanks for God's goodness, all the while seeking guidance and revelation in the ceremonial fire. Now, increasingly, church members on the Hopi side of the partition line are praying that they will not be forced away from home, away from their emotional center. Acceptance of the Native American Church does not imply rejection of traditional Navajo religion, which remains strong throughout the reservation.

Doran Bitsui's son Roman exemplifies the twin Navajo instincts to avoid assimilation into the American mainstream and to learn from the outside world. After finishing elementary school in Tuba City, Roman entered a program called "A Better Chance" and enrolled on scholarship at Northfield–Mount Hermon, a private boarding school in Massachusetts. Then he went on to Princeton, earning a bachelor's degree in political science in 1978. After graduation Roman went to work for the Navajo Tax Commission, whose program to tax energy corporations operating on the reservation is a key part of the tribe's attempt to secure an economic future. Roman spoke of the land dispute and the Native American Church in his Window Rock office.

"I guess we all hope that somehow our prayers will be answered, that maybe Congress will see the process of destruction they're creating," he said. "We pray that although it's been mishandled, it will work out." Roman explained that when he came home on vacations from school in the East his family sponsored peyote meetings to pray for his success. "It helped me to see who I am and where I came from," he said. "It gave me strength and pride in myself. In the meeting you anticipate achievement in school. You can blend in with the others, but at the same time you're yourself." Asked if he had ever thought of living in the East, Roman smiled and said, "It's not my place. This is my place over here."

A Family Thinks About Separation

Mae Wilson Tso's first child, twenty-four-year-old Larry, was working at the woodpile outside his mother's hogan, reducing the logs from Big Mountain to pieces small enough for the stove. He was wearing his Navajo Police jacket, with a small American flag sewn onto the right sleeve and the seals of the Navajo Tribe and the tribe's emergency medical services program on the left. A pig smiled jovially from a patch on the brim of his baseball cap. He carried his load into the hogan, laid it in a pile next to the door, spoke briefly with his mother and Earl in Navajo, and sat down to talk about his family and the land dispute.

"Us Indians, we live in the family. Family life is more precious to us than anything else. We stay as a group. In the outside world, when you're eighteen, you get away from your parents if you want and never come back if you don't want to. But here it's different. Like me, I'm married and I got two kids. I work in Tuba and I live in the barracks over there during the week. But I come back here on the weekends. I'm young enough to live with the outside world, but I don't want to. I'd rather be here with the family and the stock.

"Right now I don't have a home of my own. So I come here and stay with my parents, or we stay with my wife's parents over by Hardrock. Now Washington says we don't have the land. They tell us not to build our houses or graze our sheep. It seems like they think of us as animals. It seems like they control us. The Hopis control us, and Washington controls us. It really bothers the people. A lot of them get sick about it. My mother has the sickness. The relocation is always on her mind. She starts crying and gets short of breath; it's like asthma or something like that. We take her to the hospital, and they say there's nothing wrong with her, so now she's been seeing a psychiatrist. They think about it so much it's affecting their mind. Like my grandfather, we have to check on him all the time. He talks about how it might be if we have to leave. I was on a horse and came up to him one time and he was by himself crying. He said it was because of all this problem he didn't know what to do. He said he didn't want to lose his grandchildren. We're a close family, and we just don't want to get separated."

Larry spoke calmly, evenly, without gesture. He knows the outside world and has accommodated himself to it, finding a career as a policeman. He spent the last three years of high school on the Mormon Church's placement program in Utah, an experience he recalls as pleasant and broadening. But the camp near Dinnebito pulls him surely to his center. He still wants to return, to affirm his allegiance to family and land, to walk the earth he walked as a child, to dream of making things better. Perhaps it's instinct, part of his emotional equipment for survival. As strongly as his mother, who herds sheep, this man who enforces laws regards the family camp as the most palpable expression of who he is. It is Larry's answer to everyone's yearning for belonging, for being a part of something greater than oneself, something supportive and constant and inherently good.

In July 1974, when the Senate was preparing to act on the land dispute, Senator Fannin released a statement in which he said, "It is not the will of this Congress or any of its members to disrupt the Navajo way of life or to create any economic, cultural, or social hardship on these Americans."[5] Senator Goldwater joined Fannin in a "dear colleague" letter urging the Senate not to be influenced by the "emotional campaign put on by the Navajo Tribe to prevent the relocation of any Navajos living in the Joint Use Area. There is no relocation problem. This is a once in a lifetime opportunity for their families to better their living conditions as well as educational and job opportunities."[6]

When the bill reached the Senate floor, James Abourezk cited the observation of Thayer Scudder that "almost without exception people resist forced relocation." Scudder had spent twenty years studying relocation projects around the world, but Fannin was not impressed. He scornfully interjected that Scudder had spent only four days on the Navajo Reservation "and became an instant expert." Then Abourezk resumed his final plea against partition and relocation. "Now, the talk about relocation money, the talk about the BIA and the government helping relocate these 8,000 Navajo or 6,500, whatever the figure might be agreed upon, the talk about making it easy for them to move is meaningless, as well, when we talk about people whose only relationship to anything is a relationship to the land, where money means so much less than land."[7]

The arguments of the senators from Arizona prevailed in the Senate and were made into law. But they were not the last word on relocation. In 1979 the Mental Health Branch of the Indian Health Service on the Navajo Reservation reported that Navajos marked for relocation were asking for psychological counseling at eight times the rate of Navajos on the Navajo side of the JUA partition line. In its report on a twenty-five-week study of the mental health effects of partition, the IHS study team found no reason to share the optimism of Senators Fannin and Goldwater. It warned that the resettlement communities being planned by the relocation commission "may indeed become behavioral sinks populated mostly by older Navajos who have very little to do with their time and who are cut off from their traditional sheepherding lifestyles."[8] One of the Navajo members of the team summarized an interview with a medicine man who lived on the Hopi side of the line:

> He feels very bad and says everyone's health is going bad now. He says he notices also people's minds are sad, even the livestock notices this, even nature knows this, that's why there's no rain for a long time. He says sometimes he thinks about this and feels silly when he cries like a baby when he remembers the time when he was a little boy. He says those days are gone, the happy ones. They are replaced by sad and angry ones, people going crazy everywhere, even fighting over sacred land which has been good to us, all of us people.[9]

In the northwestern corner of the Hopi partition area Lutie Begay leaned against the hood of a battered old pickup and talked about her feelings of hurt at what Washington was doing. "God put us here," she said. "He helped us with the livestock so we could live here. He gave this land to us and gave us a different language. He made our skin the color of the earth which is our mother. Our grandparents have taught us how to live. How can they cripple all this, ruin our life? What is so great that they would get out of it, that they want us out of here? This is what we think, and we have a lot of grief and sorrow."

The Ahasteens

Sixty miles southeast of Dinnebito, in the southern portion of the JUA, the family of Jim Ahasteen live in a wide valley among massive formations of volcanic rock, mighty necks and shoulders raised from the earth like islands in the emptiness of the South Pacific. When night comes here uninhibited by moon or stars, the earth disappears, breathed in by the darkness that seeps around the rocks like black fog; then morning, and the sun makes the earth anew, reshapes the land in its chiseled contours, rugged and austere and serene. For most of the year only gramma grass, sage, and pygmy pine mat this earth. But in the spring the yucca hoist yellow flowers from clusters of green leaves as slender and sharp as sabers; the prickly pears cap their barbed plants with strawberry red blossoms. Both the yucca and the prickly pear are cactus flowers, as sturdy as the people with whom they share the desert. This is the Teesto chapter, where several hundred Navajos live on lands partioned to the Hopis.

Since 1970, the Ahasteens have lived in a house built by the Navajo Professional Vocational Training Program, a federally funded program that teaches construction skills while improving reservation housing. There are two rooms, one large room holding three beds, a sofa, crib, chest of drawers, and wood burning stove; and a smaller room that is kitchen and storage area. The Ahasteen house is more modern than the Tso hogan. It has plaster walls, a gas oven, and a screen door. But like the Tso hogan, it is heated by wood and lighted by a Coleman lantern. Like the Tsos, the Ahasteens haul their water and chop their wood. Near the house is a hogan they use for ceremonial sings and for storage.

James, the oldest child at twenty-nine, lives in Fort Defiance where he owns his own cartographic business, making maps for the tribe and the BIA. Jack, a year younger, lives near James and is a talented free-lance artist. Barbara lives at home and works as a secretary for the Teesto chapter. Four other children are still in school, either the BIA school nearby or the public school in Winslow.

Jim Ahasteen leans forward on the couch, thoughtfully stroking his chin, talking about the land dispute. His wife sits on the edge of the bed spinning wool for the rug that is halfway up her loom. A complex pattern of red, grey, black, and white wool, the product of painstaking artistry, it may bring her $200 at the trading post and then be retailed for several times that. Gary and Leon kneel on the floor, tossing a football back and forth; their spirited chatter in Navajo is interrupted frequently by cries of "Touchdown!" Little Wanda sits in the light of the Coleman, reading from a book that carries pictures and names of things for each letter of the alphabet. "Hammer, house, horse; igloo, ink, Indian," she reads aloud. Fourteen-year-old Sarah, in high school now and old enough to know the meaning of the land dispute, sits next to her mother and follows the discussion with the visitor in two languages. The house is crowded, but there is no feeling of being cramped.

Jim Ahasteen, who speaks no English, says he was born in 1916 or 1917; there is no exact record. He never attended school because his mother thought it was more important that he stay home and help herd the sheep. It is a loss that he regrets, explaining that he sometimes wonders what sort of job he might have now with an education. During World War II he worked along with hundreds of other Navajos loading trains with ammunition at an army depot near Flagstaff. Then he worked several years as a migrant farm worker, picking mostly sweet potatoes in Colorado. Since 1976 he has been custodian at the chapter house and brought home $196 every two weeks. Together with Barbara's salary and the money from the eight or so rugs Mrs. Ahasteen weaves each year it supports the family. All but ten of the sheep have been sold to the stock reduction program.

Like nearly all people of this land, the Ahasteens are deeply religious, seeking to harmonize their energies with the earth and shifting economic circumstances. Life without faith here would be intolerably bare. They still attend sings, and for some physical problems they seek out the medicine man in preference to the Indian Health Service physician. And through the Native American Church they embrace the news of the benevolent God of Christianity.

"There are times when we really get down and worried," Jim

said through Jack's interpretation. "That is when we turn to the peyote meetings. The roadman helps us with his prayers, and it makes us feel better again. When I look into the fire, sometimes I see lots of sheep and cattle and horses in green pastures."

Veterans Feel Especially Hurt

Time after time a visitor to the people of the land dispute hears of the hurt and anger of the Navajo veterans. Some thirty-six hundred of them fought in World War II, the most illustrious of whom were the Navajo Code Talkers, Marines who used their language to make a combat code that baffled the Japanese in such battles as Guadalcanal, Saipan, Tinian, Tarawa, and Iwo Jima. The code word for submarine was Béésh łóó', "iron fish" in Navajo. Aircraft carrier became "Tsídii neiyéhé," which means "bird carrier." The Navajo word for "potato" meant "grenade," and the word for "egg" meant "bomb."

Together with a missionary's son who had grown up speaking Navajo on the reservation and who suggested the idea to the Marines, the Code Talkers developed an alphabet to spell words for which there was no Navajo term. The letter A was "Wóláchíí'," Navajo for "ant;" B was "Shash," Navajo for "Bear," and so on. Saipan was thus spelled: Dibé (sheep), Wóláchíí' (ant), Tin (ice), Bisóodi (pig), Wóláchíí' (ant), Neeshch' íí' (nut). Major Howard Connor, signal officer for the Fifth Marine Division at Iwo Jima, described the effectiveness of the Navajos in that brutal battle. "During the first forty-eight hours, while we were landing and consolidating our shore positions, I had six Navajo radio nets operating around the clock," Connor said, "In that period alone, they sent and received over 800 messages without an error." Of the strategic importance of the Navajo Code Talkers, Connor said, "Were it not for the Navajos, the Marines would never have taken Iwo Jima." The Japanese had displayed an astounding ability to break conventional American codes, but they never cracked the one from the reservation.

To a man, Navajo veterans are proud of their military service and regard the relocation program as a rude insult from the government they served well. Jim Ahasteen's brother, Yazzie Charley, was stationed with the Army in Berlin in 1962 and remembers the mobilization in fierce weather after the Russians made threatening gestures toward that city. "That time I went into the Army I took an oath that if it needed be I'd die for my country," he said in heavily accented English. "I had my hand on a Bible and there was a U.S. flag there. If anything happened, it was going to be for my people, my country, my religion. These days they want us out of here, and it don't seem right to me. I was raised herding sheep, and that's how I got used to it here. If I went somewhere else, I don't know how it would be, I don't think I'd feel good about it. Like I say, it don't look good to me. I got kids now, and we're trying to bring them up right. I want them to get a good education so they can get a good job. One day I want them to be able to have a place of their own right here next to me."

One of the Navajo workers for the relocation commission's field office at Teesto wrote down in English what Allen Chee wanted the people in Washington to know. "One of our sons, David Chee, is in the military service. They gave him weapons and said to him, 'You are a soldier now. Stand up and fight for your land and your people.' He has been through a lot of work and sweat and a lot more. So why are you talking to us about our land. We got a lot of military boys in the service today. I hope you can think about this and leave our land alone. We don't want to move out no matter what."

Navajo women also show a strong pride in their veterans. "My son, he went to Vietnam," said Laura Nez. "He thought we could live here forever, but now they're going to chase us off. I heard on the radio there might be another war, and I told my friend I hope they leave us alone. They should go get the Hopis." Yazzie Charley's sister-in-law was incredulous that the government could expel men who had served in the military. "A lot of the young people around here are veterans," she said. "And they say they'd rather stay here and fight it out. They took an oath in the service, and they feel they got a right to live here on this land."

Roger Attakai's Army picture hangs at his home near Star Mountain, where he said quite angrily he would resist relocation. "If I was born and raised in town and was adjusted to that kind of life, yes, I could do it," he said. "But we're not adjusted to that kind of life. Here we have the freedom—no air pollution, no bumping into each other, no forcing each other. We're out here calmly. So I'm willing to fight for it. What they'll have to do if they want to move me is move my carcass. I ain't leaving this place alive. My roots are way down in the land, and my feeling for living is in it too. Do you think it's right for the government to make a law like this, pushing us around, shoving us around? I got nothing to do with relocation." His voice was at a strained high pitch now, and he pushed his hands away from him, as if to remove the whole problem from his life. "I got nothing to do with moving. All this good stuff they're trying to feed us, I don't want to hear about that bonus. Five thousand dollars sounds like a lot of money, but it won't last long."

Chilson McCabe is an auto mechanic in Flagstaff who comes home to Red Lake every weekend. He was drafted into the Army in 1968 and served with the 101st Airborne Division in Vietnam. "I fought for my land and their land," he said. "And when I come back they say I've got to move. What will that accomplish? I was raised on the land, I know every square inch, I can picture what's going on out there right now. So now I'm going to have to fight for my land again."

Seeking to Remain in a Sacred Place

The fence crew that Pauline Whitesinger confronted at the end of 1977 was dividing the range into management units, in preparation for turning it over to Hopi control. In midsummer of 1979, when BIA crews were at Big Mountain, fencing the 289-mile border between the Navajo and Hopi partition areas, Katherine Smith fired a shot of her .22 caliber rifle at one of the crew members. Before her trial in a special BIA court, Mrs. Smith said she had not intended to hit anyone but wanted to show her anger and frustration with the land dispute law. Her attorney, Michael Stuhff, told the jury that Mrs. Smith could not be held criminally responsible for her actions because at the time of the incident she was experiencing "a temporary overwhelming wave of emotional distress and despair." Stuhff said his client had been pushed beyond an emotional threshold by the land dispute law that had brought the fence makers to Big Mountain. "She knew the law was not merely unacceptable, it was morally wrong—in direct violation of the traditions in which she had been raised and which she had practiced all her life." When the prosecuting attorney failed to challenge Stuhff's defense of "temporary diminished capacity," the judge issued a verdict of acquittal, citing the legal principle that when the defense presents such a defense, the prosecution is obligated to challenge it.[10]

When Congress passed the Navajo-Hopi land dispute legislation, it had no understanding of the havoc it would cause among a group of people whose apprehension of the sacred all about them remains a vital principle in their lives. Traditional Navajos pray to the trees and springs near their homes as Christians pray at shrines. Theirs is a religious sensibility that is receding inevitably in the modern world. But as Mircea Eliade pointed out, "The wholly desacralized world is a recent discovery of the human spirit. . . . desacralization pervades the entire experience of the nonreligious man of modern societies and . . . in consequence he finds it increasingly difficult to rediscover the existential dimensions of religious man in archaic societies."

Eliade said that religious man seeks to remain in a sacred cosmos. But even if Congress had known of Ashike Bitsi of Big Mountain, it could not have understood why she explained that the half-dozen variously shaped rocks spread out on the dirt floor of her hogan had been dropped by the Holy People on their journeys through the sky and that the rocks could be used to pray for health and well-being. They could not have understood the feelings of traditional Navajos for the land. "The people feel that if they are forced to leave, the mountain will feel like a mother whose children have been taken away from her," said Nancy Walters. Nor could Congress have understood the religious sense of Walters's mother, Katherine Smith, who held in her hand a pouch of gray buckskin known as a Mountain Earth Bundle, which was a sign of her right to remain on Big Mountain. The bundle is also a sign of how Navajo myth has shaped the minds of the traditional people of the JUA.

The size and shape of a large onion, the Mountain Earth Bundle bulged thickly at its center and tapered off to the buckskin ties that drew it tight, holding its sacred contents secure. Mrs. Smith explained that a medicine man had placed soil from Big Mountain at the center of the bundle, and within the outer folds he had placed soil from the four sacred mountains of the Navajos, which define the Navajo homeland and mark the boundaries within which medicine men have the power to cure. Mrs. Smith received the Mountain Earth Bundle from her mother, who told her the bundle tied her spiritually to the land and would protect her family and livestock. Speaking in Navajo, she used the word "Beehaz'áanii" to explain its meaning. Beehaz'áanii means "things to go by." In its most common English translation it means "the law." Mrs. Smith called the land dispute legislation "Bilagáana Bibeehaz'áanii," "the law of the white man."

"It wasn't made like the Bilagáana Bibeehaz'áanii," she said of the bundle, "but it was made for us at the beginning." The Mountain Earth Bundle is made according to strictly defined ritual procedures. The buck whose skin will be used may not be shot. He must be run down, roped, and suffocated with pollen by men praying to the animal as their brother, asking that he understand their need. The skin is folded to form inner pouches, like the bud of a flower. In addition to the mountain earth, it holds turquoise, jet, abalone, and shell. The shell represents White Shell Woman, the mother of Child Born of Water and Monster Slayer, the hero twins of Navajo myth who received the aid of their father the sun to make the world safe for the Diné, the People, the Navajos. To Mrs. Smith and Ashike Bitsi the story is no myth. Its characters are as real to them as saints are to devout Christians.

Medicine man Frank Mitchell tells of a trip to gather earth for the Mountain Earth Bundle in his autobiography, *Navajo Blessingway Singer.* Before his group climbed the mountain, they undressed, bathed, and put on silver belts, bracelets, and buckskin skirts worn by dancers in the nine-night sing known as "Yei Bi Chei." An elderly medicine man led the group up the mountain, each man holding bits of the four sacred stones.

> We all followed him until we came to a waterfall. That is where we put the jewels as a gift to Mother Earth for what we were going to take from her. We left the jewels there and in return gathered up some of the earth from the mountain. After we gathered up as much as we needed, we smoothed out the place; we did not want to leave it disturbed. We fixed it up so that it looked just as it had before, and then coming back we sang more songs until we reached our starting out place at the bottom. Then we finished with the singing and passed the pollen around so that each one of us could bless himself. Then we dressed in our ordinary clothes and started back home.[11]

Mrs. Smith said a white friend of hers, a missionary at Hardrock, once urged her to burn the Mountain Earth Bundle because it was a pagan symbol. "She said, 'Come on, Katherine, believe in God.' They wanted me to burn this, but I never did. I didn't say 'Throw your Bible into the fire.' "

In the same metal footlocker where she keeps the Mountain Earth Bundle, Mrs. Smith keeps a document she received from the Bureau of Indian Affairs, entitling her to twenty-six acres at the foot of Big Mountain for "as long as beneficial use, as determined by the General Superintendent of the Navajo Service, is made of it." The paper is signed by K. W. Dixon, Acting General Superintendent, and carries a gold seal embossed with the words "By Authority of the Secretary of the Interior." Mrs. Smith received the document in 1960, fourteen years before Congress passed the Navajo and Hopi Land Settlement Act. She calls the act "a misunderstanding made of law." To her Big Mountain is the center of everything. Now everything is falling apart.

Epilogue

In June 1980 Congress finally passed legislation embodying a compromise between Morris Udall and Dennis DeConcini on the issues of land and life estates for Navajo relocatees. Dubbed the Navajo and Hopi Indian Relocation Amendments Act of 1980, it combined a provision for outright transfer to the Navajos of up to 250,000 acres under the administration of the Bureau of Land Management with a provision directing the secretary of the interior to take in trust as part of the Navajo Reservation an additional 150,000 acres purchased by the tribe. It thus required no federal expenditure and avoided the veto threatened by officials in the Carter administration in 1979. In addition, at the insistence of Udall, it prohibited Navajo acquisition of public land northwest of the Colorado River — the location of the House Rock Valley and the Paria Plateau; at the insistence of the New Mexico congressional delegation, it set a limit of 35,000 acres on land the Navajos could acquire in New Mexico.

In its other key provision the new legislation allowed for up to 120 life estates of ninety acres each for Navajos who were at least forty-nine years old when the 1974 Land Settlement Act became law. Preference was to be granted to those who were at least 50 percent disabled and — in language inserted by Senator Goldwater — to residents of Big Mountain.

Senator DeConcini agreed to the compromise with some reluctance. When it was brought to the Senate floor for a vote, the Arizona Democrat repeated his charge that the 1974 act was "harsh, inhumane, and should be repealed," but he acknowledged that there was "not sufficient support in Congress" for repeal. Not only

213

would Senator Goldwater oppose a repeal attempt, but Senator John Melcher of Montana, chairman of the Senate Select Committee on Indian Affairs, who had voted for the 1974 act as a member of the House of Representatives, was also likely to insist that the government stand by its program to divide the disputed lands and relocate Navajos.

In the House of Representatives, Morris Udall remained steadfast in his defense of the Hopi victory. Perhaps no one in Congress had felt more ambivalence about the land dispute in 1974 than Udall, but after passage of the partition legislation he defended it as a just culmination of years of turbulent litigation and congressional debate. The persistent Navajo attempt to have Congress reconsider the legislation both worried him and offended his sense of fair play. In a suprisingly terse statement preceding the House vote in 1980, Udall said the amending legislation sought to remedy the "defects and oversights" of the Land Settlement Act and expressed confidence that it would "go a long way toward easing the burdens and trauma of relocation for these Navajo families."

Congressman Dan Clausen of California offered a more poignant assessment of the land dispute and the federal government's role in it. Clausen said the dollar cost of relocation would be "staggering" and the human cost "immeasurable." "It should not be forgotten that the principal cause of the long and often bitter dispute between two of America's ancient Indian tribes was the consistent failure of the federal government to pay appropriate attention to the administration of its responsibilities in Indian affairs," he said. He concluded somewhat lamely that there was a lesson to be derived from the dispute: "The federal government must exercise its responsibilities over Indians with great care." Manuel Lujan of New Mexico found no silver lining or comforting moral in relocation and bluntly said he thought it was wrong. "I still believe that the solution imposed upon us by the legislation in 1974 is a bad solution," he said. "When people have to be moved from places where they were born and raised, it is not an equitable solution, so far as I am concerned." Like DeConcini, however, Lujan knew that Congress was not willing to consider an alternative solution to the land dispute. "I therefore bow to the will of the majority as expressed in 1974 and at least support this [the amending legislation] as the only way that we can implement the carrying out of that policy."

The 1980 legislation broadened the work of the relocation

commission considerably, directing that the commission administer the land acquired by the Navajos until relocation was complete and that the commission screen applications for life estates to determine who would receive them. While the provisions for land acquisition would certainly facilitate the work of the commission, they would also draw the commission into emotional debates — and almost certainly litigation — with relocatees over a number of questions for which the legislation offered no guidance. How many acres should each family receive? Should families who depend heavily on livestock be granted more land than those who have other means of support? Would it be possible to keep the extended family system intact on a common land base? What were the commission's responsibilities in developing the land acquired for relocatees?

Some Navajos were cynical about the land acquisition program, fearing that they would encounter the same sort of opposition that had pressured Morris Udall into blocking the tribe's attempt to buy land in the House Rock Valley and on the Paria Plateau. Navajo officials also complained that in having to purchase 150,000 acres for relocatees they were being made to pay for the mistakes of the federal government. They wondered how the tribe, with an annual budget of about $26 million, would be able to come up with the estimated $20-25 million needed to pay for the land. The Navajos remained bitter and angry. Even if all went well and the land was acquired, they said, they were in for an enormous upheaval.

Questions about the life estate program were more fundamental than those about land acquisition, suggesting that Congress was naive and uninformed in its belief that life estates would ease the pain of partition. Life estates are often granted in the United States to allow people to live out their lives on land acquired by the government — for a national park, for instance. But when applied to the land dispute settlement, the Anglo-Saxon legal concept highlighted the cultural distance between Washington and the former Joint Use Area. Navajo officials Roman Bitsui and Percy Deal, who had the job of translating the law to those whose land was partitioned to the Hopis, explained that life estates are a hollow euphemism that come across in the metaphysics of traditional Navajos as "death estates."

"When you implant something in someone's mind you cause it to happen," said Bitsui, who resigned from the tribe's Tax Commission in early 1980 to become assistant director of the Land Dispute Commission. "So with life estates in essence what we'd have to say is, 'You're going to die.' " He described the reaction to the new law at Navajo chapter houses. "When I translate about life estates they feel uncomfortable. They don't like to hear that kind of talk. But the law is written that way." Deal, director of the Land Dispute Commission, talked about the psychological effects of knowing that after you die, your children must leave the land. "It is very disturbing to know that your livelihood and traditions on the land are going to end when you die," Deal said. "When there is going to be nothing you can leave for your children, nothing of the land where you were raised, for a Navajo that is very hard."

Another problem with life estates is that they will isolate their occupants on fenced-off islands within Hopi land from which their relatives have been relocated. The law provides that "such persons who are necessarily present to provide for the care of the life tenant" may live on the estate. But for an elderly Navajo, "care" means the shared presence of the extended family. Having Washington's permission to have someone there to haul the water and chop the wood is likely to be a barren comfort. And as others relocate, trading posts may have to shut down, necessitating even longer trips for supplies. Relocation commissioner Sandra Massetto said in 1979 that she did not regard life estates as a realistic means of reducing hardship because they would "isolate the people that much more." Percy Deal said six weeks after passage of the new legislation that he had not detected much enthusiasm to take advantage of the program. If interest in life estates does develop, Navajos not living in Big Mountain are likely to be upset with Senator Goldwater's provision granting preference to Big Mountain residents.

For Abbott Sekaquaptewa the 1980 legislation was a gratifying confirmation of the 1974 Hopi victory, a further expression of congressional intent to put the Hopis in control of the 911,000 acres partitioned to them. At a press conference in Phoenix, the Hopi chairman said the legislation "brings the Hopi Indian people one, step closer to emancipation and freedom after 100 years of domination by the Navajo Tribe and the Bureau of Indian Affairs."

Back on the Hopi mesas in the early part of 1980 formal discussions were under way on the question of how the tribe would make use of the land. In April *Qua Toqti* reported on the first of three workshops reviewing the land's possibilities for industrial, residential, agricultural, mineral, and recreational development. The workshops offered no indication that Sekaquaptewa's sense of triumph and emancipation was widely shared. *Qua Toqti* reported that forty to fifty people attended the first meeting, including "tribal administrative personnel, many members of the Hopi Tribal Council, and many interested persons." At the second meeting ten people showed up; only two came to the third workshop. In an editorial bemoaning the light turnout, Susan Sekaquaptewa, who continued to publish the paper after her husband's death, said the turnout "would indicate that there are no pioneers around the reservation who are either ambitious enough or miserable enough to go out and make a new life on free land; or are even interested in mining for coal or developing industry for jobs or thinking about economically bettering our society and lives." Mrs. Sekaquaptewa also expressed disappointment at the lack of response to a coupon *Qua Toqti* had printed seeking suggestions for ways to use the land. "In the three weeks we ran the coupon we only received back three responses," she wrote, "and one of them was from a Navajo."

In the same editorial Mrs. Sekaquaptewa voiced the abiding fear of the Hopi chairman and his supporters in the land dispute — that Congress might yet reconsider its 1974 action and decide that partition and relocation were not worth their cost in dollars or human suffering, that those in Congress who argued that the Hopis needed the land for their cultural and economic survival had been wrong:

> Repeatly [*sic*] you hear at these meetings that it is politically necessary to use the H.P.L. [Hopi Partition Lands] to secure it for the Hopis. Otherwise someday the "great white father" in Washington, D.C. will look over it and say "I don't see any Hopis or Hopi livestock or activity on the land, so we'll give it back to the Navajos or just keep letting the Navajos stay." The Hopis always respond that they use the land in a special sense, that it has spiritual value and meaning and that by hunting for eagles and foxes and servicing the shrines they are using the land. It is a different definition of "land use" than the bahana [white man] one but it is just as valid and important in context of Hopi culture and religion. Unfortunately bahanas are in charge and are very practical and pragmatic, and if they have

an excess of Navajos who need land, or stoves without fuel they might easily bulldoze over this gentle passive type of land use and seize it for their own purposes.

The editorial was layered with irony, not only because it was probably *Qua Toqti*'s first editorial statement of concern for Hopi traditionalists but also because an inevitable use of the land, and a use eagerly anticipated by *Qua Toqti*, was coal strip-mining.

Perhaps the most striking irony, however, was in the article on the first land-use workshop. Speculating on a possible way to make use of Big Mountain, the reporter wrote, "A big wilderness recreation area (hunting, hiking, etc.) could be exploited there."

Among the Navajos the hope for a congressional turnaround on the land dispute remained strong, almost pathetic in view of its urgency and lack of prospects. "They have a lot of faith in justice, even though it's not being given to them," said Tribal Councilman David Clark of Teesto. Clark said the relocation program was causing "unbelievable strain" among his people. "They just break down and cry while I'm talking with them. The feelings are just below the surface. All you have to do is touch it and it comes out. One of the expressions I hear a lot is that the government is tearing their hearts out while they're still alive. They say, 'I'm not an animal. I'm not a prisoner. But that's the way I'm being treated in my own country.'"

Clark and other tribal leaders were under a different kind of strain in 1980, the raw political strain felt by elected officials whose constituents feel their interests have not been protected. Out of their own sense of grievance against Washington and, no doubt, mindful of the mood of their people, they continued to voice hope that relocation might somehow be stopped. But in their political sophistication the councilmen recognized a sobering truth in a message from their staunchest ally in the land dispute, Dennis DeConcini. "I hate to hold out hopes for repeal to anyone out there," DeConcini said. "It's not going to be me saying, 'Keep your hearts pounding; repeal is on its way.' If that developed and could be put together, yes, I would certainly participate and do what I could to see it happen. But I don't want to leave anybody with some impressions that are going to make people feel worse when it doesn't come."

Morris Udall said he believed that the Navajo leadership had finally adopted the "statesmanlike" position of accepting partition and relocation. "I just have the feeling that both tribes have reconciled themselves to this as a reasonable settlement," Udall said in an interview just before passage of the new legislation. Asked if Congress might be willing to take another look at the program to settle the land dispute, Udall responded ruefully, "I doubt that anyone is going to want to open this can of snakes again."

Udall's reading of the Navajo position may have been wishful thinking. Peter MacDonald remained defiant in pledging that the tribe would pursue every possibility for repeal. "We will not rest, we will not be satisfied, we will not stop our efforts until the homes and lives of the Navajo people in this area have been preserved," the Navajo chairman said in an address to the tribal council. Invoking an old Navajo theme in the land dispute, he said, "We must carry to the American people the message that forced relocation is wrong, that a double standard, under which white people who take Indian land are allowed to keep the land but Navajos who are accused of taking Hopi land are forced to leave their land, is wrong."

The Navajo conviction that Congress had erred grievously in its plan to settle the land dispute was echoed in mid 1980 by Professor Thayer Scudder, the California Institute of Technology anthropologist who has made the study of compulsory relocation his life's work. "Congress was and is still terribly uninformed on the negative impacts of compulsory relocation on the majority of Navajo relocatees," Scudder wrote to President Carter, urging repeal of the 1974 legislation and the substitution of a development program for the Hopis and the Navajos of the former JUA. Such a program, he said, would "cost less financially and in human terms" than the relocation program.

"Mr. President, I cannot believe that the United States government would proceed with this relocation exercise if the true costs of the compulsory relocation were better understood," Scudder wrote. Contrasting the relocation program with the government's plans to provide financial settlements of Indian claims in New England, Scudder said, "I believe that we are following a double standard here which is reprehensible. . . . Mr. President, I believe that if we continue this compulsory relocation it will prove embarassing to the United States, especially granted your own stand on human rights."

Another 1980 development demonstrated the fact that, whatever grief it has caused the two tribes, the land dispute has been a bonanza for lawyers on both sides. Norman Littell, general counsel for the Navajos from 1947 to 1966, had worked under a contract entitling him to 10 percent of the value of land he "recovered, saved, or obtained" for the tribe. Although the *Healing* decision was generally regarded as a defeat for the Navajos, it did establish for the first time the tribe's legal rights to the disputed land. In 1980, after a long fight in and out of the federal courts in which Littell sought a $2.8 million settlement, he finally agreed to accept $795,000. Noting that John Boyden had received $1 million for his work in the *Healing* case, George Vlassis called the case the only one in his knowledge which neither lawyer had lost. Boyden, certainly one of the dominant figures in the history of the land dispute, died in mid 1980.

Lawyers for the Navajos and Hopis were still at work in 1980 preparing for trial in the dispute over land around the Hopi village of Moencopi, west of the former Joint Use Area. The Hopis had sought a direct partition of 240,000 acres in 1974, but the Land Settlement Act directed that the dispute be litigated in the federal court in Phoenix. Fortunately for both tribes, the act also directed that the federal government would pay the legal expenses for this court fight, which threatened the homes of several thousand Navajos in and around Tuba City.

The relocation commission remained hard at its task, working on the plan that was due in Congress in April of 1981; finding new homes for Navajos ready to move — who continued to be mostly young and educated; trying with little success to establish contacts with the chapters and tribal offices whose help they would need; preparing for a series of hearings on the regulations it would adopt to administer life estates; and examining lands available for Navajo acquisition. The commission's professional staff members were for the most part conscientious, hard-working people who felt deep ambivalence about their work. They were reluctant to be a part of a program that was causing so much pain. But they wanted to help the relocatees through the difficult transition. One staff member said privately he was considering resigning because he didn't want to be known as a second Kit Carson.

But in its monthly "Program Updates and Reports," the commission projected a far different mood, an official mood of confidence and progress, as seen in this introduction to its report for July:

Two hundred and thirty-four (234) households have relocated
— 8 during July and 112 this fiscal year. The Commission has
thus reached its revised goal of moving 110 households during
Fiscal Year 1980. Voluntary relocation will continue during
the remaining quarter of the fiscal year, and it is estimated
that the total number of households relocated by the end of
the fiscal year will equal 136% of the fiscal year's goal.

The current operational case load for each of the activity
centers in the relocation program is as follows. The Certifica-
tion Office is evaluating 987 applications. Relocation Advisory
Services staff are counseling 185 households who have been
certified as eligible for relocation benefits. Technical Supportive Services staff are providing assistance to 221 households in
identifying replacement homesites and acquiring replacement
dwellings. Real Estate Services staff are working with 72 households — 36 of whom are seeking replacement dwellings and
36 of whom are in the process of closing escrows or having
homes constructed. Postmove contact is maintained by Relocation Advisory Services staff with 227 of the households who
have relocated.

For those who followed the work of the commission, the report
was little more than an impressive statistical facade. It was an
attempt to reduce relocation to a problem of logistics, a challenge
to the organizational capacities of the federal government. Behind
the facade lay the ugly reality that the Navajos were bending to the
relentless will of the law at a staggering cost — and the frightful
possibility of violent resistance. In mid 1980 the worst fears of
those who had warned against relocation were being confirmed. At
the same time, while the Hopis pondered what to do with the
911,000 acres partitioned to them, the justification for the relocation
program remained open to grave doubt. But six years before the
program was scheduled to be completed, important men in Washington continued to insist that relocation was necessary to achieve a
just settlement of the Navajo-Hopi land dispute.

Afterword, 1987: The Navajos, the Hopis, and the Press*

At widely scattered intervals since the Joint Use Area was partitioned in 1979, the *Washington Post*, the *Los Angeles Times*, and the *New York Times* have splashed their front pages with extensive pieces on the Navajo-Hopi turmoil, summarizing the dispute's history and noting its simmering passions.

In May 1985, for example, Iver Peterson, the *New York Times*'s Denver bureau chief, traveled to Big Mountain, where he met Katherine Smith, one of the Navajo matriarchs leading the resistance to relocation. Smith told him, "If they come to push me out, I will just say, O.K., it is better if you just kill me now and leave me here."

But while the dramatic stories from Arizona have implicitly recognized the dispute as a fascinating and still-evolving issue of national significance, national editors have refused to take it seriously. They have slighted or ignored completely recent initiatives to avert confrontation. "Every so often they come up with an exotic story with nice pictures," relocation commissioner Sandra Massetto said in mid-1986. "I would think they would look at it from a substantive

*Adapted from the author's article in the *Columbia Journalism Review*, July/August 1986.

standpoint rather than a glamour standpoint. I mean, this is the biggest Indian issue in the last fifty years."

Of the big three, only the *New York Times* paid attention in 1985 when President Reagan took the extraordinary step of sending former interior secretary William Clark as his personal emissary to the two tribes. The *Times* account noted that the talks failed but neglected to report on their substance: that Clark and his deputy, Richard Morris, called for land exchanges that would minimize forced relocation. Morris says he was surprised at the press's indifference to the story, adding, "It could have helped bring about a better resolution if they had covered it."

In May of 1986, when Congressman Morris Udall called representatives of both tribes to Washington for a hearing on his bill to end forced relocation by enacting land exchanges, the three big papers took a walk on the story. Shortly thereafter, a reporter at one of the big three acknowledged that his paper had slighted the issue. There was a sense, he said, that, having published a number of pieces on an Indian tribe two years before, "we had 'done Indians' for a while. It was as if to say, 'What more is there to say about Indians?' "

Generally speaking, the big three have hurried past the Navajos and the Hopis the way some tourists hurry across the reservations en route to the Grand Canyon. They have regarded the dispute and its people as little more than material for colorful features about the "plight" of the Indians. The rest of the world has issues deemed worthy of sustained coverage and thoughtful analysis. Indians have "plights" to be lamented, as if they are out of reach in the historical past like the Cherokee Trail of Tears. Newspapers take solemn note of the injustices and then move on to the real news. Joan La France, a Chippewa, identified the problem in testimony to the U.S. Commission on Civil Rights when she said Indians "are treated as people of the past. . . . There is a gross lack of information about us being a contemporary people, a people who still live in this country."

But at least the feature-type stories have conveyed some sense of the drama of the dispute in places like Big Mountain. The real failure of the big three has been their reluctance to follow up the field reports with coverage of the less colorful but equally significant developments in Flagstaff, home of the relocation commission, and Washington. Five years ago, relocation commissioners Sandra Massetto and Roger Lewis—who joined the commission after the

death of Rev. Urbano and the resignation of Robert Lewis—called
for land exchanges between the two tribes. The two commissioners
wanted to reduce the number of those who live on the "wrong side"
of the partition line. Then Lewis resigned after saying—in an aston-
ishing moment of candor—that in relocating elderly Navajos he sometimes felt "as bad as the people who ran the concentration camps in
World War II." At the request of Senator Barry Goldwater, the
Reagan administration replaced Lewis with a man whose only qual-
ification was that he had run "Democrats for Goldwater" in the 1980
election in which Goldwater had eked out a narrow victory.

The few reporters who have lingered over the story have found
it as intriguing as the desert itself. "It's so complex, so persistent in
making you uncover layer after layer, that it's probably the most
fascinating story I've ever worked on," said Bill Walker of the *Denver Post*, who wrote a series on the issue in 1986.

The two papers closest to the two tribes—the *Navajo Times*
and the Gallup, New Mexico *Independent*—have provided generally excellent coverage of the dispute. The most significant regional
development, however, has been the *Arizona Republic*'s recognition of the inadequacy of coverage that for more than a decade had
concentrated on spot reports of congressional hearings, meetings of
the relocation commission, and press conferences organized by public relations experts employed by both tribes. "We had given it a
snapshot look, instead of helping people understand why it was
important," said city editor Richard Robertson, who coordinates news
coverage "There we were, spending a lot of time with wire coverage of the West Bank, but missing a similar story right here in our
own backyard."

The *Republic* hired Paul Brinkley-Rogers to man its northern
Arizona bureau, in part because of his interest in the Navajos and
Hopis. Brinkley-Rogers, who covered the Vietnam War as a correspondent for *Newsweek*, calls the land dispute "overwhelming, almost
to the same extent that living in Saigon was. In terms of its color,
emotions, complexity and consequences, I think it's without equal
among national issues."

In putting Brinkley-Rogers on the story, the *Republic* sought
to position itself for a widely anticipated confrontation on July 6,
1986, which Congress had originally established as the deadline for
relocation. (Over a thousand families—all but thirteen of them
Navajo—have already been relocated. Another 1,500 Navajo fami-

lies are scheduled to be relocated.) The defiance of Navajo grandmothers had been joined by rumblings from Navajo veterans of the
Vietnam War and pledges of solidarity from non-Navajo members
of the militant American Indian Movement. Many observers expected July 6 to be an Indian D-day, and the regional and national press
took note with big stories that focused on Navajo anguish under
powerful headlines: U.S. DRIVING OFF 10,000 INDIANS in the *Sac-
ramento Bee*; MOVING MEANS TRAIL OF TEARS FOR NAVAJO in the
Los Angeles Times; WAR OF TWO WORLDS: NAVAJO ELDER IS EYE
OF STORM in the *Arizona Republic*; TWO TRIBES, ONE LAND in
Newsweek.

Emily Benedek reported the story for *Newsweek* in mid-1985.
By the end of the year she was back in Northern Arizona to write a
book that will focus on the differences in attitudes and thinking
between the people of the land and the federal government. "Here
was a society of more or less self-sufficient people whose cultural
identity was strong," she said, explaining what impelled her to
take on the book project. "The government decides that to settle
a land dispute it will move a whole lot of them out of their own
world and into modern times. The people engineering that move
ruled from afar, and the law was made in Washington and administered in Flagstaff by people who had no understanding of the
Navajo culture. Yet the lawmakers and administrators thought they
were doing what was right. I wanted to show through stories how
the relocatees felt about what was happening to them and to understand how the decisions made by the government for them had been
so wrong-headed."

Congress and the Bureau of Indian Affairs have taken action
that will extend the relocation deadline by about seventeen months.
In the meantime the spate of stories on Navajo anguish in the national and regional press had created a public relations problem for Hopi
Tribal Council Chairman Ivan Sidney, who called press conferences
in Albuquerque and Phoenix to remind reporters that relocation,
unpleasant though it was, represented the culmination of a string
of Hopi victories in the courts and Congress. Wherever he went,
Sidney carried a series of posterboard maps that drove home another
key point: the Navajo Reservation has been gradually expanded
to surround the Hopis. Sidney then began publishing a tabloid newspaper devoted to telling the Hopi side of the dispute and fighting
"Navajo misinformation." The difficulty of his job doubled in early

1986 when *Broken Rainbow*, a film highly critical of the relocation program, won the Academy Award for the best feature documentary.

While both tribes have launched public relations efforts to bring national attention to the issue, the most provocative publicity has been generated by a group that calls itself the Big Mountain Legal Defense/Offense Committee. Comprising mostly youthful volunteers whose garb and idealism recall protesters against the Vietnam War, the committee has raised enough money to send Navajo elders and Hopi "traditionalists" (those who do not regard the tribal council as legitimate and who oppose relocation) on cross-country speaking engagements. The committee explains the government's relocation policy as the result of a conspiracy on the part of greedy coal interests, despite the lack of solid evidence to support the charge, and labels Sidney and his supporters "puppets" of the federal government. Sidney has responded furiously, denouncing the committee for disseminating "half-truths, innuendo, and outright falsehoods."

Regardless of what one thinks about relocation, there is plenty of reason to find fault with those who say it is the result of a conspiracy between energy interests and the federal government. Conspiracy theories have the advantage of simplifying complex issues. They also undoubtedly thrill some part of our brains that was most active when our ancestors believed the world was alive with gremlins and evil spirits that were the cause of all their problems. But they are almost always the result of intellectual laziness and political opportunism. The energy conspiracy theory of the land dispute is no exception. Relocation is a failed policy derived from ignorance and indifference. There is certainly not sufficient evidence to charge that it is the result of conspiracy.

The countercultural ideals and rhetoric of the Big Mountain Committee's members have inspired cynical reporters to call them members of the "Wanna-be Indian" tribe. No one can deny their effectiveness and commitment, however. They have generated a flood of letters to Capitol Hill. What is more, they have organized dozens of chapters across the United States, including one in Berkeley, California, that calls the fight against relocation "a facet of the greater international struggles . . . for indigenous self-determination, to end growing militarism and nuclear madness, and the day-to-day struggle in each of our lives for justice and equality."

The committee has gained a ready hearing abroad, especially in Europe, where, the historian Ray Allen Billington observed, the

United States has long been pictured as "a merciless enemy of a helpless minority, fracturing the Indians' social structure and relentlessly eroding their numbers by warfare, vice, and starvation, with the avowed purpose of eliminating the entire race."[1]

Such a picture is, of course, nonsense. Over the past twenty years the federal government has done much to shield Indians from the economic pressures that in other countries are forcing native peoples off the land and into the turbulent misery of cities. Washington has, in fact, subsidized Indian cultures with a wide range of programs to provide free food, housing, education, and medical care. But there appears to be no knowledge of these policies among Europeans, who see relocation not as the aberration it is, but as the sinister continuation of a genocidal federal Indian policy.

A March 1986 article in the West German *Frankfurter Rundschau* quoted an unnamed Indian spokesman as calling Navajo relocation America's "final solution" to its Indian problem. An article in the Austrian *Alpenpost* printed the claim of a local support group that "over 10,000 Navajos are standing on the brink of a massacre." The most outlandish commentary on relocation was a fabricated statement attributed to President Reagan that appeared in 1986 in at least three Dutch newspapers, including the respected *Volkskrant.* "This is not going to be another Wounded Knee," the president was quoted as saying about the once-anticipated July 6 eviction of Navajos by federal marshals or the National Guard. "The whole operation will be over in thirty minutes." It can't be long before the relocation story is picked up by the press in the Soviet Union, where government officials have countered U.S. claims of Soviet human rights violations with taunting reminders of our treatment of Indians historically and of the recent controversial murder conviction of Sioux militant Leonard Peltier.

With the retirement of Barry Goldwater, the legislation Arizona's Morris Udall and John McCain cosponsored in the House of Representatives is likely to be revived in 1987 and will have good prospects of passage. McCain is taking Goldwater's place in the Senate and will join Arizona's other senator, Dennis DeConcini, in opposition to forced relocation.

But should attempts to forestall relocation fail, the possibility of violent resistance cannot be denied. Given the size of the area awarded to the Hopis and the numbers of defiant Navajos and their supporters, the violence could easily be more widespread and intense than the confrontation at Wounded Knee in 1973. American Indian Movement members have camped at Big Mountain under the banner "WK 1973," a reminder of their capacity for defiance of federal authorities.

If there is a confrontation, and if federal marshals sent to evict Navajos do battle with an unlikely guerrilla force of AIM members, Navajo veterans of Vietnam, and grandmothers in calico skirts, the press will descend like Tom Wolfe's fruit flies, just as they did at Wounded Knee. They would feast on the violence of a tragedy that was spawned by competing tribes, compounded by the federal government and neglected by the national press.

Note

1.   Ray Allen Billington, *Land of Savagery, Land of Promise* (New York: W. W. Norton & Co., 1981), p. 134.

Notes

Chapter 1

1. *Navajo Times*, December 8, 1977.
2. Charles Wilkinson, "Shall These Islands Be Preserved," *American West*, May/June 1979.
3. Vine Deloria, Jr., *We Talk, You Listen* (New York: Delta Publishing Co., 1970), p. 175.
4. President Johnson's Special Message on "The Forgotten American," March 6, 1968.
5. *Arizona Republic*, May 12, 1978.
6. *New York Times*, December 21, 1977.
7. Gladys A. Reichard, *Navaho Medicine Man* (New York: J. J. Augustin, 1939), p. 14.

Chapter 2

1. Clyde Kluckhohn and Dorothea Leighton, *The Navajo* (Cambridge, Mass.: Harvard University Press, 1948), p. xv.
2. E. H. Spicer, *Cycles of Conquest* (Tucson: University of Arizona Press, 1970), p. 215.
3. *Santa Fe New Mexican*, December 12, 1863.
4. L. R. Bailey, *The Long Walk* (Los Angeles: Western Lore Press, 1964), pp. 148–49. See also Gerald Thompson, *The Army and the Navajo* (Tucson: University of Arizona Press, 1976), p. 11.
5. Thompson, *The Army and the Navajo*, p. 28.
6. Carleton to Thomas, September 6, 1863, National Archives, Office of Adjutant General, Record Group 94, Letters Received.
7. Carson to Capt. Ben Butler, assistant to Carleton, January 3, 1864, quoted in Lawrence Kelly, *Navajo Roundup* (Boulder: Pruett Publishing Co., 1970), pp. 92–93.
8. U.S. Office of Indian Affairs, Report 1867, p. 190, quoted in Dee Brown, *Bury My Heart at Wounded Knee* (New York: Holt, Rinehart and Winston, 1972), p. 16.
9. U.S., Congress, House, *Executive Document 263*, 49th Cong., 1st sess., p. 15.
10. James F. Downs, *The Navajo* (New York: Holt, Rinehart and Winston, 1972), p. 16.
11. Frank McNitt, *The Indian Traders* (Tucson: University of Arizona Press, 1970), p. 79.
12. Ibid., p. 80.
13. Robert Young, personal communication, August 28, 1979.
14. For a discussion of the conditions leading to establishment of the 1882 reservation, see 210 Federal Supplement, 126, pp. 132–38.

15. *Prescott Miner*, quoted in Platt Cline, *They Came to the Mountain* (Flagstaff: Northern Arizona University, with Northland Press, 1976), p. 109.

16. Welsh to Secretary of the Interior, September 26, 1888, National Archives, Bureau of Indian Affairs, Record Group 75.

17. Morgan to R. V. Belt, National Archives, BIA, Letters Received 36001/1890.

18. Commissioner of Indian Affairs to Secretary of Interior, January 30, 1891, cited in 210 Federal Supplement, 126, p. 148.

19. Burton, in Annual Reports of the Department of the Interior, containing the Report of the Commissioner of Indian Affairs, Fiscal Year ended June 30, 1900.

20. Murphy to Commissioner of Indian Affairs, July 10, 1908, National Archives, BIA Classified File 50594-08-313, Moqui.

21. H. F. Robinson to Commissioner of Indian Affairs, May 26, 1914, National Archives, BIA Classified File 60400-14-308. 2, Moqui.

22. U.S. Congress, House, Committee on Indian Affairs, *Indian Appropriations Bill: Hearing Before a Subcommittee of the Committee on Indian Affairs*, 65th Cong., 2d. sess. 1917–18, pp. 119–20.

23. Crane to Commissioner of Indian Affairs, March 12, 1918, U.S. House of Representatives, Committee on Indian Affairs, Washington, 1919–20, vol. 3, pp. 787–93.

24. H. F. Robinson to Commissioner of Indian Affairs, September 10, 1918, National Archives, Bia Classified File 60400-14-308.2, Moqui.

25. Annual Report of Supt. Daniels, 1920; cited in letter from Commissioner Charles Burke to L. A. Dorrington, Inspector, Indian Service, November 28, 1921.

26. Report of Miller, National Archives, BIA Classified Files, 1907–, File Mark 99561-21-150, Moqui.

27. Ibid.

28. Burke to Senator Cameron, April 13, 1926, National Archives BIA Classified Files, 1907–, File Mark 99561-21-150, Moqui.

29. John Collier, *On the Gleaming Way* (Denver: Sage Books, 1962), p. 44.

30. U.S., Congress, Senate, Subcommittee of the Committee on Indian Affairs, *Survey of Conditions of the Indians in the United States* (hereafter referred to as *Survey of Conditions*), 75th Cong., 1st sess., Part 34, pp. 17931–33.

31. Collier, *On the Gleaming Way*, p. 64.

32. *Survey of Conditions*, p. 17933.

33. John Collier, *From Every Zenith* (Denver: Sage Books, 1963), p. 252.

34. Gladys A. Reichard, *Navajo Shepherd and Weaver* (1936; rpt. Glorieta, N.M.: Rio Grande Press, 1968), p. 6.

35. *Survey of Conditions*, p. 17976.

36. Ibid., p. 17988.

37. Ibid., p. 17916.

38. Ibid., p. 18015.

39. Ibid.

40. *Navajo Livestock Reduction: A National Disgrace* (Tsaile, Ariz.: Navajo Community College, 1974), p. 47.

41. Kenneth R. Philp, *John Collier's Crusade for Indian Reform* (Tucson: University of Arizona Press, 1977), p. 243.

42. *Survey of Conditions*, pp. 18010–12.

43. David Aberle, *The Peyote Religion Among the Navaho* (Chicago: Aldine Publishing Co., 1966), p. 87.

44. *Navajo Livestock Reduction*, p. 159.

45. Ibid., p. 172.

46. *Navajo Times*, August 4, 1966.

47. *Gallup Independent*, June 7, 1977.

48. Hutton Report, National Archives, BIA Classified Files, 1907–, File Mark 8970-30-308.2, Western Group.

49. Fiske Report, National Archives, BIA Record Group 75, Classified Files, 1907–, File Mark 41043-30-150, Hopi.

50. 210 Federal Supplement 125 (1962), p. 156.

51. Ibid., pp. 155–66.

52. Ibid., p. 166.

53. MacDonald's address at a conference on The Rise of the Southwest, April 21, 1977; reprinted in *Navajo Times*, April 28, 1977.

54. Navajo Tribe, Office of Program Development, "Briefing Paper for the Navajo Tribal Cou⸱ ⸱il," 1978, pp. 3–33.

55. Navajo Tribe, Division of Economic Development, "Navajo Nation Overall Economic Development Program," 1978, p. 22.

56. *Chemical Week*, June 28, 1978.

57. Brigham Young University, Center for Business and Economic Research, "A Study to Identify Potentially Feasible Small Businesses on the Navajo Reservation" (Provo, Utah, 1975).

58. Navajo Tribe, Office of Program Development, "The Navajo Nation Overall Economic Development Program," 1974, p. 36.

59. Staff Report, Office of General Counsel, U.S. Commission on Civil Rights, October 1973, p. 67.

60. *Gallup Independent*, December 31, 1979.

61. *Arizona Star*, October 16, 1960.

62. 210 Federal Supplement 125 (1962) p. 184.

Chapter 3

1. Frank Waters, *Book of the Hopi* (New York: Viking Press, 1963).

2. *Qua Toqti*, July 25, 1974.

3. *Qua Toqti*, March 3, 1977.

4. Mischa Titiev, *Old Oraibi*, Papers of the Peabody Museum of American Archaeology and Ethnology, vol. 22, no. 1 (Cambridge, Mass.: Harvard University, 1944), p. 68.

5. Oliver La Farge, *Running Narrative of the Organization of the Hopi Tribe of Indians*, in the La Farge Collection, The University of Texas at Austin, pp. 59–60.

6. Hopi Constitution, Article 3, Section 1.

7. Ibid., Article 3, Section 3.

8. U.S., Dept. of the Interior, Bureau of Indian Affairs, Transcript of hearings on the Hopi Reservation, July 15–30, p. 5.

9. *Qua Toqti*, June 2, 1977.

10. *Qua Toqti*, November 24, 1977.

11. Charles Lummis, *Bullying the Hopi* (Prescott, Ariz.: Prescott College Press, 1968), pp. 89–90.

12. Annual Report of the Commissioner of Indian Affairs, U.S. Dept of the Interior, 1886.

13. Lummis, *Bullying the Hopi*, p. 13.

14. William Pfaff, "Reflections (Westernization)," *The New Yorker*, February 19, 1979.

15. Lummis, *Bullying the Hopi*, p. 20.

16. Heinrich Voth, "Historical Notes on the First Decade of the Mennonite Mission Work Among the Hopi of Arizona," 1923; reprinted in Harry James, *Pages from Hopi History* (Tucson: University of Arizona Press, 1976), pp. 153–54.

17. Dan Talayesva, *Sun Chief: The Autobiography of a Hopi Indian* (New Haven: Yale University Press, 1974), p. 178.

18. Ibid., p. 280.

19. Laura Thompson, *A Culture in Crisis: A Study of the Hopi Indians* (New York: Harper & Brothers Publishers, 1950), p. 72.

20. Laura Thompson and Alice Joseph, *The Hopi Way* (1944; rpt. Ann Arbor, Mich.: University Microfilms, 1962), p. 37.

21. Thompson, *A Culture in Crisis*, p. 134.

22. Crane to Commissioner of Indian Affairs, June 22, 1914, National Archives, Bureau of Indian Affairs, Record Group 75, Classified Files, 1907–, File Mark 60400-14-308.2, Moqui.

23. Crane to Commissioner of Indian Affairs, March 12, 1918, National Archives, BIA, Record Group 75, Classified Files, 1907–, File Mark 60400-14-308.2, Moqui.

24. Transcript of 1955 BIA hearings, p. 289.

25. James, *Pages from Hopi History*, pp. 130–39; for a more subjective report on the Oraibi conflict and on the entire history of Hopi Resistance, see Richard Clemmer, *Continuities of Hopi Culture Change* (Ramona, Calif.: Acoma Books, 1978).

26. *Qua Toqti*, November 29, 1973.

27. *Qua Toqti*, December 29, 1977.

28. *Qua Toqti*, March 14, 1974.

29. *Qua Toqti*, November 3, 1977.

30. 1 Nephi 12:23.

31. 2 Nephi 30:5–6.

32. *Los Angeles Times*, February 10, 1979.

33. Ibid.

34. *Qua Toqti*, August 9, 1973.

35. *Qua Toqti*, January 25, 1979.

Chapter 4

1. *Annual Report of the Commissioner of Indian Affairs for 1851* (Washington: U.S. Government Printing Office, 1851), p. 189.

2. Capt. J. G. Walker and Maj. O. L. Shepherd, *The Navajo Reconnaissance* (Los Angeles: Western Lore Press, 1964), p. 65.

3. Frank Mitchell, *Navajo Blessingway Singer*, edited by Charlotte J. Frisbie and David P. McAllester (Tucson: University of Arizona Press, 1978).

4. U.S., Congress, House, *Commissioner of Indian Affairs, Annual Report*, 48th Cong., 2d Sess., House Exec. Doc. 1 (Serial 2287), p. 181.

5. Albert Yava, *Big Falling Snow* (New York: Crown Publishers, 1978), p. 125.

6. Ibid., p. 137.

7. Helen Sekaquaptewa with Louise Udall, *Me and Mine* (Tucson: University of Arizona Press, 1969), pp. 198–99.

8. *New York Times*, February 18, 1979.

9. Richard Clemmer, *Continuities of Hopi Culture Change* (Ramona, Calif.: Acoma Books, 1978), p. 8.

10. U.S., Department of the Interior, Bureau of Indian Affairs, Transcript of Hopi-Navajo Conference, August 6–7, 1963, p. 4.

11. Ibid., p. 168.

12. Ibid., p. 160.

13. Ibid., pp. 186–88.

14. Ibid., p. 143.

15. *Arizona Republic*, May 6, 1948.

16. *Petroleum Today*, Winter 1965.

17. Ibid.

18. Alvin Josephy, "The Murder of the Southwest," *Audubon Magazine*, July 1971.
19. *Gallup Independent*, May 24, 1974.
20. *Wall Street Journal*, April 13, 1971.
21. Ibid.
22. Ibid.
23. Josephy, "Murder of the Southwest."
24. *New York Times*, May 28, 1971.
25. *Washington Post*, July 23, 1972.
26. *Albuquerque Journal*, June 7, 1972.
27. Hamilton speech reprinted in *Navajo Times*, February 3, 1972.
28. Wiman speech to the Arizona Advisory Committee on the Environment, March 24, 1972.
29. *Arizona Star*, May 29, 1971.
30. *Washington Post*, July 21, 1974.

Chapter 5

1. *Congressional Record*, May 29, 1974, p. 16784.
2. *Washington Post*, July 21, 1974.
3. *Race Relations Reporter*, January 1973.
4. *Gallup Independent*, June 2, 1972.
5. *Arizona Sun*, March 1, 1972.
6. *Arizona Republic*, April 16, 1972.
7. *Arizona Star*, March 26, 1972.
8. *Washington Post*, July 21, 1974.
9. U.S., Congress, House, Subcommittee on Indian Affairs, Committee on Interior and Insular Affairs, transcript of hearings, Washington, D.C., April 17–18, 1972, p. 23.
10. Donald Riegle, *O Congress* (Garden City, N.Y.: Doubleday & Co., 1972), p. 173.
11. Ralph Nader Congress Project, *The Environment Committees* (New York: Grossman Publishers, 1975), pp. 41–42.
12. Theodore H. White, *The Making of the President, 1960* (New York: Mentor Books, 1961), p. 402.
13. *Gallup Independent*, March 13, 1972.
14. U.S., Congress, House, Subcommittee on Indian Affairs, Committee on Interior and Insular Affairs, transcript of hearings, April 17–18, 1972, p. 30.
15. Ibid., p. 78.
16. Ibid., p. 149.
17. Ibid., p. 184.
18. Ibid., p. 192–93.
19. *Gallup Independent*, August 3, 1972.
20. *Washington Post*, August 5, 1972.
21. U.S., Congress, Committee on Indian Affairs of the Committee on Interior and Insular Affairs, transcript of hearings, Washington, D.C., September 14–15, 1972, p. 103.
22. Ibid., p. 208.
23. 18 Indian Claims Commission 241; for a full explanation of Schifter's position, see Schifter and West, "Healing v. Jones: Mandate for Another Trail of Tears?" 51 *North Dakota Law Review* 73 (1974).
24. *Washington Post*, November 2, 1972.
25. *Washington Post*, March 4, 1973.
26. Calvin Trillin, "U.S. Journal," *The New Yorker*, May 12, 1973.
27. U.S., Senate, Committee on Indian Affairs, transcript of hearings, Winslow, Ariz., March 7, 1973, p. 58.
28. Ibid., p. 120.

234 NOTES

29. Ibid., p. 52.
30. Ibid., p. 115.
31. Ibid., p. 34.
32. Ibid., p. 120.
33. *Arizona Republic*, May 5, 1973.
34. U.S., House, Subcommittee on Indian Affairs, Committee on Interior and Insular Affairs, transcript of hearings, Washington, D.C., May 14 and 15, 1973, p. 35.
35. Ibid., p. 64.
36. Ibid., pp. 41–42.
37. Ibid., pp. 39–42.
38. Ibid., pp. 68–71.
39. Ibid.
40. *Navajo Times*, September 27, 1973.
41. House Subcommittee on Indian Affairs, transcript of meeting, November 2, 1973, in committee files at National Archives, p. 127.
42. Barry Goldwater, *The Conscience of a Conservative* (Shepherdsville, Ky.: Victor Publishing Co.: 1960), p. 54.
43. Lynn A. Robbins, "Energy Developments and the Navajo Nation," *Native Americans and Energy Development*, pp. 39–41; personal communication from Richard Schifter.
44. Letter from Lujan to members of House of Representatives, March 16, 1974.
45. *Qua Toqti*, March 21, 1974.
46. *Gallup Independent*, March 28, 1974.
47. *Arizona Republic*, April 13, 1974.
48. *Gallup Independent*, April 11, 1974.
49. *Gallup Independent*, May 9, 1974.
50. *Qua Toqti*, April 25, 1974.
51. *Phoenix Gazette*, May 24, 1974.
52. Navajo press release issued May 25, 1974.
53. Meeds letter, May 24, 1974.
54. Steiger letter, May 24, 1974.
55. Goldwater-Fannin letter, May 8, 1974.
56. Owens letter, May 16, 1974.
57. *Congressional Record*, May 29, 1974, p. H4517.
58. Ibid.

Chapter 6

1. *Washington Post*, July 23, 1974.
2. U.S., Senate, Committee on Interior and Insular Affairs, transcript of hearings on the Navajo-Hopi land dispute, Washington, D.C., July 24, 1974, p. 218.
3. Ibid., p. 204.
4. *Arizona Republic*, November 7, 1974.
5. *Arizona Star*, November 24, 1974.
6. *Gallup Independent*, December 28, 1974.
7. *Gallup Independent*, December 31, 1974.
8. *Congressional Record*, December 2, 1974, p. S 20334.
9. Ibid.
10. Ibid.
11. Ibid., p. 20320.
12. *Arizona Star*, February 23, 1975.
13. *Newsweek*, December 30, 1974.
14. *Gallup Independent*, February 27, 1976.
15. *Gallup Independent*, March 3, 1976.

16. *Gallup Independent*, February 16, 1977.
17. *Arizona Republic*, February 17, 1977.
18. Ibid.
19. *Navajo Times*, January 26, 1978.
20. Goldwater to Ivins, March 2, 1979.
21. *Navajo Times*, July 6, 1972.
22. *Navajo Times*, October 11, 1979.

Chapter 7

1. *Congressional Record*, May 29, 1974, p. H4513.
2. Ibid.
3. *Arizona Republic*, June 19, 1975.
4. Steiger to Morrall, June 27, 1975.
5. *Gallup Independent*, April 28, 1977.
6. Ibid.
7. *Arizona Republic*, August 3, 1975.
8. *Arizona Republic*, February 28, 1976.
9. *Gallup Independent*, June 13, 1975.
10. *Gallup Independent*, October 8, 1976.
11. *Arizona Star*, August 13, 1975.
12. *Qua Toqti*, October 16, 1975.
13. *Arizona Daily Sun*, July 9, 1975.
14. *Qua Toqti*, October 16, 1975.
15. Steve Rich, written statement submitted to Interior Dept. Task Force on Navajo Land Selection.
16. *Arizona Republic*, November 19, 1976.
17. A. D. Findlay, statement delivered at public hearing on Navajo land selection, Page, Arizona, July 9, 1975.
18. Report of William Simkin, December 1975, vol. 2, p. 23.
19. *Gallup Independent*, April 30, 1977.
20. *Farmington Daily Times*, May 5, 1974.
21. *Navajo Times*, May 27, 1974.
22. New Mexico Advisory Committee to the U.S. Civil Rights Commission, "The Farmington Report: A Conflict of Cultures," July 1975, p. 9.
23. See Philip Reno, "The Indians Come to Town," *The Nation*, August 31, 1974.
24. *Time*, June 24, 1974.
25. *Navajo Times*, May 27, 1974.
26. *Farmington Daily Times*, March 10, 1977.
27. *Gallup Independent*, April 29, 1977.
28. Pearson H. Corbett, *Jacob Hamblin, Peacemaker* (Salt Lake City: Deseret Book Co., 1976), p. 111.
29. Ibid., p. 165.
30. U.S., Department of the Interior, Bureau of Indian Affairs, draft of *Environmental Impact Statement on Navajo Land Selection*, 1978, vol. 1, p. 226.
31. Ibid., p. 122.
32. *Arizona Republic*, December 2, 1979 (reprinted from *Washington Post*).
33. U.S., Department of the Interior, Bureau of Indian Affairs, transcript of public hearing on the Navajo Land Selection draft EIS, November 3, 1978, p. 68.
34. Ibid., p. 74.
35. *Empire Magazine*, Sunday *Denver Post*, March 5, 1978.
36. EIS hearings transcript, p. 25.
37. Draft EIS on Navajo Land Selection, Dept. of the Interior, 1978, p. 124.

38. Corbett, *Jacob Hamblin*, p. 328.
39. EIS hearing transcript, p. 18.
40. Ibid., pp. 49–50.
41. Ibid., pp. 95–97.

Chapter 8

1. *Gallup Independent*, March 27, 1975.
2. *Gallup Independent*, April 17, 1975.
3. William Simkin in *The Chronicle, Journal of the National Academy of Arbitrators*, October 1977.
4. Ibid.
5. *Navajo Times*, January 24, 1977.
6. *Gallup Independent*, December 18, 1975.
7. *Arizona Republic*, December 19, 1975.
8. *Gallup Independent*, March 4, 1977.
9. *Gallup Independent*, March 9, 1977.
10. *Gallup Independent*, March 18, 1977.
11. Hopi press release, March 30, 1977; see also *Gallup Independent*, March 31, 1977.
12. *Gallup Independent*, May 5, 1977.
13. *Navajo Times*, February 16, 1978.
14. *Navajo Times*, September 15, 1977.
15. *Navajo Times*, February 16, 1978.
16. Ibid.
17. Ibid.
18. Ibid.
19. *Gallup Independent*, March 31, 1977.
20. John J. Wood, Walter M. Vannette, Michael J. Andrews, *A Sociocultural Assessment of the Livestock Reduction Program in the Navajo-Hopi Joint Use Area* (Flagstaff: Dept. of Anthropology, Northern Arizona University, 1979).
21. *Navajo Times*, August 31, 1978.
22. Ibid.
23. Ibid.
24. *Arizona Star*, August 31, 1978.
25. *Navajo Times*, September 28, 1978.
26. *Navajo Times*, October 5, 1978.
27. *Navajo Times*, April 12, 1978.
28. *Navajo Times*, May 17, 1979.
29. *Navajo Times*, June 26, 1979
30. *Navajo Times*, July 3, 1979.
31. *Navajo Times*, June 14, 1979.
32. *Navajo Times*, October 4, 1979.
33. *Arizona Republic*, December 6, 1979.
34. *Navajo Times*, January 4, 1979.

Chapter 9

1. Phoenix newspapers Primary Candidate Survey, July 12, 1976; in the file on Hawley Atkinson of the *Arizona Republic* library.
2. *Gallup Independent*, June 14, 1976.
3. Ibid.
4. *Gallup Independent*, November 5, 1976.
5. *Arizona Republic*, January 9, 1978.
6. *Gallup Independent*, June 28, 1976.

7.   Ibid.
8.   *Gallup Independent*, July 1, 1976.
9.   *Gallup Independent*, July 12, 1976.
10. Ibid.
11. *Gallup Independent*, October 14, 1976.
12. Ibid.
13. *Gallup Independent*, May 26, 1976.
14. *Gallup Independent*, November 26, 1976.
15. *Gallup Independent*, November 30, 1976.
16. *Arizona Republic*, January 1, 1978.
17. *Arizona Republic*, December 20, 1977.
18. *Arizona Republic*, May 10, 1978.
19. *Phoenix Gazette*, March 3, 1978.
20. *Gallup Independent*, May 24, 1977.
21. Goldwater to Kleppe, November 17, 1976.
22. Goldwater to Kleppe, December 2, 1976.
23. *Navajo Times*, January 27, 1977.
24. Ibid.
25. *Arizona Republic*, January 15, 1977.
26. *Arizona Republic*, September 5, 1978.
27. *Navajo Times*, November 9, 1978.
28. *Gallup Independent*, December 13, 1976.
29. Ibid.
30. *Gallup Independent*, November 4, 1976.
31. *Navajo Times*, June 16, 1977.
32. Indians Against Exploitation flyer, 1975.
33. *Gallup Progress*, February 22, 1979.
34. *Navajo Times*, June 16, 1977.
35. Interim Report of the Navajo and Hopi Indian Relocation Commission, 1979.
36. Ibid.
37. Geneva Lewis, report to the Navajo Paralegal Training Program, September 1979.
38. *Gallup Independent*, February 17, 1979.
39. *Arizona Sun*, March 4, 1979.
40. *Arizona Sun*, March 11, 1979.
41. *Navajo Times*, November 22, 1979.
42. Annual Report of the Navajo and Hopi Indian Relocation Commission for 1979.

Chapter 10

1.   David Aberle, *The Peyote Religion Among the Navaho* (Chicago: Aldine Publishing Co., 1966), p. 15.
2.   Ibid. p. 113.
3.   *Navajo Times*, September 16, 1967.
4.   *Navajo Times*, May 25, 1978.
5.   *Navajo Times*, August 1, 1978.
6.   Goldwater-Fannin letter, November 25, 1974.
7.   *Congressional Record*, December 2, 1974, p. S 20319.
8.   Martin D. Topper, "Mental Health Effects of Navajo Relocation in the Former Joint Use Area," Navajo Area Office, Indian Health Service, March 1979.
9.   Ibid.
10. *Navajo Times*, November 1, 1979.
11. Frank Mitchell, *Navajo Blessingway Singer*, edited by Charlotte J. Frisbie and David P. McAllester (Tucson: University of Arizona Press, 1978), p. 202.

Index

Phoenix Indian School, 16
Pittsburgh and Midway Coal Co., 102
Polilema, Otis, 62
Price, Hiram, 27
Princeton University, 201
Prescott Miner, 28–29
Public Law 93-531 (Navajo-Hopi Land
  Settlement Act), 146, 159
Pueblo Lands Act of 1924, 99
Pyne, Joe, 94

Qua Toqti (The Eagle's Cry), 50, 54, 56,
  62, 64, 114, 216, 217, 218

Rachford, C. E., 40
Randolph, Elmer, 92
"Range War," 93
Red Lake, 177
Red Shirt, 3
Reese, Billy, 190
Regula, Ralph, 111, 139
Reichard, Gladys: *Navajo Shepherd and
  Weaver*, 35; *Navajo Medicine*, 19
Relocation benefits, 14, 130, 191
Rhoads, C. J., 40, 47
Rich, Bonnie, 149, 150–51
Rich, John, 149–50
Rich, Steve, 149, 151
Riegle, Don: *O Congress*, 94
Roberts, Neal, 132
Rocky Ridge School, 9, 15, 195
Roosevelt, Theodore, 57, 149
Rudzik, Bob, 136
Ruzow, Larry, 178

Sagebrush Revolt, 149
Sahu, Winifred, 54
Salt River Project, 79, 85
Sand Clan, 54, 55
Sand Springs, 70
San Francisco Peaks, 40, 59, 194
San Juan County, New Mexico, 144–46
Save the Arizona Strip Committee, 139,
  144, 170, 175
Schifter, Richard, 99–100, 110, 115, 119,
  135
Scott, Hugh, 129
Scott, Marlin, 176
Schweiker, Lowell, 129
Scudder, Thayer, 182, 203–4, 219
Sekaquaptewa, Abbott: calls *Healing*
  decision a compromise, 103; Civic
  Center controversy, involvement in, 56;
  criticizes New Mexico congressional
  delegation, 114; extent of support for,
  71; impoundment of Navajo cattle, 156;
  justifies relocation, 96; lobbyist in
  Washington, 120; oil leases in District 6,

78; on extent of Hopi use of JUA, 74; on
  mining future, 162; profile of, 73–74;
  reacts to partition line, 155; refuses to
  release Navajo stock, 157; rejects further
  negotiations, 104; responds to critics,
  53; seeks appropriation for lobbying,
  109; seeks dismissal of Benjamin,
  158–59; warns of possible violence, 113;
  Winslow hearing, 1973, 103; Winslow
  hearing, 1978, 162
Sekaquaptewa, Emory, 72, 73
Sekaquaptewa, Emory, Jr., 73
Sekaquaptewa, Eugene, 73
Sekaquaptewa, Helen: *Me and Mine*,
  72–73
Sekaquaptewa, Susan, 64, 217
Sekaquaptewa, Wayne: anti-Navajo
  editorials, 64; Mormon Church, views
  on, 62–64; on Goldwater, 99; profile of,
  61–64; views on traditional religion, 62;
  mentioned, 50, 51, 56
Senate Select Committee on Indian
  Affairs, 168, 214
Senatorial courtesy, 126
Seventh Cavalry, 101
Seyestewa, Jesse, 68
Shearin, Lee, 133
sheep unit: defined, 33
Shelton, Joseph, 13–15
Sherman, William T., 24
Shipaulovi, 72
Shungopavi, 55, 71
Sigler, Louis, 96
Silversmith, Barbara, 192
Simkin, William, 143–44, 154–56, 188
Sioux, 24
Skeet, Wilson, 178
Smith, Katherine, 209, 210–12
Snake Dance, 51, 59
Southern California Edison, 78–79
Southern California Gas, 136
Spicer, Edward: *Cycles of Conquest*, 21
Staats, Elmer B., 131
Stafford, Robert, 129
Steiger, Sam: contrasted with Owens,
  108–9; criticizes Lujan letter, 113;
  criticizes union role in land dispute
  debate, 110; exchange with Lujan, 109;
  House Rock Valley controversy,
  involvement in, 139–41; loses Navajo
  vote, 5, 125; profile of, 93–95; quotes
  Udall, 116; warns of need for partition,
  93; mentioned, 117, 131, 134, 138, 160
Stock reduction: Benjamin comments on,
  158; Collier's program, 32–36; federal
  policy after 1937, 36–37; legislative
  provision for, 130; mandated by
  Navajo-Hopi Land Settlement Act,